D1499837

SHADOW WARRIOR

FELIX I. RODRIGUEZ
AND JOHN WEISMAN

SIMON AND SCHUSTER
NEW YORK LONDON TORONTO SYDNEY TOKYO

Simon and Schuster
Simon & Schuster Building
Rockefeller Center
1230 Avenue of the Americas
New York, New York 10020

Copyright © 1989 by Felix Rodriguez and John Weisman

All rights reserved
including the right of reproduction
in whole or in part in any form.

SIMON AND SCHUSTER and colophon are registered trademarks
of Simon & Schuster Inc.

Designed by Lynne Kopcik/Barbara Marks Graphic Design
Manufactured in the United States of America

10 9 8 7 6 5 4 3 2

Library of Congress Cataloging in Publication data

Rodriguez, Felix I.
Shadow warrior / Felix I. Rodriguez and John Weisman.
p.   cm.
1. Rodriguez, Felix I.   2. Spies—United States—Biography.
3. United States. Central Intelligence Agency—Biography.
4. Espionage, American—Central America.   5. Guevara, Ernesto,
1928-1967—Assassination.   6. United States—Relations—Central
America.   7. Central America—Relations—United States.
I. Weisman, John. II. Title.
E840.5.R63A3 1989
327.12'0973'092—dc20
[B]   89-19727
            CIP

ISBN 0-671-66721-1

All photos copyright © Felix Rodriguez, except for the following:
4, 20, 21, 22 - Wide World Photos
25 - John Weisman
28 - Dick Swanson

To
Donald P. Gregg
with profound respect and gratitude . . .
to
Rosa, Rosemarie, and Felix
with all my love . . .
and to
Susan Povenmire Weisman
with many thanks

SHADOW WARRIOR

PROLOGUE

The helicopter was small—a single engine and a Plexiglas bubble. Above me, the sky was an intense blue. Five hundred feet below, the inhospitable Bolivian jungle was a thick carpet of thorny green vegetation. I sat on a narrow canvas bench behind the pilot, occasionally shifting my weight to help keep the chopper steady.

Below and just to my right, tied to a stretcher and attached securely to the chopper's skid, was the dead body of Che Guevara.

On my wrist was his steel Rolex GMT Master with its red-and-blue bezel. In my breast pocket, wrapped in paper from my loose-leaf notebook, was the partially smoked tobacco from his last pipe.

There were stains on the army fatigue trousers I was wearing—Che's blood caked dark against the khaki-green material.

It was October 9, 1967, 2:15 P.M. local time, and it was as if I were in the middle of a dream. Except it wasn't a dream. The chopper was real. The blood was real.

Che Guevara was dead.

My gaze moved from the sky to the jungle, to Che's body, then to the blood on my uniform. Back in the United States, the adopted country I was not yet even a citizen of, my family had no idea where I was or what I was doing, although at CIA headquarters in Langley, Virginia, the word was probably circulating by now that Che had been executed. I'd had the opportunity to radio a short, coded message before the helicopter arrived to pick up the body. It had been impossible to contact the CIA station at our La Paz Embassy because of interference caused by the mountains, but I was sure my message had been relayed there from Langley.

I was twenty-six years old, the father of two young children, and, like many of my fellow Cuban exiles, I had been at war for almost a decade. At war against Fidel Castro and everything he stood for. At war against Che Guevara and the revolution he wanted to spread throughout the Western Hemisphere.

I looked down at Che's body and then up into the blue again.

I thought about Che Guevara, about the slight, thin-boned little man whose liquid eyes held an unspeakable sadness; whose days of revolutionary glory in Havana, Moscow, and Peking had ended squalidly in a wretched mud-brick schoolhouse in La Higuera, his clothes tattered and torn, his feet shod in rotting leather, his hair matted and filthy, his dream of a peasant uprising an utter failure.

It was all so . . . surreal. My mind was going at top speed, fragments of thoughts jumping in and out of my consciousness. I recalled my childhood in Cuba, of going out to the barn where I laced my strong morning coffee with frothy milk right from the cow. I thought about my prep school friends from Perkiomen Academy in suburban Pennsylvania and how different their lives must be from mine.

Before my eyes flashed my first trip to the anti-Castro training camps high in the rough, steaming Guatemalan mountains, camps carved out of jungle very much like the one I was flying over now, and remembered the directions we were given to get there by joking veterans: "Go as far as the third cloud and take a right."

Had I only been nineteen then? It seemed a century ago.

I relived the final seconds on the ground in La Higuera, where Che died, when, with the chopper rotors already churning, a Catholic priest hurriedly rode up on a cranky mule and gave the last rites of the Church to the corpse of a man who had long before renounced God.

I thought of my parents and my family and wondered how much about this day I could ever tell them.

I thought about how Che had died with courage, and second-guessed myself about whether or not I could have succeeded in keeping him alive, as the CIA had instructed, although it would have meant taking on a responsibility that I might later have come to regret. Had there been anything more I could have done?

Even today, I do not know the answer.

The orders had come down by telephone in the code the Bolivians predetermined. I took the call from Vallegrande myself and heard the words, "Five hundred—six hundred." Five hundred meant Che. Six hundred meant execute him. If the Bolivians had wanted him kept alive I would have heard the number seven hundred. I asked that the order be repeated. It was.

I informed the senior Bolivian officer on the scene, Colonel Joaquín Zenteno Anaya, that the general staff wanted Che executed. I also told him that my instructions from the United States government were to keep Che alive at all costs. I knew that our people had choppers and planes ready to evacuate the revolutionary *comandante* to Panama for subsequent interrogation, and that no expense or effort would be spared if the Bolivians gave their consent.

But it was not to be.

Zenteno turned to me. "Felix," he said, "we have worked very closely, and we are grateful for all the help you have given us. But don't ask me to do this. If I don't comply with my orders to execute Che I will be disobeying my own president and I'll risk a dishonorable discharge."

The Bolivian colonel looked at his watch. "I know how much

harm he has done to your country. It is eleven in the morning. I will leave in the helicopter now. At two P.M. I will send it back. I would like your word of honor that, at that time, you will personally bring back the dead body of Che Guevara to Vallegrande. The manner in which you deal with Che is up to you. You can even do it yourself if you want."

I looked Zenteno in the face. "Colonel," I said, "please try to get them to change their minds. But if you cannot get the counterorder, I give you my word of honor as a man that at two P.M. I will bring you back the dead body of Che Guevara."

The Bolivian and I embraced, and then he left.

A few minutes later I found myself inside the small dark room where the wounded Che lay bound on the dirt floor. I looked down at him and said, "Che Guevara, I want to talk to you."

His eyes flashed. "Nobody interrogates me," he replied sarcastically.

"Commander," I said, "I didn't come to interrogate you. Our ideals are different. But I admire you. You used to be a minister of state in Cuba. Now look at you—you are like this because you believe in your ideals. I have come to talk to you."

He looked at me for some seconds, wondering whether I was being sincere. He must have been a good judge of men because he realized I was speaking from the heart.

Finally he spoke. "Would you untie me? May I sit?"

"Of course." I ordered one of the soldiers outside to enter. "Take the ropes from Commander Guevara," I commanded. The soldier looked at me incredulously. How could I be treating an enemy with such dignity? I gave the command a second time and Che's arms were unbound.

The guerrilla groaned as the ropes were untied. His joints were probably frozen, as he had been tied up for almost a whole day by now, and it took the soldier and me some effort until we finally sat him up on a broken-down wood bench.

He asked me for tobacco for his pipe. We had none so I got a cigarette from one of the soldiers and gave it to him. Carefully he stripped the paper and tamped the tobacco into the bowl of his pipe, lighted it, and inhaled deeply.

We talked for a long time—not about strategic matters but about Cuba, and communism, and about our different philosophies of life.

Toward noon, a helicopter bringing food and ammunition arrived. Before it took off, carrying dead and wounded Bolivian soldiers, the pilot, an air force major named Jaime Nino de Guzmán, showed me a camera he had been given by the Bolivian division intelligence officer, Major Saucedo. Nino de Guzmán asked to take a picture of the prisoner.

I asked Che if he minded having his picture taken. He agreed to permit it, and we helped him limp out to the front of the schoolhouse. Nino de Guzmán gave me the camera, which was set correctly. Although my Bolivian hosts had been tremendously kind to me and I certainly didn't want to get Major Saucedo in trouble, something inside me instinctively made me surreptitiously change the speed and the lens opening, ensuring that the pictures would never come out. I pointed the camera and snapped Che and Nino de Guzmán.

I, too had a camera—a Pentax. I set the exposure, gave it to Nino de Guzmán, watching carefully to make sure the settings were not tampered with, then stood next to Che. I knew as Nino de Guzmán snapped the shutter that the CIA would have the only picture of Che that day.

We stood posed somewhat formally against the mud schoolhouse in the bright Bolivian sunlight, the two of us squinting into the lens. I told Che, "*Comandante*, look at the little bird," and at that instant he cracked the hint of a smile. But he quickly became serious just as the shutter clicked. My hand was around his left shoulder, and the two of us were surrounded by Bolivian soldiers. It is the only picture of Che alive on the day of his execution.

Back inside, I asked him about the people he had put in front of firing squads. He said the only ones put to death were foreigners—imperialistic agents and spies who had been sent by the CIA.

I looked at him. "Commander, how ironic for you to say that! You're not a Bolivian. You are a foreigner. You have invaded sovereign Bolivian territory."

Che glanced at me sympathetically. "These are matters of the proletariat that are beyond your comprehension," he said adamantly.

He pointed at his bandaged right leg, which still oozed blood. "I'm spilling my blood here in Bolivia," he said. "I feel Argentinian, Cuban—and Bolivian."

He pointed to the corpse of a Cuban guerrilla captain named Antonio that lay on the packed mud floor behind me. "Look at this one," Che said. "In Cuba, he had everything he wanted. And yet he came here to die like this. To die because he believed in his ideals." Then he rubbed his face with his hands and was silent for some seconds.

The conversation continued. Sometime later, because of the tack of my questions, he realized I might not be a Bolivian. He turned to me and said, "You are not a Bolivian."

"No, I am not. Where do you think I am from?"

"You could be a Puerto Rican," he said. "Or a Cuban. But whoever you are, by the sorts of questions you've been asking me I believe that you work for the intelligence service of the United States."

"You're right, Commander," I said. "I am a Cuban. I was a member of the 2506 Brigade. In fact, I was a member of the infiltration teams that operated inside Cuba before the invasion at the Bay of Pigs."

He looked at me with new interest. "What's your name?" he asked.

"Felix," I said.

It did not mean anything to him. And there was no use going any further. "Just Felix."

"Ha," he replied cryptically.

I spent almost three hours with him, shuttling between the schoolhouse and other areas in La Higuera where I had intelligence work to complete. Perhaps I was putting off the inevitable, perhaps it was just a busy time. I am not sure even today. Still, I knew what was coming. It became more obvious after a schoolteacher came up to me as I was photographing Che's diary.

"*Mi Capitán,*" she asked, "when are you going to shoot him?"

I turned to her in surprise. "Why are you asking me that?"

"Because," she responded, "the radio is already reporting that he is dead from combat wounds."

So—it was useless to wait any longer. I walked down to his room at the schoolhouse just before 1 P.M. I turned toward him and looked him squarely in the face.

"*Comandante*," I said, "I have done everything possible in my power, but orders have come from the Supreme Bolivian Command..."

He understood immediately. His expression at that instant showed he had lost all hope of surviving. He didn't move a muscle, but his face turned white as writing paper. He stared at me, his eyes liquid and sensitive, his face stable and serene. "It is better like this, Felix," he said. "I should have never been captured alive."

I looked at him; his wounded leg did not seem to hurt him anymore. His hair was dirty and matted. His clothes were torn, his arms still stiff from lying bound on the damp, cold floor. It was an instant of incredible, conflicting emotions. Here in front of me was the enemy I had fought against for so long. And yet I couldn't bring myself to feel hatred for him. I felt pity for him and even, perhaps, admiration.

He pulled out his pipe. "I would like to give this pipe to a *soldadito*—a little soldier—who treated me well," Che said.

At that instant, Sergeant Mario Terán, who must have been listening outside, burst into the room. "*Mi Capitán, I* want it, I want it!" he shouted.

Instantly, Che pulled the pipe toward his chest. "No—not to you. I will not give this to you," Che said.

I ordered Terán out of the room. "I want it," he insisted again. "Out! Get out!" I commanded. Finally he left.

Che still held the pipe close to his chest. I looked at him. "Would you give it to me, *Comandante*?" I asked.

He thought a few seconds. "Yes. To you, I will."

"*Comandante*," I said, "do you want me to say anything to your family if I ever have the opportunity?"

He was silent for some time. Finally he said, "Yes. Tell Fidel that he will soon see a triumphant revolution in America. And tell my wife to get remarried and try to be happy."

It was a tremendously emotional moment. Both of us were visibly moved.

Spontaneously he held out his hand to me and I took it. Then he embraced me, holding tight. It was the *abrazo* of a man who knows he is about to stare death in the face.

He stepped back and stood at attention. He thought I would be his executioner. I approached him, shook his hand, and embraced him the way he had embraced me. Then I walked outside. Neither of us said another word.

I walked into the bright sunlight, not looking back. I looked at my watch. It was 1 P.M. Outside, Sergeant Mario Terán and Lieutenant Pérez were waiting for me. They were surrounded by a crowd of anxious Bolivian soldiers. I didn't remember seeing such a crowd when I'd entered Che's room.

I looked straight at Terán and gave the order. "Sergeant, shoot him. But remember—he is supposed to die from combat wounds, so—" I ran my hand under my chin—"shoot from here down. Not in the face."

Terán answered, visibly excited, *"Sí, mi Capitán,"* and looked anxiously toward the doorway. I turned away. I had neither the will nor, if truth be known, the courage to witness what was about to happen. I walked up the hill to my left, to the little command post I'd set up for myself and began making the notes I would radio to CIA headquarters, when I heard a short burst from the M-2 carbine Terán had borrowed from Lieutenant Pérez.

It had been done. Che was dead.

I checked my watch. It was 1:10 P.M. local time.

I felt drained, emotionally exhausted. It was over.

I sat in the chopper, Che's body tied to the right skid, and thought about my wife, Rosa, and my children, three-year-old Rosemarie and my year-old son, Felix, and I wondered whether I would someday be able to explain to them why I did what I did; why I chose to become a soldier, then a CIA agent, and fight, rather than accept, Cuba's fate and Castro's totalitarianism. I had made a commitment to those who started with me in 1959 in the Dominican jungles and those who died for their ideals in Cuba in 1961. The oath we took was to free Cuba—and Cuba was not yet free.

Below, the rough jungle carpet started to thin out, replaced by foothills and then mountains. We were coming into Vallegrande, where we would set down at the Pando Regiment's barracks, far from any prying eyes.

I leaned forward and tapped the pilot on the shoulder. "Landing soon?" I shouted over the engine's noise.

He nodded affirmatively. "But not where you thought. They ordered us straight to Vallegrande airport."

That was bad news. Since the middle of September, when the Bolivian hunt for Che had intensified, journalists and others had begun to flock to Vallegrande, a mountain city of seven thousand inhabitants, and I, for one, had been worried about the publicity surrounding the Bolivian army's operations in the region. In fact, and unknown to me at the time, stories about Che's possible capture already had appeared in two Bolivian newspapers, *El Diario* and *Presencia*, this very day he was executed.

I saw the airfield ahead and below us. It was absolute chaos. There must have been at least two thousand people there. Press. Photographers. And planes—I counted several Bolivian air force C-47s. It was an agent's nightmare, and it shook me from my reveries.

Although the Bolivian government had requested the Central Intelligence Agency's assistance in tracking down Che (indeed, my Agency colleagues and I had even been received by the Bolivian president, René Barrientos, shortly after our arrival in La Paz), my mission was a clandestine one.

As far as most of the locals knew, I was simply a Cuban named Felix Rámos Medina—a pseudonym whose initials reflected my real name, Felix Rodriguez Mendigutia. I wanted very much to keep things clandestine, both for the Agency's sake and for my own safety. No, it would not be good for me to be photographed or identified arriving on the helicopter that carried Che's body.

We flew lower, the chopper turning into the wind for its approach and landing. As we descended, the throng started to move toward us, a sea of people all waiting to catch a glimpse of the legendary dead revolutionary.

I knew I would have to act quickly. There were already rumors circulating about Agency involvement in Bolivia's counterinsurgency programs, and if Castro had any agents in the crowd they would be looking for CIA people. So the instant we touched down I bolted out the door on the left side of the helicopter, away from Che, pulled my Bolivian army cap over my face, and melted into the crowd, safely anonymous.

In fact, until the afternoon of May 27, 1987, when I stood, my right hand raised, and took an oath to tell the truth before the Joint House-Senate Iran/Contra committees, my life was mostly one of anonymity. That was the way I had wanted it. That was the way the Agency had wanted it. For fifteen years as a CIA agent I had worked under an assortment of aliases, assembled a thick file of false identity documents, and shunned publicity. Often when I traveled, my wife and my family had no idea where I was going or what I was doing.

It was better for them not to know—and safer for me. Since 1967, Fidel Castro has put a price on my head. He has a long memory. Indeed, when my old friend Roberto Martín Pérez was released in May 1987, after twenty-eight years of torture and hell in Castro's prisons, he was given a message specifically for me.

A lieutenant colonel named Peralta, one of the heads of the DGI (Dirección General de Inteligencia—Cuban intelligence) came to Boniato prison and had Martín Pérez brought to his office. Peralta told him that he might be released.

"But if we do let you go, you shouldn't get too close to your old friend Felix Rodriguez Mendigutia," the officer said. "We haven't been able to get him—yet. But we will. He's one of Prime Minister Castro's top priorities. If we release you you can tell Rodriguez we've sent cruel emissaries after him."

"Cruel emissaries" is another way of saying Palestinian assassins. So you make accommodations. My house has an Agency-installed $25,000 security system (the CIA even has a lien on the only piece of land I own to cover the cost). In Miami I have a concealed-weapons permit and I always carry a pistol. I also have a mobile phone nearby. I don't telegraph my moves. I keep a low profile.

But with my testimony on May 27 all anonymity disappeared forever. Whether or not I wanted it I became a public figure—my face in the newspapers and on television screens.

Moreover, what I said was often quoted—accurately in some stories and incorrectly in others. I learned, sometimes painfully, in the weeks and months following my initial Capitol Hill testimony, that people tend to deal not in the truth as it really is, but the truth as they want to see it—and the facts be damned.

That is one of the primary reasons for this book. I write it to set the record straight—to clarify the distortions both about myself and about some of the things I have done.

Most importantly, however, I write this book to say emphatically that what I have done I am proud to have done, both as a Cuban and as an adopted American. I believe that my actions when I served with the Agency, and throughout my private battles against Castro and communist totalitarianism have been always correct and, more important, always honorable.

Sometimes I feel a little bit like Ulysses, the ancient Homeric soldier from Ithaca. Like him, I am from an island nation. Like him, I went to war. And like him, I am having a hard time getting home.

When I sat in that chopper, Che's body tied to the skid, more than twenty years ago, I had no idea where my own personal odyssey was going to take me. But I did know, even then, that the values my family had instilled in me were the most important elements of my life.

As a child I was taught that there are things much more important than money or power or comfort. Honor, duty, devotion, mutual respect—these things can never be bought. They have no price.

Those values have not changed for me in more than four decades. They are the values my wife, Rosa, and I have tried to instill in our children, Rosemarie and Felix, Jr.

I have never been a rich man   nor, I believe, will I ever be. But I am wealthy beyond measure in intangibles: I have the advantage of being able to look myself in the mirror every morning and be happy with whom I see. I have my friends, my family, and, most important, I have my honor.

On October 5, 1986, at precisely 9:50 A.M., a vintage C-123 transport plane filled with ten thousand pounds of ammunition, some six dozen automatic rifles, and seven RPG (rocket-propelled grenade) launchers lumbered off Runway 33 at Ilopango Air Base just outside the city of San Salvador on its way to a supply drop for the FDN (Nicaraguan Democratic Front) anticommunist resistance fighters inside Nicaragua. The pilot, Bill Cooper, was a veteran of CIA air operations in Southeast Asia. So were the copilot, Buzz Sawyer, and the dropmaster, a red-haired, lanky Midwesterner named Eugene Hasenfus.

Cooper, Sawyer, and a Contra security officer were killed when the C-123 was shot down by a Sandinista soldier's Soviet-made SAM-7 ground-to-air missile later that morning. Hasenfus alone parachuted from the stricken aircraft and survived. When the Sandinistas discovered the bodies of Cooper and Sawyer, they carefully went through their personal effects. On Cooper's body was a notebook containing my name and phone number.

The name in the notebook read Max Gomez.

It struck me odd at the time—and still strikes me odd today—that of the hundreds and hundreds of stories that have appeared about my involvement in what has come to be known as the Iran/Contra affair, only a handful ever explained the history and significance behind the particular *nom de guerre* I assumed in El Salvador. Because, for Cuban-Americans, the name Max—short for Máximo—Gómez evokes the same feelings of dedication toward freedom and democracy that the Marquis de Lafayette's name does for Norteamericanos.

Gómez was a Dominican who left his homeland in order to become a Cuban general and fight against Spain for Cuba's independence in the nineteenth century. His name is universally revered—there is even a Boulevard Máximo Gómez in Miami.

Yet few of the reporters who call themselves experts on Latin America ever bothered to research my pseudonym or explain the background of "Max Gómez" to their readers, as far as I can tell. Their apparent blindness toward Cuban history represents to me the arrogance of the press when it comes to understanding, reporting, and interpreting the complexities of Central and South America, as well as the tendency of journalists to stereotype people they neither know nor understand.

Moreover, for me, the name of Máximo Gómez has its own personal evocations. On the wall of my home in Miami is a letter from the famous *Generalisimo* to one of my ancestors, whose husband fought with him during the war against Spain. Even today I cannot look at it without being moved. Since my childhood, Máximo Gómez has been one of my heroes and one of my role models.

Indeed, people continually ask me why I have spent so much of my adult life fighting against communism, fighting for the freedom of Cuba and for democratic principles. The answer is that it was bred in me. It has always been an integral part of my family's history.

My great-great-grand-cousin, Rafael Rodríguez García, was a sergeant in the army expedition of the generals Serafín Sánchez and Roloff, which landed in Cuba in July 1895 to fight for liberation against Spain. Another great-great-grand-cousin, General Alejandro Rodríguez Velasco (1852–1915)—he was the one whose wife got the letter from Máximo Gómez—was the first popularly elected mayor of Havana. My paternal great-grandfather, Ignacio Rodríguez, was deported by the Spanish for revolutionary activities to a concentration camp on the Isle of Pines. The Spanish executed two of his brothers. My maternal grandfather, a dentist named Don Felix Mendigutia, was also involved in anti-Spanish activities. He would have been arrested but managed to flee to Mexico ahead of the Spanish authorities. Another relative, General Manuel de Mendigutia Navarro, who died of typhoid on a battlefield in Oriente Province on July 4, 1871, at the age of thirty, was even cited as a national hero in one of Fidel's newspapers. In April 1972, an article in *Vanguardia* described Mendigutia Navarro's "magnificent service to the Revolution" against Spain. If I am a freedom fighter, I come by it honestly.

I was born May 31, 1941, in a hospital in Havana but within days was taken back to my family's hometown, Sancti Spiritus, a city of roughly 50,000 people situated in Las Villas province about 250 miles southeast of Havana, so I consider myself an Espirituano. By American standards it would be considered a conservative place—life in Sancti Spiritus was often more akin to life in Spain than it was to Havana's freewheeling style. But by conservative I do not mean reactionary in the political sense. In fact, Espirituanos were, from the city's very first days, political mavericks.

Our family combined two strains of Sancti Spiritus's tradition of self-determination. My mother was a Mendigutia, whose ancestors came from the fiercely independent Basque region that lies between Spain and France. My wife, Rosa, tells me I probably inherited my stubbornness from her genes. My father's family, Rodriguez, was traditional Spanish—although there was a lot of Espirituano influence as well.

My father, Felix, was a merchant whose store was on the ground floor of the two-story building he had been given by his father as a wedding present. My mother, Rosa, helped out in the store and also kept the house.

Our house was a wonderful place. It was well situated, right on the city's oldest square, a wide plaza filled with palm trees and an octagonal bandstand in the center. On balmy nights, as a child I could push open one of the two sets of French doors in the parlor that opened onto a narrow balcony and watch as people strolled below. As this was a traditional town, single men always strolled in a clockwise direction and single women, walking in twos or threes, always went the opposite way. There was little talk between the sexes during those evening strolls—but a lot of eye contact.

Our house was a continual adventure for me because there was always something new to discover. The floors were inlaid with intricate tile patterns; the walls were filled with vitrines—glass-fronted cabinets inside which were fabulous treasures of porcelain, china, and marble.

There were big marble columns atop which sat classical busts, and in the formal dining room lots of sparkling crystal and huge candles —they must have been almost three feet tall—to light the linen-covered table. Our furniture was heavy wood, always polished to mirror-brightness, and from the walls huge paintings of my ancestors looked down on me. In my parents' bedroom the ceiling was made of ornately stamped tin, from which hung small crystal chandeliers. It was like living in a museum, with my parents as the curators and me the perpetual tourist.

I was an only child, which was uncommon in Cuba. My father had two sisters. My mother had six brothers, and as a child I spent a lot of time with my various uncles and aunts. My favorite was Felix Claudio Mendigutia (both my mother and father's family are heavy in Felixes and Rosas—it's sometimes hard to keep us straight). Uncle Felix Mendigutia ran the farm that belonged to my mother's family, and I spent most of my vacations with him. The other uncle to whom I was close was named Raúl Mendigutia. He was a judge, and occasionally I went to watch as he presided over a court session in Sancti Spiritus, and listened to his experiences when he traveled the nearby countryside to settle disputes between the farmers. From Raúl I learned fairness. He was known for that quality, and the stories he told when he came to our house affected me.

I was, my parents told me, somewhat precocious as a child, although not the best of students. I preferred my time at the farm, where Uncle Felix Mendigutia taught me to ride a horse and shoot a .22 rifle by the time I was about seven, and I was even driving a car by the age of ten—although only on the farm. The farm meant a lot to me. Sometimes I would go out early in the morning and hunt for birds, which I would bring back and have dressed for lunch or dinner. In the warm evenings I'd accompany the workers as they herded the cattle back to the barns on horseback. Uncle Felix had cows, and one of my favorite treats was running down to the dairy shed early in the morning with a cup of hot, thick, sweet Cuban coffee and watch as a farmhand milked the cow, the milk all foamy and warm and creamy, right into the cup for me.

In many ways, being an only child prepared me for an agent's life. I spent a lot of time alone and learned at an early age to be self-sufficient, to work on my own, to deal with and solve problems by myself. My Uncle Fernando Mendigutia, a lawyer who lives in Miami now, says I was a headstrong child. I was also somewhat mischievous. At about the age of eight I managed somehow to convince a man who was tutoring me to sit in a chair in our parlor while I bound him up tightly with a long cord. I left him there and went out to play—and caught hell from my father for doing so. Still, I would have liked to see my parents' faces when they came home and found the poor guy all tied up, explaining why he'd sat still while a little kid did that to him.

Our family was comfortably middle class. My paternal grandfather had the idea to market bottled drinking water and his brand, Villa Lolita, was the first commercially sold drinking water in Sancti Spiritus. He became quite successful in time. My uncles were all professionals: there were two engineer-architects, two lawyers, and two accountants among them. I myself grew up wanting to become an engineer-architect. I was pretty good at drafting and making pictures.

I began school in Sancti Spiritus, continued in Havana when my Uncle Toto—José Antonio—became Minister of Public Works for the

Batista government and my mother went to help him set up his house. My father stayed in Sancti Spiritus and commuted to Havana on weekends. At ten I was enrolled in the Havana Military Academy, and I did pretty well there—with some encouragement from my family. Uncle Toto always used to tell me, "Do well at school or I'm going to take you out and put you on the streets to sell eggs and chickens." I believed him. So I worked hard—I even got a good conduct medal at the end of my first term. We lived pretty well in Havana. José had a big house right on Fifth Avenue in Miramar, a fashionable part of the city. I felt like a pretty lucky eleven-year-old.

I should say a few words here about Fulgencio Batista y Zaldívar. I never really knew him, although I saw him twice at relatives' homes. But he only stopped to say a perfunctory hello—I was, after all, a child at the time. When I testified before the Iran/Contra committees, the Senate chairman, Senator Daniel Inouye, asked me what sort of person Batista was, commenting, "He has been described by some as the worst tyrant in the Caribbean."

Somehow, I think that those who survived the brutal regimes of Rafael Leonidas Trujillo in the Dominican Republic and François "Papa Doc" Duvalier in Haiti, or the Cubans who live under Castro's tyranny might dispute the good Senator from Hawaii. On the other hand, Senator Inouye perhaps wanted to score a political point with his liberal constituency by endeavoring to hint that all anti-Castro Cubans are in favor of repressive right-wing dictatorships—something that isn't true at all. MRR—the Movement of Revolutionary Recovery—which has worked vehemently and militantly against Castro since 1959, for example, began as an anti-Batista underground organized by college students in the fifties. Most Cubans detest all dictators, whether they come from the right or the left.

Fulgencio Batista came from a extremely poor family. As a youth he worked as a laborer on the Cuban railroads; after that he joined the army. Even then he must have had charisma: as an obscure army sergeant he rose to power after the overthrow of the dictator Gerardo Machado in 1933. But Batista stayed behind the scenes until 1940, when he was elected in what my cousin Miguel García, the family historian (and no fan of Batista's), calls "a clean election." He ruled for four years, after which he allowed free elections. He sponsored a man named Carlos Saladrigas Zayas for the presidency. Saladrigas lost to Ramón Grau San Martín, and Batista, after turning over the reins of power, went into self-imposed exile in Daytona Beach, Florida. He returned to Cuba in 1948 as an elected senator for Las Villas Province, having run a successful campaign from outside the country. Then, on March 10, 1952, he staged a coup at the behest of the Cuban armed forces, who requested his assistance, as they were discontented with the way President Carlos Prío Socarrás was neglecting the army, and disturbed over rumors about Prío's tolerance of Cuban organized crime.

It was only during the years following the 1952 coup that Batista's activities convinced many Cubans—some of them would later become my good friends in the anti-Castro movement—that the former army sergeant had gone too far. They organized anti-Batista movements such as the MRR.

Yet many other Cubans—good people from all classes—were either in favor of Batista or remained neutral. As much as many loathed Batista's corruption, the Cubans' innate fear of communism was stronger than was their distaste for dictatorship.

The father of my closest friend, Papo Reyes, is a good example of this. Papo's father, Anselmo Alejandro, was a barber with a tiny shop in the town of Colón, southeast of Havana. He was a poor and simple man all his life and he had no love of dictators. On the contrary, Anselmo was a real student of American-style democracy. Although he never lived to see *Los Estados Unidos* himself, he spent much of his time reading about the United States and telling stories about American history to his six children.

Anselmo, who was black, knew that there were problems of segregation in the U.S. (In that respect, Cuban society was better than American. In fact, it was not until after Castro's ascendancy that Cuban blacks first encountered any real discrimination.) But he remained a strong proponent of the American way of life, even with its flaws. Papo still loves to talk about the way his father kept a map of Europe on the wall of his home during World War II, eagerly charting with pins the progress of the American army campaigns against Hitler and Mussolini. Papo's old man was a big fan of generals like Eisenhower and Patton, and he admired Franklin D. Roosevelt.

And although he couldn't stomach dictators, Anselmo hated the communists worse than Batista. "I've read a lot of books about the Russian Revolution," he used to tell young Papo, "and the one thing I've discovered is that if the communists get in, they'll take even the little that you or I have. They will steal the country."

Why is it that dictators such as Batista (and others in the region—Perón, Somoza and Trujillo come to mind immediately) can rise to power in nations that have fierce nationalistic and independent tendencies? One answer, I believe, lies in a Spanish word that defines the sort of leaders we often find in Latin America: charismatic, nationalistic, paternalistic, patriarchal leaders. That word is *caudillo*.

It refers to a man who governs not necessarily because he was elected, but because he, better than others, is able to govern by force of personality, by sheer presence. A *caudillo*'s power is absolute—it is never shared.

Fulgencio Batista was one of these *caudillos*.

When I was about twelve, Uncle Toto—José Antonio Mendigutia, the Minister of Public Works—offered to pay for my education if I agreed to go to the United States to study. I must admit I didn't pay much attention to him. Nor did I especially want to think about going to the U.S. It was almost summer-vacation time, and our family had, as was its habit, rented rooms in a house named Casa La Rosa at Varadero, a town with what was generally accepted as the best beach in Cuba, on the north coast not too far from Havana. Casa La Rosa was an old two-story wood house that sat right above the sandy beach. In the front, steps led from a huge raised courtyard, thick with trees and benches on which to sit during the afternoons, to the street. From the rear of the house we'd go down a flight of wood steps to the white sand fifteen feet below. In June or July we'd all gather there for a month or so—Mendigutias from my mother's side and Rodríguezes from my father's. I would swim all day, and lie in the sun, and take long walks with my parents and my uncles, listening as they talked among themselves. It was a wonderful place to be, very informal.

One day my Uncle Manolo Jiménez took me aside. The husband of my father's sister, he was a proud man who had been educated in

Paris. We walked down from our rooms to the courtyard and sat under a big, lush tree and he looked me in the face.

"Uncle Toto says he offered to pay your way at a school in the United States," he said, his face serious.

I nodded.

"So? what have you decided?"

I shrugged. "Nothing really."

He shook his head. "Felix," he said, "let me tell you some things. You are young now, and you don't realize what it means to have an education outside Cuba. But it's important."

"Why?" I asked. "We've got everything we could ever want right here."

He paused to look up at the sky. "You're right. We do have everything we could ever want right here. But, Felix, nothing is forever."

I really had no idea what he was talking about.

"Money comes," my uncle said, "and money goes. Today we're all comfortable. Tomorrow—who knows?"

He took my hand. "My father was the mayor of Sancti Spiritus, right?"

"Uh-huh."

"But he wasn't rich. In fact, he had to make a lot of sacrifices to send me to medical school in Paris."

I nodded.

"So now I'm comfortable. I have a nice house, and I can afford to come here to the beach in the summer. And even if I didn't have any of those things, I am a doctor, a professional, and I can go anywhere to work."

That made sense.

"The most important thing, Felix, is to have an education. And to have an education abroad is something that very few of us ever get the opportunity to do. If Uncle Toto wants to send you to *Los Estados Unidos*, I would think very seriously about his offer, because if you don't go, you may regret it later in your life."

Something about what he said took root in my consciousness. Indeed, until that conversation, I really hadn't paid much attention at all to anything having to do with what I'd do, or what I'd grow up to be. I'd lived my life—like most twelve-year-olds—day to day. Education was an abstraction. A career was something I couldn't really fathom. But there was an urgency in my uncle's voice that I had never really heard before, a tone that made me pay attention.

So the next time I saw my Uncle Toto, I told him that I wanted to study in the United States.

"Are you serious?" he asked me.

"Yes, sir," I answered like the cadet I was. "I am decided. I will go to school there."

It was a decision that would affect the rest of my life.

Ultimately we chose a place called Perkiomen Preparatory School, which was located in the tiny town of Pennsburg, Pennsylvania, roughly forty miles northwest of Philadelphia. In September 1954, I registered as a seventh-grader.

It wasn't easy at first. After my father left, I was terribly lonely. The only cures for my homesickness were the frequent visits of Agustín Rodríguez, his wife, Emma, and his sister-in-law, Esperanza, who drove from Philadelphia to see me, and the time I spent with Nick Navarro, a Cuban in his mid-twenties who worked near Pennsburg. (Nick and I would remain friends to this day. He would move to Florida, where he is currently the elected sheriff of Broward County.) My loneliness was cultural as well as physical. One of the things that struck me early on at Perkiomen was the provinciality of so many American students, and the overall limitations of the American system of education. It was a good school academically, but there was a distinct insufficiency of courses that dealt with things non-American. For example, many of the kids I met at prep school had absolutely no idea where Cuba was. One of them once asked me how long it would take to drive to Havana—he had no idea that it was a separate country, with its own history and culture and society. Only later would I realize that most American kids grow up pretty naive, with very little comprehension of, or understanding about, the rest of the world. And only later would I realize that this deficiency translates into the policies set by the U.S. Government—a government of men and women too many of whom grow up with only a minimal understanding about the rest of the world.

I spent most of my vacations in Cuba: summers at the beach in Varadero, Christmas and spring vacations with my family, either in Sancti Spiritus, Havana, or at my Uncle Felix Claudio's farm. Things were good. Life was a game, full of surprises and challenges. On one vacation I brought a classmate from Perkiomen home with me and we sampled the nightlife in Havana, borrowing Toto's huge Buick sedan to tour the nightclubs, and spent a few days lying on the beach at Varadero looking at beautiful women.

There were political changes taking place all during this time, of course, but like most teen-agers I didn't take much notice of them. I do, however, remember listening to a lot of conversations about Fidel Castro and his guerrilla movement in the Sierra Maestra. There had been warning signs that his populist, democratic propaganda was just a facade, and my family worried that, because of the precariousness of Batista's regime, the guerrillas could conceivably splinter our society. One memory remains strong: we were convinced—despite what Castro was putting out at the time—that Fidel was, underneath it all, a communist. While few of the student groups who worked in the anti-Batista underground came out behind Castro, most of Cuba's known communists supported his insurrection. And that alarmed my family, as they were all very much anticommunist in their philosophy.

In retrospect, two points occur to me about Castro. The first is the naiveté with which he and his "revolution" were greeted by the United States; second is the amount of time it took Americans to realize that he was indeed a communist, and the dangers that an expansionist communist regime ninety miles from the U.S. can portend.

Perhaps it was the corruption of the Batista regime in its final days and—as was learned only later, its laissez-faire policies concerning the U.S. organized-crime syndicates that controlled many of the Havana hotels and casinos much the same way they did in Las Vegas—that made Fidel Castro, the seeming underdog, such a favorite here in the United States.

Maybe it was the articles by the writer Herbert Matthews that depicted Fidel as a romantic guerrilla hero, majestic in his fatigues, with his beard and florid speeches. Maybe it is just that Americans are altogether too trusting. The fact is that Fidel was not what he appeared to be—and many of us in Cuba knew it.

He wasn't even a member of the proletariat, despite his many efforts to "dress down" and speak for the common man. Like other revolutionary terrorists (Yasser Arafat comes to mind) he was a member of the upper class. His father, Angel (who once worked for the United Fruit Company), owned a 23,000-acre farm in Oriente Province.

When Batista and his family fled, early in the morning of New Year's Day, 1959, I was in Mexico with my parents, who had gone there on an extended vacation. (It turned out to be more extended than they or I ever guessed at the time!) They never returned to Cuba again, although I did (under very different circumstances). The beautiful house in Sancti Spiritus remained with our maid Minina— who was over one hundred years old, and so infirm that we hired a maid to take care of her—the big house's sole permanent resident.

Finally, in 1964, Castro appropriated our house and everything in it. That almost killed my father. He told me at the time, "I never want to go back to Cuba—even if Castro is gone. That way, the house will always be as it was. Fidel stole everything, but he can't take away my memories."

What I remember about those chaotic first days was the worrying. We worried about whether my Uncle Toto had escaped. As a member of Batista's government he was certainly on Castro's wanted list, and my parents were relieved when they heard, on January 3, that Toto had fled to Key Marathon in the Florida keys. We also feared that those in the family who stayed behind, either out of choice or because they were unable to escape, would be singled out for retribution. But there was something else as well. It was the gnawing realization that Castro was trying to strip my family not only of its material wealth, which was considerable, but also to deprive us of our history, our pride, our whole way of life. He may have succeeded in his first goal. But our pride, our honor, our history, and our values we did not have to pack up in boxes. They came with us in our hearts and to this day remain intact.

There is something indescribable about having your roots torn out; about losing your past; about becoming a refugee. So many Americans came to this country as refugees—from the pogroms in Eastern Europe, from the civil wars in Italy and Spain, from the famine in Ireland. Most of those who escaped to this country in the nineteenth century are well integrated into the American fabric now: Italian Americans, Irish Americans, Jewish Americans they call themselves. And, having pulled themselves up by the bootstraps, as they used to say in the Horatio Alger novels, we Americans often tend to forget what an incredibly wrenching experience it can be to have to leave your homeland with only what you can carry on your back, and start your life again from scratch. We were not the first, and certainly were not the last, to be uprooted. After us came Haitians, Russians, Vietnamese, Cambodians, and Nicaraguans, to name only a few.

I'd read about refugees and immigration in American history classes at Perkiomen but hadn't given the subject much thought. Now, in 1959, I was a refugee myself. More than anything else it made me mad. Castro had no right to take my life and uproot it. So, like thousands of other Cubans, I began making plans to do something about it. And up to this day I continue the fight for the liberation of my homeland. There are too many friends of mine who died for the freedom of Cuba. I will be betraying them if I stop now. For me it is a never-ending commitment that will end only when Cuba is free. Then, and only then, will I be really free.

By the time I went to Mexico to visit my parents at the end of my junior year, I'd decided to act. Mexico City was filled with Cuban exiles—hundreds of them—and there were stories circulating about a force called the Anti-Communist Legion of the Caribbean, which was being formed in the Dominican Republic to fight Castro.

It made sense to me that the so-called tyrant and dictator Rafael Leonidas Trujillo would back an anti-Castro army. He had good reason: by June 1959, Castro had already launched an attack on the Dominican Republic, sending an estimated 250 Cubans to invade and fight a guerrilla war against Trujillo.

One interesting confidential memorandum sent on June 4, 1959, from Castro to one of the rebel leaders, Captain Enrique Jiménez Moya, outlined two civilian operations that would run parallel to the military campaign. The first of these, Operation Rome, was the elimination of the Catholic Church in the Dominican Republic—including what Castro referred to as "clerical elimination." The second phase, Operation Agro, entailed the systematic destruction "of statues and monuments that idolize Trujillo and, generally, those of his family." (The Dominican operation was only the first of Castro's revolutionary activities. Soon thereafter he would send Cubans to Venezuela and Nicaragua as well. It didn't take long for him to begin his communist expansionism.)

Not that Trujillo was any great lover of democracy—quite the opposite. But he was willing to provide anti-Castro Cubans a base from which to operate, and so I made up my mind to go down there, join the Anti-Communist Legion, and fight. The only problem was that, being seventeen, I was a minor, and the Dominicans ruled that before they would authorize my visa I'd have to provide a note of consent from my parents.

My father refused. "I won't sign what might be your death warrant," he told me, as we sat in my parents' room at the Hotel Ontario in Mexico City, the consent form on a table between us. "For God's sake, Felix, you're only seventeen—a child. Think of what it would do to your mother if something happened to you."

"I understand your concern," I said. "But I have made up my mind to go and fight."

"And," my father added, "what about school? You have only one more year before you finish. Go back to Perkiomen and graduate. Then I'll think about giving you permission."

"I can't wait, Father. I don't want to wait."

"The matter is closed, Felix. I will not sign the consent form."

I looked at him. I understood his concern and his worry. But I was not to be denied. My Basque genes took over. "Father, I realize you believe you are acting in my best interests. But this is something I feel strongly about—and if you won't sign the papers, I'll forge your signature and go anyway."

Maybe he thought I was bluffing—I don't know. But he simply said, "That's fine—do what you want. But I will not sign it. If you do this and you get yourself killed, which is altogether likely, I don't want it on my conscience."

I took a pen from my pocket and signed his name to the form—right in front of him. It wasn't a great forgery, but how would they know? He watched but said nothing. Within two weeks I was on my way to fight against Castro, the beginning of a commitment that has not yet ended.

Because there were so many Cuban exiles in Mexico City, I'd thought—naively—that hundreds and hundreds of patriots would be going to the Dominican Republic. As it worked out, there was a lot of rhetoric and very little action. Only two of us, I and a man named Antonio Muñiz, who was a lawyer, made the trip from Mexico City back to Miami and from there to General Andrew Harper Airport in Ciudad Trujillo, the Dominican capital. We took that route because we had U.S. visas. Other volunteers made their way through Central or South America. In my passport was a green courtesy visa stamp from the Dominicans—Number 60. On the Miami–Ciudad Trujillo leg we were joined by another four exiles. Some army!

We arrived on July 4, 1959, and I remember hoping at the time that the date would eventually become as auspicious for Cubans as it was for Americans.

My first days as a revolutionary guerrilla were not bad at all. We were met at the airport by General Pedraza himself, who drove us to his house—Number 66 on the appropriately named Cordell Hull Street. He gave us strong Cuban coffee and outlined the goals of the organization. From there we went around the corner to the Hotel Paz (today it's called the Hispañiola), where I was assigned a third-floor room with an ocean view and a little terrace. Life was great. We could sign for our meals in the hotel dining room, go swimming in the luxurious pool, and walk the hot streets just like tourists. It felt like a vacation.

Wherever you went in the capital that he'd named after himself, the dictator Trujillo was there too. On the front of our hotel was a big electric sign that said in bright letters, VIVIMOS FELICES GRACIAS A TRUJILLO—"We live in happiness thanks to Trujillo." In the lobby hung a huge portrait of Trujillo in a white uniform, bedecked in ribbons and medals. The elevator in the Paz was an old-fashioned affair, one of those European-styled contraptions that looked like a cage. As it rose or descended, you could stare at the walls between the floors. There, too, Trujillo was in evidence: "Trujillo is the compass of the Navy," read a sign between the ground and the first floor. "Trujillo is the compass of aviation," proclaimed the next level. And between the second and third floors, "Trujillo is the lighthouse who brightens the path of the Dominican people." Outside the university was a statue of Trujillo dressed in a toga. It bore the legend "The First Teacher of the Republic." There were more ominous signs in every prison in the country: "God is in Heaven—Trujillo is on Earth." His influence extended even to Dominican cigarettes, one popular brand of which was called El Benefactor.

I saw Trujillo a couple of times as he came to visit his racehorses, which were kept in the presidential stables across from our hotel. He was a short man with a carefully trimmed mustache, who wore a flashy uniform and rode in a huge black Chrysler Imperial limousine with a chauffeur but no bodyguards. Of course, he didn't need bodyguards: there were policemen stationed every fifty meters around the stables complex whenever he was there.

One of the first things I was told before leaving Mexico was never to criticize Trujillo either publicly or privately. "Your rooms will be bugged," we were warned, "and no matter what you think of his totalitarian regime, keep your mouths shut, because Trujillo is the only one who's given us a base from which to fight Castro."

The advice was sound. One day I had occasion to visit the Dominican army colonel who worked as the hotel's administrator. In his office were eight Revere reel-to-reel tape recorders and a complicated switchboard system that allowed him, I guessed, to listen to conversations in any room he wanted to. There were rumors, too, about what happened to political dissidents in the Dominican Republic. I was told they simply disappeared—for good.

We stayed at the Hotel Paz four glorious days. Then we were driven by car to begin our training at the Dominican naval base officially called the José Trujillo Valdez naval station but known because of its heat and horrible conditions as *Las Calderas del Diablo*—The devil's boilers, or just Las Calderas—where we arrived late at night. There were a lot of problems to contend with. I was just a kid, after all, whose background of private schools and the good life in Cuba and the U.S. had in no way prepared me for the Spartan conditions in which we were about to live.

There were about 350 of us in all: 100 or so Cubans, about 150 Spaniards, and an eclectic mix of Europeans: Germans, Greeks—even a Yugoslavian pilot who'd defected with a MiG fighter. I was the second youngest in camp—most of the fighters were men in their thirties and forties. I knew almost nobody except my family's longtime friend, Lieutenant Colonel Lutgardo Martín Pérez, who was formerly the head of police patrol cars in Havana, and his son, Roberto, nicknamed Macho. One friend I did make was a Cuban named Orlando Rodríguez. Orlando and I later served together in Guatemala, at Fort Benning Georgia, and I saw him in Vietnam.

When I arrived, only about half the force was there. The others, including Macho, were out mopping up the last of the guerrillas Castro had infiltrated a couple of months previously to destabilize Trujillo's regime. In fact, the only combat the Legion ever saw was in the Dominican Republic—not Cuba.

Trujillo had initially come up with a novel yet effective way to deal with the invaders. He knew Castro had sent in roughly 250 guerrillas. So he put out the word to all the farmers in the areas where the Cubans had landed—Constanza, where they landed by air, using a Cuban plane painted to resemble a Dominican air force aircraft, and Puerto Plata, where they came by sea—that for each Cuban brought in, he would pay one thousand dollars cash per head.

The farmers would know the Cubans, Trujillo's message said, because they all had beards, just like Castro. Now, the Dominican *campesinos*—the peasants—they were simple people, and when Trujillo said he'd pay $1000 per *head*, they took him literally. So farmers started showing up at Dominican army posts with burlap bags of bearded heads to collect their rewards. And Trujillo ended up paying a lot more than $250,000—because a lot more bearded heads were being turned in than there were Cuban invaders. There weren't, we joked, very many Cubans left for the Legion to fight against.

Life as a revolutionary was not as I'd expected it. First of all, the food was terrible. They'd budgeted only thirty-five cents per day per person for food, and it was horrible. We had a cook named Rossini, an Italian who sweated all the time—right into the pots. The swarms of flies were unbearable. You'd end up picking them out of your plate. For the first four days I didn't touch a thing. Then hunger won out and I had to eat. But it was bad!

Breakfast was basically dirty-colored hot water that Rossini called coffee accompanied by a piece of bread so hard that if you hit someone with it you'd probably kill him. Lunch and dinner came from the same big pots—rice, over which was poured a souplike substance that had bits of bone and gristle and sometimes even a little meat.

The Anti-Communist Legion of the Caribbean was an organization run on a shoestring—a frayed shoestring at that. We received no salaries. If the officers were paid, I never heard about it at the time, although later it was rumored that some Dominican officers skimmed money from the Legion's food budget. In fact, my parents had to send me a few dollars each month so that I could buy tubes of condensed milk to put in the coffee, just to make it drinkable, and perhaps a piece of cooked chicken once a week or so if I could get to the small village that lay just outside the base for an hour or so of rest.

Mostly, we trained. The schedule was basic military; our instructors were fellow Cubans and some Dominicans. We'd get up early— six or so—and start the day with calisthenics. Then would come arms training. We worked hard learning how to break down the old M-1 Garand rifles—the same big, heavy rifles the U.S. Marines used to use—and the .30-caliber machine gun, the 30.06 Springfield rifle and the .45-caliber pistol. In time I got pretty good at being able to assemble and disassemble all those weapons. I also became proficient on the firing range, as I'd had a fair amount of experience at shooting on my Uncle Felix Claudio's farm. By the time I left the Legion, I was ranked the number three shot in my company of ninety soldiers.

We marched a lot, too. At first the officers just walked us from point to point without any equipment. It wasn't so bad. Then they started loading us down: rifles, packs, ammo. Our feet blistered and hurt as they marched us through sand and through jungle on progressively longer and longer hikes, until we could go thirty, forty, even fifty kilometers at a stretch. The longest hikes were done on a highway so an ambulance could come and get those who collapsed from the heat—and quite a few did just that.

We trained for about six weeks. Then, in early August, we were given new uniforms and equipment and told to make ready for our first mission.

I was able to get a couple of days' leave in Ciudad Trujillo, where I stayed again at the Paz, happy to eat well and sleep comfortably. One thing that shocked me, however, was the lack of operational security. I couldn't believe it—there I was, in the lobby, mixing with tourists and who knows who else, when an announcement came over the hotel's public-address system: "Will all the volunteers who are willing to fight for the liberation of Cuba please meet with Lieutenant Colonel Angel Sánchez Mosquera at the front desk." When we finally left in a gray Dominican navy bus, the maids waved goodbye telling us, "Have a good time in Cuba." Everybody seemed to know who we were—and what we were about to do.

Phase one of the plan was to load five of us into a big Sikorsky helicopter at Las Calderas and chopper to San Isidro Air Force Base. From there the small advance group would fly to Cuba in one of the three C-47 aircraft that had taken Batista and his family from Cuba the night he fled the country, land near the city of Trinidad on the southern coast, and set up a base of operations. When it was secured, the rest of the invasion force would be flown in a day or so later. We were confident the people in the Trinidad area would support us, and that within a matter of days we would be able to expand the area under our control to my old hometown of Sancti Spiritus, about forty miles away. That really excited me.

I was the youngest soldier in the advance party, and I wasn't selected because I was better than the rest—but because I was skinnier. Rossini's cooking had finally gotten to me, and I'd lost a lot of weight during training, and our officers probably figured I'd get better food on the air base than what we had at the camp. One thing disappointed me, however: I was not going to remain in Cuba with the others in the vanguard. I was assigned as a gunner on the C-47. My responsibilities were to protect the plane and assist the pilots in refueling and checking the oil. As a member of the Legion's second battalion, I would land only with the main force.

Finally we climbed into the chopper that would take us on the first leg of our journey. I sat next to my friend Roberto Martín Pérez, excited and just a little nervous, but confident that we would succeed in our mission. Then, just as the blades started to turn, Roberto's father, Lutgardo, climbed on board the aircraft and spoke to us.

"Only one of you can go," he shouted over the engine noise.

"Why?" we both demanded to know.

He looked at Roberto. "You are my son." He looked at me. "And you are like a son to me, Felix."

Then he explained that his conscience wouldn't allow him to let two boys he considered his sons fly on the same mission in the same aircraft.

"I'll go," I said.

Martín Pérez's father shook his head. "No," he said. "You are younger than Roberto—and he has more experience. He was a sergeant in the police."

I protested, but it did no good. Reluctantly I left the chopper, was replaced at San Isidro by a lieutenant named Betancourt, and watched, disappointed, as it took off.

The mission was a disaster. Castro knew of our plans and had troops waiting as the plane landed near Trinidad. Our people were all killed or captured—indeed, Roberto Martín Pérez would spend the next twenty-eight years in Cuban prisons. If I had gone with him, I probably would not have survived. In the years to come his upstanding and courageous conduct in prison was an inspiration to me. To continue what we both started has up to this day motivated my commitment to the freedom of Cuba.

In fact, we found out what had happened to our advance force not from our own people or the Dominicans, but from Cuban radio. We were in our barracks, waiting to load onto trucks that would take us to San Isidro, when we overheard a broadcast from Havana saying that the Cuban army had captured a plane and also some of the invaders on it, and killed the rest.

Shortly thereafter, we moved to a fort at Constanza because of rumors that Castro was going to send his air force to bomb Las Calderas. Our living conditions improved immensely, as Constanza had comfortable quarters and we were allowed access to the town's swimming pool. We conducted war games and maneuvers, and I succeeded in becoming one of the Legion's few military policemen, ultimately was promoted to corporal, and commanded a squad of three Greeks and five Spaniards.

Life at Constanza was as good as life at Calderas had been bad. I met a fair number of girls, went to a dance or two, and lived pretty well. But by October, the company doctor confined me to bed for a two-week period. Somehow, I'd contracted a terrible case of hepatitis, so my parents came from Miami, where they'd moved in August, picked me up and flew me back to Florida.

Looking back, I see how naive and unprepared we all were in those days. We knew nothing of the complexities involved in launching and supporting a military operation in hostile territory hundreds of miles from a secure base camp.

Today, I realize that we were doomed from the very start. Back then, I was simply heartbroken over our failure. We had trained hard; we had suffered in the jungles, endured the flies, the bad food, and the aged equipment in the hope that our sacrifices would make a contribution to the freedom of Cuba. Yet Castro had dashed our plans before most of us ever set foot on Cuban soil.

3 By the time I returned to Miami in November 1959, the influx of Cubans fleeing Castro was making itself felt city-wide. By the end of the year, more than one hundred thousand Cuban refugees had made their way north to *Los Estados Unidos*. Many were skilled workers and professionals. Mostly, we in Miami settled around Eighth Street Southwest, in an area that has come to be known as Little Havana.

As has been the case with most immigrant groups who come to the United States, we Cubans tended to live in close proximity. It helped to ease our adjustment. It also made it easier for Castro to keep an eye on what we were doing: infiltrated among the thousands of Cubans who sought refuge in Miami were—and still are—a large number of agents from G-2, Cuban intelligence, which today is called the DGI.

I recovered from hepatitis and went back to Perkiomen for my final semester at my parents' request. They insisted that I graduate. I worked hard. As I recall, I was required to pass all the exams from the semester I'd lost. So I forsook sports and extra-curricular activities and crammed. My grades weren't terrific, but in June I graduated with the rest of my class.

Although I did the schoolwork, my heart wasn't in it. By the time I left for Pennsylvania, I was already in contact with another anti-Castro group, the Cruzada Cubana Constitucional, or CCC. Unlike the Anti-Communist Legion of the Caribbean, this one was made up of people more my own age. It was headed by Pedro Luis Diaz Lanz, a pilot and the chief of Castro's air force who defected to the U.S. after making off with a plane and showering Havana with anti-Castro leaflets.

One of Diaz Lanz's top officers in the CCC was a man named Frank Sturgis, who would later become well known for his participation in the Watergate burglary; but back then he was a weapons instructor, having gained his expertise as a major in Fidel Castro's guerrilla army before he defected. Because of my experience in the Anti-Communist Legion, I was made a sort of platoon sergeant in the CCC.

Diaz Lanz's organization was one of many that had sprung up in the Miami area during this time (much later I would discover that there were ultimately scores of anti-Castro groups working in the Miami area by the end of 1961). The Diaz Lanz group was small: it was made up of somewhere between thirty and forty young Cuban idealists, most of whom I either knew in passing or were friends of mine. Our goal, similar in many ways to the Legion's, was to begin military operations against Castro.

Our problem was that we had neither weapons nor anywhere permanent to train. Instead, we would practice at shooting ranges and occasionally would go into the swamps west of Miami and spend a few hours training at being guerrillas.

Our lack of facilities was why, during spring vacation of my senior year at Perkiomen, my close friend Edgar Sopo Barreto and I, two eighteen-year-olds, found ourselves in Washington, D.C., sitting in the columnist Jack Anderson's office trying to convince him to support an invasion of Cuba.

As Sopo recalls, the whole thing was originally Frank Sturgis's idea. Sopo had been talking about trying to get U.S. Government support for our activities—but had no idea where to start. It was Sturgis who suggested to Sopo that a powerful columnist like Jack Anderson, who worked with Drew Pearson, might be the perfect person to help us out.

My English was better than Sopo's, so I became the spokesman. We'd heard of Jack Anderson. We knew Jack Anderson had connections to all the Washington bigshots—and if he was sympathetic to our anticommunist cause, we believed he could get us Government backing right away.

The question was how to get to Anderson. I mean, here we were, a bunch of young Cubans, most in their late teens and early twenties, whose primary goal in life was overthrowing Castro's communist government. Today, as I look back on it, we were naive and idealistic, and our expectation that a columnist would help us invade Cuba was completely unreal. But we were also committed. And so Sopo and I tried to figure out how to wangle an introduction to the famous man.

It was Sopo who came up with our method of entree. His father, who had recently died while incarcerated at La Cabaña Prison in Havana, had been a military doctor. He had once served in Washington, a tour of duty at the naval hospital in Bethesda, Maryland. One of Sopo's father's colleagues, a Cuban naval officer named Rodríguez Alonzo, was still living in Washington. Sopo called and asked if he knew Anderson.

"No, Edgar, I don't," Rodríguez Alonzo told Sopo. "But I know someone who might: Admiral Calvin Galloway." Sopo knew the name—Galloway had been at the Bethesda naval facility when Sopo's father was there in 1958.

"Could you call him?" Sopo asked. "Call him and tell him that we have to talk to Jack Anderson because we want to set up training camps and we need U.S. Government support, and we think Anderson's the only one who can help us do it."

To our amazement, Rodríguez Alonzo called back a couple of days later and told us we had an appointment with Anderson. We packed our best clothes, my Uncle Toto advanced us the plane fare, and off we went to Washington. The next day, we found ourselves sitting in Jack Anderson's office.

Anderson greeted us warmly. He asked us what we wanted, and didn't laugh when we said it was to overthrow Castro, and that we needed his help. As a matter of fact, he appeared to be very sympathetic to our cause. He listened as Sopo and I explained that we wanted his assistance in setting up a training camp so that we could form a brigade and invade Cuba.

Anderson nodded. He told us that it might be possible; that he had a friend who owned some land on a place called Martha's Vineyard—we had no idea where that was—and that if we got the green light from the U.S. Government, he'd try to persuade his friend to let us use it for training.

Then, somehow, the conversation turned to weapons. I told Anderson that one of our biggest problems was that we had no arms.

Anderson said he could help us in that area, too. He took us to another office in the same building, an office in which hung pictures of tanks and planes and photographs of Israeli soldiers, where he introduced us to an Israeli—a man who had a long scar running down the side of his face—who showed us the most incredible weapon I had ever seen. It was an Uzi submachine gun. The Israeli then showed us something even more amazing than the Uzi. It was an attachment that fit the submachine gun's barrel, which he said adapted it to fire an RPG—a rocket-propelled grenade. I remember handling it and thinking that if we had a few hundred of those we certainly could free all of Cuba.

"How many do you think you'll need?" the Israeli asked. "We have a large stock right here in Washington."

"Four or five hundred," I told him with a straight face. "How much would it cost us?"

He told us. Sopo and I blanched. "Don't worry." The Israeli laughed. "If you get the OK from the U.S. Government, we'll advance you the weapons and you'll pay us when Cuba is free."

To sidetrack for just a minute, it occurs to me that one question I was never asked by the Iran/Contra committees, by the special prosecutor, or by Senator John Kerry's staff was, "Who was the first contact you ever had in the arms business?" I would have had to answer that it was the famous columnist Jack Anderson!

In any case, Anderson took our names and promised us that he would talk to his influential friends. He told us he supported our cause and wished us well. We went back to Miami happily and absolutely convinced that he'd do something for us.

As a matter of fact, when, later on, the U.S. Government started to organize its anti-Castro operations, we were sure it was Jack Anderson who had managed to pull some strings for us, even though we had never heard from him again. Sopo and I actually felt proud because we thought we'd been the motivating factor behind Washington's decision.

We had no idea, of course, that as far back as December 11, 1959, the director of the CIA's Western Hemisphere Division, J.C. King, had written a memo to CIA director Allen Dulles that recommended taking action against what he described as the "far left" dictatorship of Fidel Castro.

Nor did we have any inkling that it was on January 13, 1960, months before we met Jack Anderson, that Allen Dulles first suggested direct covert action against Fidel. The evidence lies in the declassified minutes of a meeting of what came to be called the 5412 Group, which were printed in a 1975 U.S. Senate report, "Alleged Assassination Plots Involving Foreign Leaders." Fifty-four-twelve, which has also been known as the 40 Committee, the Special Group, and the 303 Committee, is made up of senior CIA, State Department, Department of Defense, and other Government agency representatives. Its function was to approve covert-action proposals. According to the U.S. Senate report, the January 23 minutes report that Dulles "noted the possibility that over the long run the U.S. will not be able to tolerate the Castro regime in Cuba and suggested that covert contingency planning to accomplish the fall of the Castro government might be in order."

I graduated from Perkiomen in June 1960 and was accepted as an architecture student at the University of Miami. My parents knew that I was more interested in joining an anti-Castro organization than I was in continuing my education, and they sought to bribe me away from my revolutionary activities with a car. So, for my graduation, Uncle Toto and my parents presented me with a turquoise-blue Austin Healy Sprite convertible. They made the six-hundred-dollar down payment, and I would find a summer job and pay the rest, then use the car to commute to the university in the fall.

I took a job—at a tropical-fish farm down in the Kendall area, south of Miami. And I had a good time that summer. I had my new car, a few dollars in my pocket, and my friends from the Diaz Lanz group. We hung out together, occasionally going to the movies or dinner, picking up girls, or just sharing sodas or fruit-juice punch.

We were a lot like most kids who have just graduated from high school, passing through that magical and somewhat mystical period between adolescence and young adulthood, when you spend a lot of time talking about your dreams and your hopes. The difference with us was that our dreams didn't have to do with jobs, or college, or that sort of thing. Instead, we talked about liberating Cuba.

The summer of 1960 was also a time of getting used to our new and much reduced circumstances. From the comfort of our life in Cuba we'd become refugees. Instead of our big houses in Sancti Spiritus and Havana, and my Uncle Felix Claudio's farm, we—my parents and I and Uncle Toto—had first moved to a small two-bedroom wood-frame house off West Flagler Street. By the summer of 1960 we'd all moved into more spacious quarters, a one-story rambler in Northeast Miami with a lovely backyard, terrace, and barbecue. We weren't poor by any means, but things were . . . different, and adjustments had to be made. My father, in fact, would soon go to work as a physical therapist for a financier named Abe Bernstein. Bernstein's nephew, Morey, a millionaire financier, was the author of the 1950s best-seller, *The Search for Bridey Murphy.* Morey would become like an older brother to me.

One of the adjustments I made on my own was a decision to fight for my country instead of attending the University of Miami. During the summer of 1960, word spread through the Cuban community that volunteers were being sought to go to fight against Castro.

Few of us had any idea who was behind the plan. Rumor had it that some rich Cuban was paying the bills, with the approval of the

U.S. Government. Now, of course, we know that the CIA ran the operation. But to be frank, I don't think one Cuban in a thousand knew what the CIA was back in the summer of 1960.

What we knew was this: you showed up at a storefront in Miami, and you gave your name and filled out an application, and then you were told that you'd be called when you were needed. The instructions were simple: When you receive the call, you show up in a designated place. Don't bring any clothes, or radios, or even a suitcase. Nothing but a toothbrush and a razor. It all sounded intriguing.

I made preparations to go secretly—not saying a word to my mother and father, who I knew would have raised hell with me. So I smuggled a set of clothes out of the house, and the day I received the call, I left just as I normally did when I went to the fish farm, wearing shorts and a T-shirt and a pair of sneakers.

But instead of going to work, I drove to a friend's house. I gave him the keys to the Austin Healy and instructed him to wait several hours, then go to my parents and tell them what I'd done.

"Tell them," I said, "that I'm already out of the country and there is nothing they can do."

A woman friend drove me to the rendezvous point and waited. I was lucky she did: I discovered to my dismay that the pickup was being delayed because of bad weather. "Go home," I was told. "It will be in a few days. We'll let you know."

That was impossible. I'd already burned my bridges. And so, even before I worked for the CIA I embarked on my first clandestine mission: hiding from my parents—a mission that ended up lasting for not one, but three days. I spent the time at the home of my friend's parents.

Finally I was picked up—one of three or four people—and we were driven by car to the Homestead area, south of Miami, where we were taken to an empty house out in the middle of the woods. First we were assigned registration numbers. Mine was 2718. Later I learned that the numbers for infantry personnel began at 2500, so that if Castro found out about our brigade, he'd believe it was larger than it actually was.

Our clothes and personal possessions were taken, we were strip-searched by Cuban officers to make sure we weren't carrying any forbidden articles, like compasses or weapons, and then we were given khaki shirts and trousers—a sort of sanitized uniform that gave no hint of who we were—by the officer in charge, a former Cuban colonel named Martín Elena. Martín Elena told us that we were about to go to a secret location, a training camp outside of the U.S. that was being financed by a rich Cuban who used to own sugar mills before Castro. He added that the camp wasn't quite finished, so we might have to help in the construction, as well as do our training. That turned out to be an understatement!

Later the same day our watches were taken away and we were put in an enclosed truck and driven for hours. Later we discovered that the truck had driven in circles so we'd have no idea where we were going. By the time we arrived, we believed we'd been taken somewhere in the middle of the state. Actually, we were taken to the Opa-locka Airport, which is due west of North Miami, and less than an hour's drive from Homestead. The truck drove into a closed hangar and we disembarked to be greeted by U.S. Immigration and Naturalization Service officials, who gave each of us a form to fill out. If we were leaving the country, we were apparently doing it with the approval of the U.S. Government.

Soon after, we heard an aircraft taxiing up to the hangar, and we were put back inside the truck, where we waited for what seemed an interminable length of time. Then, suddenly, the ramp of the truck was opened, and voices shouted at us: "Go–go–go! Move it—don't look left or right!" And off we went, directly into the airplane. I sneaked a look as I ran, but saw nothing, as two ropes hung with curtains had been stretched from the truck to the aircraft, shielding us from view.

The plane was a C-54, and inside we sat on canvas benches that ran the length of the aircraft—just like paratroopers. There were windows, but they had been painted black. As soon as the plane was loaded, the door was closed and the American crew got us airborne immediately. We flew for some hours—no one knew how long because we had no watches—and then we landed.

One of our officers opened the hatch, and we saw that it was still night. We were ordered out of the plane to stretch our legs and discovered that we were sitting at the end of a long runway, out of sight of any buildings. Soon after we arrived, a Jeep drove up. I noticed immediately that it had Guatemalan plates on it, but the plates were not attached too well, and I thought that the jeep was a trick to convince us that we were in Guatemala when in fact we were either still in Florida or we'd flown to somewhere else in Latin America. In truth, we *were* in Guatemala, at the San José military airport, where we'd landed because our final destination, Retalhuleu, had no runway lights—hence the aircraft couldn't land until daybreak.

After two hours or so on the ground, we took off, and after a flight that couldn't have lasted more than twenty minutes we touched down on a rough strip, were fed a big breakfast of bacon, eggs, toast, and coffee, all served on a clean divided army tray. Then we were loaded into trucks for the trek to our training camp. In subsequent days I'd remember that tray with increasing fondness, because it turned out to be the last clean eating utensil I'd see in months.

We were two or three truckloads of sweltering recruits who made the journey through the steamy Guatemalan countryside. We saw nothing, as the canvas sides and tailgates were closed. We simply sat, bouncing as the truck hit what seemed like every rut and pothole in existence, growing hotter and hotter. After what seemed like hours, the truck groaned to a halt, the canvas was unhitched, and we were told to jump out, which we did—into a sea of mud.

"The truck's stuck," the officer said. "We're going to march the rest of the way."

"March" was an overstatement. It was September—the height of the rainy season in Guatemala—and we slogged our way up a road that led through jungle and foothills until we started to climb and climb and climb. Finally the officer stopped us. "There," he pointed proudly. "There's the camp."

We looked at what the CIA called Trax base camp. It wasn't Fort Benning—not even close. But it was ours—a real military training camp. The buildings were all in place, but they lacked showers and indoor plumbing. The accommodations were very basic. We slept on bunk beds that were racked together in sixes—two stacks of three. On the other hand, we weren't there on vacation, but to become an army. So we built ourselves privies and showers, became accustomed to the poisonous snakes that riddled the jungle hillsides, put up with the dirty trays they served the food on, and trained to be soldiers.

We would later become known as the 2506 Brigade, named after volunteer number 2506, Carlos Rodríguez Santana, who shortly before I arrived at Trax camp had been killed during a training hike. There was a benefit arising from that rough Guatemalan jungle training camp that I didn't see at the time: most of the friends I made there I have kept ever since. It was at Trax I first met Nestor Pino, who is now a colonel in the U.S. Army (and one of the best). And José Basulto, the radio operator who would later teach me communications skills over pancakes at his mother's house. And dozens of others who, over the years, have remained close to me.

Our instructors were mostly foreigners, led by a U.S.-trained Filipino colonel named Napoleón Valeriano whom we code-named El Chino Vallejo. Valeriano was a West Point graduate—or so we were told—who during World War II had been infiltrated by submarine to conduct guerrilla activities in the Philippines against the Japanese, and later, after the war, against the Huks, communist-led terrorists based on Luzon. He was very young at the time, in his twenties probably, and he knew that the Filipino peasants he'd been sent to organize and lead wouldn't have very much confidence on him. So he invented a character named Colonel Volcano, an elderly, wise, and very experienced officer, who, he explained to everyone, was the head of the unit. He, Valeriano, was Volcano's young assistant.

No one ever saw Colonel Volcano, of course. But Valeriano was always on hand to explain what the wise old officer wanted, and help get it done. It was an effective ruse, as it allowed the young officer a lot of flexibility in his activities.

So we listened to El Chino Vallejo's stories, and also paid attention to our other teachers, who included Ukrainians and other Europeans. We gave the other foreign instructors nicknames as well. (Interestingly, we had the habit of referring to all non-Cubans as foreigners.) They became *Los Halcones*—the falcons—and they'd all had experience in resistance movements during World War II. There were also a few American "foreigners" dressed in civilian clothes, but all looking and talking like military people.

We did a lot of physical training and worked out with modern weapons: 57-mm recoilless rifles, Thompson submachine guns, grease guns, .45-caliber pistols, and the like. One thing I found curious at the time was the fact that after we'd finish our weapons training, the guns and ammunition would be taken away from us. Later I learned it was because the Americans were afraid that we'd mutiny and take over the camp.

We even received basic paratrooper training, learning how to fall correctly and roll. We never made any jumps but worked from a tower instead. And we were given instructions in explosives and military techniques, and courses in such areas as first aid, communications, and basic survival. We were even taught how to do things like gauge distance by timing muzzle-flash and sound.

To do that, our instructors took us to a precipice high above the camp at night. We were instructed to watch the crest of a mountain a couple of miles away. There was a flash of gunfire—and then the sound of the shot rolled toward us a few seconds later.

"OK," the instructor said. "What you do is, when you see the muzzle flash, you start counting in seconds—a thousand one; a thousand two; a thousand three—until you hear the sound of the weapon. Every second that the shot takes to get to you means the muzzle is half a mile away. One second, half a mile. Two seconds, a mile. Three seconds, a mile and a half, and so on."

Roughly three months after I arrived, our unit saw combat for the first time. But not against Castro. We were called in to help put down a coup attempt in Puerto Barrios, close to the Honduran border, against Guatemalan president Miguel Ydigoras Fuentes.

There were about six hundred of us at Trax; just about everyone volunteered to help the Guatemalan president, and two hundred of us were selected. We were issued weapons, then trucked to Retalhuleu air base where we were to board the planes that would take us to Puerto Barrios. We were somewhat nervous during the ride and we kept our submachine guns at the ready, pointed toward the jungle in case of an ambush. If somebody had fired a shot by mistake, we would probably have blown away a few hundred meters of roadside.

At the air base, we waited for our orders, everyone sleeping at the side of the runway because there were no quarters for us. The plan was for about a hundred of us to fly to Puerto Barrios—three C-46s of us, roughly thirty-three to a plane—take over the airfield after it had been softened up by our own Free Cuba air force of B-26 light bombers (the same planes and pilots, incidentally, that would later fly over the Bay of Pigs) and hold it until the rest of the force arrived.

The tricky part was deplaning. As far as the Guatemalans knew, Puerto Barrios was completely in enemy hands, and the airfield would be defended. So our C-46s would land quickly, and we would go down ropes as the plane taxied, rolling like paratroopers to the side of the runway to set up our defensive perimeter. I was given a .30-caliber machine gun. My role was to lay down protective fire from the doorway as the plane went down the runway, then, after the last of the men jumped, I'd toss the machine gun to an assistant and go down the rope myself.

We tried it three times—twice from a stationary C-46, then as a final test, from a moving aircraft. Then it was time to go. We piled onto our aircraft and took off. The ride was silent. Nobody did much talking although we were all pretty excited. Finally we arrived over Puerto Barrios, and the day's first screw-up occurred. The B-26s hadn't finished bombing and strafing the area, so we had to circle above the bay and wait for them to complete their mission. It was incredible to watch from the hatch of our C-46 as the bombers dived, circled, and dived again to do their deadly work. One scored a direct hit on a truckload of rebel soldiers, and from our vantage point two thousand feet away some of us said later they could see the bodies fly.

"OK," one of the officers finally shouted, "we're going in."

Our plane banked toward the field and lowered its flaps. I should have been nervous, but I wasn't. Instead, I was overwhelmed with a sensation of calmness—the resigned feeling that I'd placed myself in fate's hands, and whatever would happen would happen. There was also a tremendous excitement—our first combat experience together. I looked down the row of my fellow Cubans, all holding their weapons. Their faces were firm and serious. No one was laughing or cracking jokes. At that moment, we became brothers-in-arms, and I began to comprehend for the first time what that phrase, which I'd heard so many times before, really meant.

We were on our final approach. From the port I could see the B-26 making a protective run for us, raking the runways with lethal .50-caliber machine-gun fire.

Touchdown. Our C-46 bounced as it hit the runway, and everyone tensed. There were thirty-three of us aboard, and our officers had said that the enemy might number as many as two thousand. We were the first plane in—and if we could secure a runway, the others would follow. I hoped they'd follow quickly. I looked down the fuselage. My friend Nestor Pino was in the doorway, one hand tight on the rope, the other holding a Thompson submachine gun. He would lead the way.

The rear wheel came down and the pilot reversed the engines, the sound of the props roaring in our ears. Quickly the plane taxied down the runway, moving at perhaps forty miles per hour—too fast for us to descend. Outside I saw evidence of the battle that had been going on: a destroyed helicopter, old airplanes—and yet as I caught a glimpse of the terminal, painted green, I saw that the glass seemed to be completely intact.

Then, suddenly, a Guatemalan officer shouted above the noise: "We're taking fire! They're shooting at us!"

The plane reached the end of the runway and spun around, making a wide, fast turn onto the taxiway. I readied the .30-caliber machine gun.

All hell broke loose as everyone who had a weapon that could point out a hatch or doorway fired blindly toward the edge of the runways. Somebody stuck a Browning automatic rifle between Pino's legs as he half-dangled out of the plane and blasted away. Before anybody could jump out, the plane gained speed, and took off from the taxiway. Later, Pino told me, "I was so anxious for action that if the plane had been going five or six miles an hour slower I would have jumped—and I'd have been left behind on my own when it took off again."

Later, when we returned to Retalhuleu, I was one of the people who checked the fuselage of the aircraft thoroughly—and we discovered not a single bullet hole. Even though we hadn't actually seen any fighting, we were assembled the following day and the Guatemalan minister of defense showed up and congratulated us for our help. He said that the rebel garrison had been told that one thousand heavily armed, highly trained Cubans were coming to fight against them with sophisticated military equipment. When the rebels heard that, he said, they surrendered without firing a shot. He then told us we were all being granted honorary Guatemalan citizenship, to thank us for our work on behalf of his country. So much for all those covered trucks and blacked-out aircraft. If there were any questions left about where we actually were, the Guatemalan defense minister answered them for us that bright, hot day.

And, to be honest, it didn't matter to us where we were, who was paying for our training, or what specific organization sponsored the camps. We thought only of our final objective: to invade Cuba and free it from Castro's dictatorship. Nobody I knew at Camp Trax spent any time wondering whether the U.S. administration or the CIA, or whoever, was "behind" our operation. We didn't ask. We didn't care. We were just grateful to be allowed the opportunity to fight for the freedom of our country.

4 Soon after our abortive combat experience, the instructors began to make the first selection for 2506 Brigade's elite infiltration units, called Grey teams. Each would be comprised of five men, based on the concept used by Napoleón Valeriano in the Philippines, and similar to the U.S. Army's Green Beret combat team. Most of us who were selected for the first "cut" of roughly eighty volunteers had similar backgrounds: we were mostly former or current students; young, physically very fit, and idealistic.

Each Grey team would include a team leader and four combat specialists: weapons and demolition, communications, psychological warfare, and intelligence. Ultimately, seven five-man teams would be chosen. It was a high-risk operation: thirty-five of us went to Cuba; only fifteen survived. The original mission of the Greys was to infiltrate "in black"—that is, without any reception team to ease its way—then to establish themselves in the countryside, win the trust of the locals, and organize guerrilla and resistance activities.

The reason for a "black," or surreptitious, entry was to prevent security leaks both in Cuba, and within the anti-Castro forces. It is risky to go in without support. Yet at the same time, if no one knows you are coming, then no one can compromise you during infiltration, when a team is tremendously vulnerable.

Even though precautions had been taken when the primary selections were made, at least one Castro spy, for example, made it into the Grey teams. His name was Benigno Pérez. We knew him to be a former lieutenant in Castro's armed forces who, like many of his fellow officers, had defected to the U.S.

Pérez was a hardworking individual. I remember him as a small man who drove trucks and bulldozers, a cigar seemingly clenched permanently between his teeth. But one thing about him made me wary: the guy would never look you in the face. When you spoke to him he'd avert his eyes, as if he was ashamed of something. He was older than most of us, and I wondered why he was selected for the Grey teams. At the time I guessed it was because they believed he'd still have good contacts in Cuba as a former Castro officer.

I was happy when he was finally assigned to someone else's unit —I would have refused to have him on mine simply because I had a queasy feeling in my gut whenever Pérez's name was mentioned. But it wasn't so good for the guys he worked with, because Pérez didn't have good contacts in Cuba, but *great* contacts—many of them members of Castro's secret police—and every one of his fellow team members was captured. Today, Benigno Pérez lives the good life in Cuba as a high-ranking officer of the DGI.

After infiltration, our goal was to create, from scratch if necessary, an anti-Castro organization in Cuba. We would build networks, establish communications facilities and courier systems, and recruit people. When we had done that, other infiltration teams, known as Black teams, would arrive. They were comprised of specialized trainers, who would teach the resistance fighters how to receive air drops and set up maritime supply routes.

Ultimately, we were told our strategy was to create massive armed resistance in several areas of Cuba simultaneously, so that Castro, even though he had numerically superior forces, would not be able to concentrate them in one place. It was the old concept of divide and conquer—except in our case it would be divide and liberate.

When our operation became secure, the main force of Cuban freedom fighters would be brought to the province where we were strongest, a provisional government would be set up, and, we were told, immediately be recognized by the United States and by Latin American democracies.

That was the original concept. Whether it would have actually worked is a moot point, although I am still in agreement with the basic strategy. Yet in retrospect, the U.S. Government was also naive and unschooled in a number of areas. First, and perhaps most significantly, the Agency, for all its alleged sophistication, was curiously uneducated about Cuba and about us Cuban freedom fighters.

The CIA had won a tremendous victory in Guatemala six years earlier. In 1954, with the help of a relatively few armed Guatemalans, a good propaganda campaign, and a strong radio transmitter, the Agency managed to dislodge that country's leader, Jacobo Arbenz Guzmán, whose Guatemalan Labor Party had drifted more and more leftward until it became almost completely Marxist.

Nineteen sixties Cuba, however, had an entirely different set of dynamics, pressures, and internal realities. The Guatemalan armed forces in 1954, for example, numbered less than ten thousand. In 1960, Cuba's armed forces had about a quarter million. In Guatemala, Arbenz did not hold absolute power. In Cuba, Castro did. Yet despite the tremendous differences, the CIA decided to design its Cuban operation on the Guatemalan model and staffed it with many of the same American officers.

Moreover, the Agency had no Cubans working in high-ranking staff positions during the planning of these complex anti-Castro operations. Putting aside the racist overtones of that fact, it simply didn't make much sense to plan a costly and complex undertaking without the help of people who intimately knew both the country and the people the Agency was trying to help. The lack of Cubans in positions of responsibility and American naiveté were two elements that many of us who were there feel doomed the U.S.'s anti-Castro program from the very start.

But even the original concept of Grey team activities would be changed radically. I arrived in Guatemala in September 1960. By the time I was in that C-46 circling over Puerto Barrios in late November the United States had a new President-elect, John Fitzgerald Kennedy, and it was his administration, not Dwight Eisenhower's, that would determine our fates. Much later, we would discover that Kennedy's people had no intention of allowing an operation designed by Eisenhower to go forward. If Cuba was to be liberated, it would have to be done by an operation devised by Democrats, not Republicans. So, many of Ike's plans were scrapped.

The first outward sign of this was that our Filipino friend, El Chino Vallejo, was reassigned. In his place came a tall American named Frank who said he was an army colonel. He told us things had changed. Instead of a guerrilla movement, the U.S. was now planning a full-scale invasion of Cuba, backed by air support.

As far as the Grey teams were concerned, Colonel Frank's new ideas meant more training. By then our unit had been moved as a group to a place we called Garrapatenango (literally tick base, because of the insects that swarmed all over us), where we learned how to receive air drops—which is more complicated than it seems, as my friends in the Nicaraguan Democratic Resistance would learn some twenty-six years after I did.

It's not a matter of standing in a clearing and waving at a plane, or building a bunch of bonfires in a pattern. Clandestine air drops in hostile territory must be well-coordinated operations in which planes fly from airfields hundreds of miles away, taking circuitous routes to avoid detection, then come through enemy airspace, navigate to a precise spot on a map and drop their loads within a few yards of the target. The reception team must be able to communicate the exact coordinates for the air drop to the supply base, successfully get to the drop zone, guide the plane if necessary, and retrieve the goods —all without being discovered by the enemy.

Today, such drops have been made relatively easier with the implementation and use of LORAN (Long Range Navigation) or Omega advanced navigation systems, sophisticated, secure radios, and other communications gear, pilots' night-vision goggles, and infrared devices smaller than a pack of cigarettes that can be used to guide a plane over a drop zone. The infrareds, which were sometimes used by the Contras, and which I have helped obtain for the Salvadoran air force, are tremendously helpful. They are powered by a six-volt battery—the same kind used in most home smoke detectors. Invisible to the naked eye, they emit strong pulses of infrared light which, when seen with the assistance of night-vision goggles, can make the difference between success and failure in nighttime resupply or Medevac operations.

During the time I was helping to coordinate the Contra resupply missions from Ilopango Air Base in El Salvador, we tried repeatedly to get such infrared devices to help the American pilots and crews. We finally succeeded, but only after many of the early resupply missions ended in failure when our pilots could not locate the Contra forces they were supposed to supply, or when the Contras were unable to guide the aircraft precisely. And that was with 1980s communications. Similar exercises were much harder a quarter of a century before, in Garrapatenango—which was in the middle of a thick, inhospitable jungle filled with huge bloodsucking ticks and poisonous snakes. In such places, the reference points necessary for resupply air drops are nonexistent.

Our training was akin to a survival exercise: our only supplies of food were dropped to us by airlift. We were like guerrillas, perpetually on the run, while trying to guide the aircraft to where we were and to coordinate a clandestine supply drop. If we failed, we went hungry.

Indeed, something I discovered which would help me a lot in subsequent assignments was that accuracy *does* count. Missing a drop zone by one kilometer after a flight of several hundred miles may not sound like much, but if the drop happens to be in tough terrain, like Vietnam, El Salvador, or Nicaragua, it can take an hour or two to cover the lost ground—more if there are hostile forces in the area.

We also were instructed in tradecraft, which is the shoptalk word used by agents for describing the art of surviving in hostile territory. The truth of the matter is that despite all the instructions, all the books and pamphlets, and all the classwork, tradecraft is only really learned by experience. It is not an exact science, but what I like to think of as a survival science. There is only one rule: If it works, use it. If it doesn't work, you are usually dead or captured.

Mostly tradecraft is common sense and instinct. You have to be able to blend into your surroundings so as not to attract the attention of hostile intelligence or police agents. For example, clothes can be a problem. You can follow all the rules and still get caught because you're wearing a pair of obviously American shoes when you are trying to pass as an East German or a Yugoslavian. Or you infiltrate into Havana, but stick out like a sore thumb on the street because your shirt is more Miami than Miramar district.

We also tried to be careful when assigning Grey team members to make sure they were familiar with the area in which they'd operate.

I, for example, was first assigned to J team, which was being sent to the city of Santiago de Cuba in Oriente Province. Problem was that I'm from Sancti Spiritus in Las Villas Province. I had only been to Santiago once. I didn't know the streets or the local customs. I wasn't familiar with the dialect or the slang. So it would take a local cop about five seconds of casual conversation to find me out. It took a while to convince the Americans, but we were finally assigned to teams in which each member knew his area and would feel comfortable operating there.

Our instructors were veterans of World War II European resistance movements. They taught us some of the more technical aspects of tradecraft, such as passing messages or moving sizable quantities of equipment and weapons without being detected.

By the end of the year, we were moved to Panama for final training. We weren't supposed to know it was Panama—we went through the usual nonsense of blacked-out plane windows and closed canvas trucks. But there aren't too many places in the world where you're in a tropical area and you hear boat horns close by and occasionally catch a peek of a big liner moving slowly through a lock. We figured there were two possibilities: Panama or the Suez Canal. But we couldn't find any sand, and the flying time had been awfully short, so we guessed Panama. There were other hints that tested out newfound intelligence skills, too—like the small tags on the garbage cans, which read "Ft. Clayton—Canal Zone."

Actually, it didn't matter where we were, just so long as we got our training, which we did—most importantly, advanced weapons training, using Soviet and other East European equipment. We spent New Year's Eve 1960 in the Canal Zone. Our instructors provided Heineken beer and wine so we could celebrate. It was just about New Year 1961 that I came up with what I considered at the time a truly inspired idea: an operation that would shorten the war and save lives.

I volunteered to assassinate Fidel Castro, and the Americans took me up on it.

One day I was talking to a friend of mine with whom I had served in the Diaz Lanz group. I knew his family, which also had come from Las Villas Province. We were talking about the probability of success our infiltration teams would have, and I suggested that by assassinating Castro I might be able to save lives. He agreed, and I took the plan to the acting camp commander, an American we knew as Larry, and volunteered our services.

Soon thereafter Larry told me my idea had been accepted by the people in charge. Early in January we were all flown to Miami where we were assigned a third Cuban to be our radio operator, and where I was given a weapon. And what a weapon it was: a beautiful German bolt-action rifle with a powerful telescopic sight, all neatly packed in a custom-made padded carrying case. There was also a box of ammo, twenty rounds.

I was told that I wouldn't have to sight the rifle, as it had already been zeroed in. Apparently the resistance had obtained a building in Havana facing a location that Castro frequented at the time, and they'd managed to presight the rifle.

The Americans moved the entire infiltration unit to a place in the Homestead area while we waited for our boat. It looked like an old motel, although it was out in the boondocks, right near a bunch of tomato fields. The place had a pool, where we practiced paddling the rubber rafts we'd use to go from our boat to the shore. From our "headquarters," we drove by car down into the Keys, where at a predetermined spot we'd blink the headlights and a small boat would come to shore, retrieve us, and carry us to the yacht that would take us to Cuba.

Three times my friends and I tried to infiltrate Cuba with that damn rifle, and three times we failed. The boat we used was a power cruiser, maybe forty feet long, with air conditioning and luxurious appointments and fancy cabins. The captain was an American, but our crew were all Ukrainians. They spoke no Spanish—at least not to us—and they were tough-looking s.o.b.s who carried Soviet bloc automatic weapons.

Our problem was, we never managed to get ashore. We were supposed to debark onto a Cuban boat near Varadero Beach, an area I knew well from my childhood. From there we would be taken to rendezvous with members of the anti-Castro resistance and be driven to Havana. We would be provided a safe house, then move to the room where we'd be able to shoot Fidel, do it, and then try to escape somehow.

It sounds like a suicide mission. The truth is that escape meant very little to us. We were young, committed, and idealistic enough to try anything.

On our first try, we never saw a boat in our area. After about a week, we tried again. That time we sailed right up to the contact point—but discovered a huge ship, perhaps one hundred feet long. We sailed to within fifty or so feet of it, and checked it out with our spotlight. It was much too large to be our rendezvous boat—in fact, it looked like a ghost ship, because we couldn't see anyone aboard. We scrubbed again.

We were already well on our way to Cuba for the third time when the American captain canceled the mission. The reason he gave us was a hydraulic failure. When we got back to Florida, they took away the rifle and the ammunition, and said that they'd changed their minds about the mission.

I was tremendously disappointed and felt that the Americans let us down. I had volunteered to kill Castro, not because I was working for any American intelligence agency—which, as a matter of fact, I didn't know at the time—but because I was a Cuban soldier. I considered myself at war with Fidel, and he was a legitimate military target as far as I was concerned. And, as far as I am concerned, he still is a legitimate military target even today. My colleagues and I couldn't understand why the Americanos were denying our initiative. After all, it was our war, and it was our lives. And if we were willing to risk getting ourselves killed, it was our business.

Much later I heard about the CIA's various assassination and destabilization plans organized against Fidel under the umbrella name Operation Mongoose. These included such inanities as exploding cigars, poisoned Scuba gear, and a chemical to make his beard fall out. The plans also included supposed Mafia "hits." Operation Mongoose shows how little the Americans understood us Cuban freedom fighters. There was no need to go outside for anti-Castro activities. Anything the U.S. wanted to do would have been happily undertaken by people like me.

In 1987 I was asked by the independent counsel investigating the Iran/Contra affair, "Did you participate in Operation Mongoose to kill Castro with an exploding cigar?"

"No, sir, I did not," I answered. "But I did volunteer to kill that son of a bitch in 1961 with a telescopic rifle." I got a friendly laugh and a "You are crazy, Felix!"

My rifle team was not disbanded, however. The Americans brought in two others, Edgar Sopo Barreto (with whom I'd visited Jack Anderson), and Pepe González Castro, and told us we would become the infiltration team for Las Villas Province. Our mission would be to develop a resistance movement, stockpile weapons and explosives, and prepare to attack the Castro infrastructure when the invasion finally came.

There were thirty-five of us in all—seven five-man teams. While we remained at our motel-like safe house, the CIA tried to keep us Cubans from finding out where we were. But it was impossible. I knew precisely where we were—the Homestead area, southwest of Miami. How? Every scrap of garbage or old newspaper gave away our area, if not our precise location.

We were given more instruction in landing techniques, using rubber rafts and paddling back and forth across the swimming pool. Those exercises were useful—we learned to paddle. But we also learned that while it's easy to "land" a rubber raft at the edge of a swimming pool, it's much harder to do the same thing when you're fighting a wicked surf and trying to control a raft filled with ammunition, grenades, explosives, rifles, and other weapons, all the while attempting to watch out for people who want to kill you.

My friend Edgar Sopo recalls that our trainers instructed us to tape a grenade inside the crotch of our trousers so that if we were ever captured and threatened with interrogation we could ask to urinate, then pull the pin and blow ourselves up. We listened, but decided against it. Frankly, says Sopo, "we thought they were a little bit crazy."

We also taught ourselves countersurveillance techniques in a novel way: we discovered a nudist colony nearby. So, armed with binoculars, we'd regularly sneak through the trees and see how close we could get without being discovered. We must have been good, because no one ever complained.

We also managed to escape our instructors from time to time.

The fact of the matter was that we didn't care for the people assigned to us, and there was some friction. So we decided to let the Cuban leadership know what was going on. We were assigned four to a room, and one night after lights out, Sopo and I decided to escape. We piled clothes on the beds and covered the lumps with blankets, just as we'd seen done in the movies, slipped out the door, sneaked down the driveway, and walked quietly along a dirt road until finally we discovered a paved street. We walked for quite a while, maybe ten or fifteen minutes, and then saw a house, its lights on, in the distance.

Sopo knocked on the door and a woman answered. He told her that his car had broken down and asked if he could telephone his family to come and help him out. She was only too happy to help.

Then Sopo asked her for her precise street address. "It's so dark out we couldn't see where we were," he explained.

She gave it to us—it was a Homestead address, about four miles from the air force base.

Sopo told his family, "Come during the day so you'll be able to find the road, then come back and pick us up at night."

That's what happened. We fooled the Americans completely. And virtually all of us Cubans got to see our families, as we arranged nightly "escapes" to Miami. In fact, my whole infiltration team escaped as a unit the weekend before we left for Cuba. We knew we were about to undertake a dangerous mission, one from which many of us would not, in fact, return. We wanted the chance to see our families one more time before we left. So we pulled off a successful covert operation—we all went to Miami. We even have a picture of us, taken at Sopo's house.

If the Americans had found out about our escapes, they would have been upset. But the fact is, they didn't. Now, thinking back on it, we broke all the rules of operational security by visiting our families. Sure, *we* could keep secrets. But we had no idea who our parents and relatives might gossip to, and if I'd had the experience then that I have now I might have counseled against "going over the wall" so much.

Still, our escapades were more helpful than our American advisers might have thought. First, we were able to make contact with the Cuban political leadership and get from them a sense of what we'd be finding in Cuba—how effective the anti-Castro movements were, and to gauge the kind of political and material support we could count on in the countryside and inside the cities. And second, the clothes the Americans had given us were useless for infiltration teams. They were American-made, and would have given us away immediately. Fortunately our families had amply filled closets, and the clothes we finally packed to take to Cuba were all Cuban.

5 The first infiltration team left for Cuba on Valentine's Day—February 14, 1961. We were to be the second to go. We went in on February 28. We were driven to Key West, then we transferred to our boat. It was a rough trip. The heavy seas tossed our small boat (it was perhaps twenty-five feet long and filled to the gunwales with weapons and explosives). The trip took about four and a half stomach-wrenching hours, and at about six in the afternoon we saw the Cuban shoreline ahead. It was a tremendously emotional moment for me as I caught my first glimpse of the Cuban coastline. I was returning to my country the way I wanted to: with a weapon in my hand, to fight the communist dictator.

We had drifted to the west of our planned landing zone at Arcos de Canasi, which is close to the border between Matanzas and Havana provinces. Our captain was named Kikio Llanso; his second-in-command was a stocky man named Rolando Martínez, who now has become a close friend of mine and who would become well known as one of the Watergate "burglars" working for E. Howard Hunt. After plotting our position they turned us toward the east, and in the darkness we ran parallel to the beach perhaps one hundred meters from the sand, cruising slowly and watching for the signal to land.

To me, the whole experience was incredible, as if I were taking part in a movie. We could hear sounds from the shore as we moved slowly, silently in the darkness. We passed fishermen casting their lines off piers, watched people strolling around a small town square by the ocean, and even saw families enjoying a late picnic. We could see the lights in the houses, and an occasional car as our muffled motor chugged evenly along. Then, finally, we saw the recognition signal—three flashes of light in sequence—and the boat stopped.

We loaded our rubber dinghies, trying hard not to lose control as they rose and fell under our feet, lashed to the powerboat. We had our weapons and backpacks, but we also had to land two tons of equipment—explosives, grenades, machine guns, ammunition, and communications equipment. The landing would not be easy, either: instead of a sandy beach, we had to steer around jagged rocks and land the rafts at the base of a long, steep hill.

Once we made it ashore, we found roughly two dozen people waiting for us: local farmers and workers from the local sugar mill. Things became tremendously disorganized, which made me a little nervous. The whole operation was a not-too-secure clandestine landing, with the campesinos smoking cigarettes in the darkness as they helped us unload the rafts and carry our equipment. Finally, we stood there sweating, everything we'd brought from Florida on the sand at our feet.

I gave the order to the local guide to move out. Our objective was a road that was perhaps three kilometers away. The first problem was moving everything off the beach. At the edge of the sand was that damn hill—almost like a cliff—perhaps 150 feet to the top, all of it covered with thick, brambly vegetation. There was one narrow path, and with the help of ropes we managed to lug everything to the crest. There I dispatched all the weapons, explosives, and ammunition—even our own weapons—with our volunteers, to be hidden away for future resistance operations.

I turned and looked out to sea. Our boat was nowhere to be seen. Kikio and Rolando had probably left the moment we'd floated our final load ashore. Then I turned away from the water and, taking the point with our guide, began our trek inland through the countryside.

It was frightening and exhilarating at the same time: I was back in Cuba, breathing the air of my childhood. And yet I was back as a soldier, a stranger in my homeland, not knowing whether or not we were being betrayed by the campesinos who carried our explosives on their shoulders. Yet I believed I was in God's hands, and that I had no choice but to trust those who were helping us. I'd even left my M-3 submachine gun with one of the people who greeted us on the beach that warm night. Still, I was wary. The area we were traversing was perfect for an ambush—a path surrounded by heavy vegetation. And we were making enough noise as we moved through the countryside to alert the nearby farm dogs, who set up a howl as we passed.

Finally, after a couple of hours, we reached the Matanzas-Havana highway. We had only the clothes on our backs. Quietly, whispering our conversation, we waited near the side of the road for our vehicles. The pickup method was rudimentary, but, as is the case with so much tradecraft, it worked—so we used it. The anti-Castro resistance known as the MRR was in charge of moving us from Matanzas to Havana. They knew our approximate time of infiltration, but not exactly when we'd arrive at the highway. So they put a number of cars on the road at fifteen-minute intervals, driving back and forth on the Matanzas-Havana highway. When we were in position, we were instructed to leave a rock in a certain position at the side of the highway. The car would see the recognition signal and stop, we'd jump in, and be off.

We had verbal recognition signals as well. Each car would take either two or three of us. When it stopped, the driver would call out "Two," or "Three." Our answer would be the number ten, minus the number of passengers—so we'd answer "seven" or "eight."

My team split into two groups on the highway. Three of us, Segundo Borges, Javier Souto, and Pepe González, went straight to Las Villas Province. Borges was to instruct the resistance on how to receive air drops and maritime pickups. Pepe's assignment was action and sabotage, and Javier was the communications man—the link with Miami. Edgar Sopo and I would first go to Havana to link up with the resistance leaders. From there we would go into Camaguey, where we'd coordinate the reception of a large shipment of arms— one thousand weapons were expected from the Americans. The car for Sopo and me cruised by first. The driver saw our recognition signal, stopped, and we piled in. He sped off, then turned to look at us.

"Jeezus," he said, "are you guys crazy?"

"What the hell are you talking about?"

"You don't wear fatigue uniforms or army boots here. Do you want to get us killed?"

Sopo and I had to laugh—the Agency had made us wear military uniforms and boots for the infiltration, so here we were looking like a couple of paramilitary revolutionaries, when we were supposed to be passing as civilians. Quickly we scrambled out of our green fatigues and changed into the Cuban clothes we'd gotten at our homes in Miami.

We drove for about an hour and a half. It was late, and there was little other traffic on the road. Still we were somewhat nervous, and I was happy to arrive at our destination, the home of an elderly couple just outside Havana. They were lovely people, who fed us and asked us about life in the United States, and then gave us a comfortable room in which to sleep.

I was surprised to find such a well-coordinated resistance movement waiting for us. The Agency had not told us about any of this. In fact, we'd planned to hide out in the jungle and forage for ourselves. But instead, there was an organization to support us, safe houses in which to live, closets full of clothes for us to change into, and a network of messengers, drivers—everything we would need to prepare our operations.

The CIA prepared the resistance as best it could. Their weapons were M-3 World War II-vintage submachine guns. They had also been given .45 automatic pistols, which would have been fine if they were operating in the U.S. But here in Cuba, Castro's forces carried 9mm pistols, and .45s would present a problem if they ran out of ammunition. It was, as Sopo says today, not much better an operation than if we'd called a few of our friends, bought guns on the street and a powerboat or two, and mounted our own clandestine invasion.

Still, U.S. Government involvement had its benefits. Castro, for example, believed at the time that the infiltrations were being carried out, with the help of the U.S. Navy, from submarines, and that we infiltrators were receiving heavy American support. If he'd only known the truth!

The next morning we awoke refreshed and had a cup of the strong sweet coffee I remembered from my childhood. Then it was time to meet the head of the Cuban resistance and talk over our assignments with him. His code name was Francisco, and he arrived midmorning accompanied by the MRR's chief of security, Cesar Baro.

Francisco's real name was Rogelio González Corso. I expected him to be elderly, but he turned out to be just a little older than me— perhaps twenty-seven or twenty-eight. He was handsome, with wavy hair, dark eyes and a medium build. He showed up wearing an open-necked shirt and a pair of light-colored trousers. Seeing him on the street you'd mistake him for a student. He had a degree in engineering and he spoke eloquently. Francisco was the kind of guy who naturally inspired people. He was the number one target of Cuban intelligence, and so he was very cautious about the way he moved around the country. He lived in a series of safe houses used only by him, never spending two nights in the same one. No one knew his schedule, and only a very few the locations of his safe houses. His networks included armed resistance groups that carried out sabotage in the cities and guerrilla activities in the countryside, intelligence operations against Castro for the Americans, and support of our infiltration units.

Ultimately, G-2 captured Francisco, but only by chance. Castro's intelligence people raided a house just outside Havana on April 1, 1961. As luck would have it, Francisco and some of his top people, including Cuba's former chief prosecutor, were at a meeting three doors away. They would have gone undiscovered, but the maid in the house being searched panicked and—inexplicably—ran straight to the house where Francisco was holding his meeting. The police followed and started to search the house she'd fled to. There was a gunfight, and everyone at the meeting was captured. They didn't know they had Francisco until a couple of days later, after they'd had ample time to interrogate—and probably torture—everyone. Francisco was executed on April 17, the day of the Bay of Pigs invasion.

The morning we met Francisco, he gave Sopo a big *abrazo*, since he'd known him a long time, and he shook my hand warmly. Instinctively I liked this man. Then we all sat at the table talking animatedly, and made our plans. Our team would form a northern guerrilla front in Las Villas, the goal being to force Castro to split his troops and eventually to divide the island in half. Borges, Souto and Pepe were already in Las Villas to set up their operations. Sopo and I would follow. First, however, we'd go to the town of Morón, in Camaguey Province, where that huge shipment of weapons from America was scheduled to arrive.

Although we remained in Havana for almost two weeks, we didn't see much of the city. We stayed indoors for the most part, venturing out for meetings (even then only in closed cars), and for security's sake always moving from safe house to safe house. We weren't afraid of being spotted by Castro's security people so much as we were nervous about being seen by our own friends and family. There was also a problem with the documents we'd been given by the CIA. As I put in a report to the Agency some months later, "We had to ask [the MRR] for [new] identity documents since the ones we had were old and nonvalid."

We learned tradecraft by living it. For example, most of the safe houses had closets full of clothes. We would clean up and exchange the shirts and pants we were wearing for a new set. But once in a while we'd see somebody on the street wearing yesterday's outfit. Even though you didn't know him, you'd know that he was another guy from our organization.

Even though we didn't spend a lot of time on the streets I noticed changes in the two years since I'd been in Havana. First was the large number of soldiers on the streets. And second, there were signs everywhere proclaiming the victories of the Cuban revolution, and revolutionary propaganda heralding Castro's achievements for the country. It was similar to Trujillo's self-promotion in the Dominican Republic—and I think the people took it for the fiction it was.

I also had the sense that Castro's position was still, if not downright precarious, somewhat shaky. The campesinos who had met our boat, for example, had no great love or loyalty toward Fidel—in fact, they were some of our greatest supporters. There were hundreds of officers in his military who were working against him. And Cuban moderates of all classes had already realized that Fidel's claim that he was no communist was a bald-faced lie.

Finally we went to Morón to wait for the weapons shipment. At first we stayed in the city itself. But Morón is a small place, and within a couple of days the MRR members who gave us our safe house said we'd have to move because word was spreading quickly that "foreigners" were in town. In fact, they weren't the only ones with warnings. A man who knew Sopo's family showed up at our door and said, "Look, friend, this is a small town—there's only one road in, and one road out, and it's getting dangerous for you."

We decided to move. After dark, we moved to a deserted farmhouse a few miles outside the city, where we waited for the weapons. And waited. And waited.

The place was barren—a house in the middle of nowhere. The floors were made of dirt. There was no electricity, no plumbing—no running water whatsoever. We were unarmed, with no way to protect ourselves. In fact, we took to running to the fields surrounding the house for cover every time we'd see the dust raised by someone approaching. We were bored to distraction. There was absolutely nothing to do except sleep, or sit on the floor and wait. We had no radio. No telephone.

Each day at about noon a farmer riding a broken-down horse arrived carrying two pails of beans and rice, some Cuban steaks, fried bananas, and two canteens of water. After five days or so, another man showed up unannounced. He said he was a farmer, and a member of the 30th of November movement—another anti-Castro organization—and he wanted to work with us.

The arrival of our uninvited volunteer was the last straw. Not only did we have no communications, no plan, no weapons—but now we had no operational security. If this farmer knew we were infiltrators, how many others knew? And when would Castro's secret police find out and raid our hideout?

I was really furious, and I decided to act. The frustration had gone on too long. A couple of days after our volunteer farmer showed up I formulated my plan and announced to Sopo, "I'm going to Havana to find Francisco and tell him this whole operation is screwed up. Then I'm going back to the States. I'm gonna find those fucking weapons and carry 'em back here personally."

I contacted Francisco through a woman I knew as Margarita Rosas. She was the wife of a prominent physician, and very active in the MRR. Francisco agreed with my proposal and helped make arrangements for me to leave the country. But leaving was easier said than done. Three times I made the long drive from Havana to the north coast, where I was supposed to rendezvous with an American boat. And three times the boat failed to show up. It was not an easy trip for me to make. Traveling along the highway was fairly simple, but the last stretch, from the road to the coast, meant slogging through three to five kilometers of rough countryside. The possibility of being discovered and captured was high. At any time we might have been seen by one of the local farmers, or by a Castro patrol.

Indeed, coordination is one of the most important elements of any clandestine mission. There are so many variables that can cause disaster. The weather can be a factor: rain or mud can double the amount of time you need to move overland. Transportation can go awry. An accident on a street half a mile away can tie up traffic and cause a missed rendezvous.

Luck can be an element, too. A soldier at a roadblock might pick the moment you cross to light a cigarette and his attention be diverted. Or he could be having a bad day and decide to hassle everyone he checks on his shift. Knowing these things, you try to make as much work in your favor as you can. If every possible move is well planned in advance, then the variables will hurt you less.

We also had an additional major problem with our infiltration: the boats the Americans gave us were largely inappropriate for clandestine operations. They were ill-maintained, often breaking down. Further, they were usually too small to accommodate the large numbers of weapons we were trying to bring into Cuba. Boats weighed down to the gunwales are unsafe and unmaneuverable, and we faced both these problems on a regular basis. So, the Americans had trained us, equipped us and dropped us off. But they did not follow through, either in support or logistics. This lack of coordination ultimately was a factor in our failure.

Just after the second abortive rendezvous I was almost captured by Castro's people.

We'd driven from Havana and hiked five kilometers in the darkness through tough countryside. We waited three hours, insects eating us all the while, for the boat that was supposed to take me back to the U.S. When it didn't show, we made the long hike back to the car and started toward Havana again.

It was one in the morning when we came upon the roadblock. There were five of us driving west in a big black Chevy Otis rent-a-car. Our adrenaline was high and we were ready to fight, but we were also frustrated, exhausted, and sorely underequipped with weapons: among us we had only one revolver. Not to mention the fact that I was carrying a thick envelope of documents prepared for U.S. intelligence by the MRR.

The package included details about Castro's military installations, information about Soviet bases and advisers—even microfilm and photographs. It was not something to be captured with. For some inexplicable reason, the MRR officer who sealed the envelope had written on it: "For Clarence"—the name of the CIA recipient in Miami—and then, in big block letters, the word SECRET was written across the envelope.

My colleagues were not happy about the prospect of being captured either—they were on Castro's wanted lists. So the options were severely limited—which is why, when it comes to tradecraft, there are no rules. I had only seconds in which to make a real life-or-death decision.

One possibility was to run the roadblock—which I immediately discounted because the patrol probably had radios and could call ahead to have us intercepted. Another was to talk our way through. If we saw things were going badly we could try to take the soldiers' weapons. But they outnumbered us eight to five, and they were armed with FAL automatic rifles.

My intuition told me to bluff our way through. First, we were in a big black Chevy—the same type of car used by Castro's intelligence people. Second, we were all males dressed in civilian clothes—we might well pass for secret police. Third, and perhaps most important, I knew that roadblocks such as these were usually manned by inexperienced, uneducated soldiers who didn't want to be out in the middle of the night and didn't want any trouble.

We were moving so fast that we actually skidded about one hundred feet past the roadblock before we came to a complete stop. On my instructions, the driver put the car in reverse and we started to ease slowly backward toward the soldiers. I ordered everyone to roll down the windows. When we were perhaps twenty feet away, I leaned out of the car and asked, in a voice that I hoped radiated authority, *"Pasa algo, compañeros?"*—Is anything wrong, comrades?

After a second or two, the officer answered: "No—nothing wrong. You may continue."

Later, thinking about it, I guessed at two thoughts that might have crossed the soldiers' minds. The first was that we were indeed from G-2. The second was that we were exactly the sort of people they were looking for, but they believed we were probably heavily armed.

Did we fool them? Perhaps. Did they want to be fooled? Probably.

This was not our only close call. At one point, Sopo and I were contacted in Havana by a man we didn't know, who had been introduced to us by the MRR's chief of security, Cesar Baro. The man told us he had to move a cache of weapons for the resistance. Although he had reached us through the MRR, we were still cautious—Castro had infiltrated the resistance movement just as he'd managed to place agents in the infiltration teams. Still, we wanted and needed the weapons.

Our new contact behind the wheel, and Sopo and me with him, we drove to his house to pick up the weapons late one afternoon. Two other MRR cars followed behind us. There were supposedly a lot of weapons.

As we approached, I started to get nervous. We were headed directly for the headquarters of Castro's secret police. As we drove right down Fifth Avenue, straight toward the G-2 building. Edgar Sopo began to nudge me and whisper, "Felix, it's a trap!"

But at the last minute the driver went right past G-2, turned the corner and parked in front of a big colonial house. We went in and discovered our three carloads of guns. The weapons were stored in the cellar, against a wall that was common to the G-2 dungeons. There must have been two hundred guns down there, and we carried them out to the cars in plain sight of anyone who might have passed. Luckily, no one from the secret police saw us.

Moving around Havana was often a problem. One of the things you face when operating inside a hostile totalitarian state is the regimentation. For example, single males traveling alone often arouse suspicion, especially when they arrive at a hotel with virtually no baggage. Couple that with the fact that in states such as Cuba, where the hotels are government owned, hotel employees report to the intelligence apparatus on a regular basis. So on the few occasions that there were no safe houses to go to, we had to improvise ways to escape detection.

One of the best ruses was picking up women. Sopo and I did that one night when, after a long session with a group of resistance leaders, we found ourselves in a strange section of Havana at one in the morning. This was in March, when the resistance was engaged in heavy sabotage, and Castro's security forces cruised the streets all night. So we ducked into a piano bar, saw a number of "ladies" sitting by themselves, tipped the bartender generously, and asked if he'd make us a couple of introductions.

"Sure," he said. "And don't worry—they're all real clean girls, too."

We chatted for a while, then Sopo and I asked them, "How about spending some time together?" We'd been months in the Guatemalan jungles, then Panama, then Florida—all without the company of a woman.

They, of course, were more than willing—and they had a convenient motel to go to. The next day Sopo and I had a big laugh about the whole thing. He told me, "You know, she was also one hell of an anti-communist—spent the whole night going on about how bad Castro is."

"Mine said the same things," I told him. "But I defended Fidel a little—because you can't be too sure whether they're trying to provoke you or not."

Another time it might have been easier on our nerves to have had a couple of women along with us. Sopo and I were driving in Las Villas Province one day. We decided it would be nice to stop for a good steak lunch, so we pulled over in the town of Manacas, where we knew there was a terrific beer garden. But just as we were cutting into our meat, two big black Chevys festooned with antennas pulled up, and eight rough-looking men sporting pistol bulges marched into the restaurant.

I shot Sopo a look. They were probably coming to check the identity cards of everyone in the place.

We had IDs, of course, but they were forged, and they looked it. Worse, both Sopo and I were from Las Villas Province, and there were people in that restaurant who, if they didn't know us, knew our families.

Luckily for us, all the G-2 men wanted was steak and beer. They sat down a few tables away from us and ordered. We finished up and got out.

I was finally able to exfiltrate on March 25—my fourth try. Even that attempt was screwed up. Rolando Martínez picked me up in his boat—and ran out of gas about a mile short of Key West. He had to radio for another Agency boat to come out and help us make our landfall.

I spent three days in a safe house, being debriefed and trying to arrange for the weapons we needed for the resistance. Having learned the scope of the anti-Castro movement inside Cuba and having seen firsthand the enmity in which Fidel was held by most of the people with whom I'd come in contact, I was optimistic about the chances of success. I told my debriefers what I knew and what I felt.

On one of those days I managed to get away from the safe house for a few hours and visit my family. My Uncle Fernando Mendigutia (now a lawyer in Miami) had kept his house in Havana, and during this brief visit he told me that if I ever needed a car in Cuba to go to his house and ask the chauffeur, Oscarito, for transportation.

I didn't consider visiting my family or Fernando's offer a security breach. First, my family knew I was an infiltration team leader and that I'd been in Cuba for three weeks. Second, virtually everyone in

Miami knew there would be an invasion soon. And third, it would be safer to use my uncle's car and his trustworthy driver than to rely on taxis or other public transportation in Havana if an MRR car was unavailable.

Later, back at the safe house, the Americans gave me a new set of orders to pass to all the infiltration teams once I returned to Cuba.

"No matter how ridiculous the instructions you receive might seem," I was told to tell my colleagues, "follow them to the letter—because they're elements of an overall plan."

I was also told that something would be happening within the next thirty days, and to make sure that my team was prepared to move quickly.

Finally I was driven to the Keys by a lanky Texan named Sherman. There I received the weapons I'd waited a month for. Sherman also presented me with something special to take to Cuba. It was a miniature flamethrower—it fit very comfortably in one hand, yet it threw a fifteen-foot, yard-wide column of white phosphorus flame. Sherman told me the flamethrower was highly classified, but that he wanted me to have it anyway.

From what Sherman told me on our drive south I knew something would happen soon. He talked about shipping bombs to the training camps in Guatemala, and arming our planes, and was generally positive about operations.

I had no problems transporting the weapons back to Cuba, but getting them ashore was something else. Once again, faulty coordination prevented me from landing with anything except my mini-flamethrower, a box of .45 pistols and ammunition, and a crate of hand grenades. Everything else was left aboard the boat and delivery was rescheduled for a week hence. I don't think the resistance ever got the hundreds of rifles, machine guns, mortars, and munitions I brought.

I made my way back to Havana from Morón in an old Buick Roadmaster, the flamethrower securely hidden under the dashboard. (I never had the chance to use it; I gave it to one of my MRR contacts. I never discovered whether or not he put it to use.) I was saddened to learn of Francisco's capture, but there was work to be done. I had to inform the other Grey teams about the new instructions. The MRR assigned me a car and a female companion. Tradecraft again, as a man and woman aroused less suspicion than two men or a man alone. She was a widow with five children, an attractive and well-educated woman named Maria, from a respected and wealthy family named Comellas. She was one of the most dedicated members of the resistance I ever met.

I was responsible for passing new orders on to resistance groups. The first was in Camaguey, where our infiltration team leader was a former Castro army captain named Oliverio Tomeu. His safe house was right in the middle of Camaguey, and as I walked in, all I could think of was that it looked just like the set from the movie *Casablanca*, filled with ceiling fans and beaded curtains, and Oliverio sitting in his underwear on a creaky chair next to a creaky table.

I gave him his new instructions: he was to take his fighters and cut off the road to Havana.

He looked at me as if I were crazy. "How the hell can I do that?" he asked. "The land here is absolutely flat—you can't hold positions. We'll be massacred."

I shrugged. "Look—all I know is it's supposed to be part of a master plan."

He gave me a big *abrazo*. "OK, Felix—but it is crazy." That was the last time I ever saw Oliverio in Cuba. Like so many others in our infiltration teams, he followed his instructions to the letter. He was captured, but he survived and now lives in Florida.

One day, Maria's brother, an infiltration-team member, whom we called Cawy, said that if I didn't have anything pressing to keep me in Havana, "I think you might want to think about leaving for a couple of days, because it's about to get hot as hell."

I had nothing planned, so Maria and I went with a friend of hers to a little town outside Havana where the friend's family owned a small sugar mill. We stayed there for the weekend and drove a borrowed green Mercedes south to a lovely, secluded beach. On the radio we heard that the El Encanto, Havana's biggest department store, had burned to the ground.

According to Fidel, the CIA was responsible for the sabotage. We knew better. Cawy's group may have used Agency explosives, but the plan was theirs alone.

It would also have made the CIA nervous to know that I made

one personal visit while I was in Havana—to the home of the woman I would later marry.

I had known Rosa Nodal since I was about fourteen. We'd corresponded occasionally when I went to prep school. We became friends over the years, but not at all involved romantically. And yet, I always felt that we would someday become so. I hadn't seen Rosa in three and a half years. Then, one day after my return to Havana, I decided to pay her a visit. I used my Uncle Fernando's car, and Oscarito drove me to her home.

Rosa's father, Patricio, opened the door. His eyes went wide as saucers—he knew I had left Cuba and thought I was living in Miami. He told me Rosa had gone to Cienfuegos, their hometown on Cuba's southern coast. I left quickly, knowing he must have thought I was crazy to be back on the island.

I never told the Agency what I'd done. They probably would have regarded it as an unacceptable breach of security. On the other hand, I was probably safer visiting the Nodals' home than moving from safe house to safe house. One day early in April, for example, I arrived at a safe house after a meeting with some resistance people, only to discover a fire raging next door. Police and firemen were everywhere. Since I was not carrying any identification at the time, Maria, who was driving, thought we should wait until the authorities left before returning me to the house.

It was a lovely day, so we drove a few blocks to enjoy the clean, white sand and clear water on a nearby beach. As we approached the seashore we came upon a militiaman. Not thinking, I waved to him and asked, "Is it OK to use this beach, or is it private?"

"Private? Hey, *compañero*, where you been? There ain't no more private beaches in Cuba since the Revolution. They all belong to the people."

I could have kicked myself. "Right, *compañero*. Power to the Revolution! Thanks."

We drove onto the sand at the most secluded part of the beach, climbed out of the car and sat watching the water for a while, talking about nothing in particular. A short distance to the east we saw a small guardhouse manned by a single soldier. Farther down the beach was a large green house. We didn't give it much thought. It was a beautiful day, and the beach brought back childhood memories for me.

But after a while, the soldier from the guardhouse sauntered over to where we sat. "Hey, *compañero*," he said to me, indicating the villa, "make sure you don't move across to that side of the beach."

"Why?" I asked. "Hey, *compañero*, I thought there were no private beaches in Cuba anymore."

"There aren't," he said. "But this beach is special. It belongs to Fidel." He pointed toward the big house, "That's Fidel's place—he's there now."

That got my attention. I told him we would stay put. We waited about ten minutes before leaving, then climbed into our car. But when we tried to drive away, the wheels kept spinning. We were stuck in the sand. The more we tried to move, the deeper they sank. The deeper the tires sank, the more nervous we became.

We were finally rescued by a lieutenant in Castro's personal body-guard unit, who saw our predicament and was anxious to help—especially after he got a look at Maria.

He called for a jeep to tow us out, but there wasn't one available. So he ordered four of his men to push us onto firm ground.

When we were finally able to drive away, Maria smiled and thanked him graciously. I was very grateful too. "Thank you, *compañeros*," I said. And, thinking ahead to our planned invasion, I added, "If there's ever anything I can do to help you, just call on me!"

I did a lot of moving around during those two and a half weeks, setting up operations, coordinating my own team's efforts, and waiting for some message from the U.S. about the invasion. No such message was ever sent.

6 I first learned about the Bay of Pigs invasion on Cuban radio the morning of April 17. When we turned the receiver on, we discovered all the Cuban stations had switched to the same emergency network. They were broadcasting government instructions, ordering military personnel to report to their bases, and other defense information. I turned the dial to "The Voice of America" and heard there had been an invasion. According to the U.S. broadcast, our freedom fighters had already successfully crossed the main highway to Havana. That claim, of course, turned out to be untrue.

I made frantic phone calls to people in the resistance, only to discover to my horror that many of them had already been picked up in wholesale sweeps by Castro's forces. Castro's intelligence appeared to have been better than ours! At least *he* seemed to have had some warning of what the Americans had planned.

Since it was still early in the morning, I decided to go to church to take communion. It might, after all, be my last one. Maria drove me to the church of San Juan de Letrán, where my parents had been married. I asked to see a priest. When he appeared, I whispered what I wanted—and told him why.

He nodded sagely. "My son," he said, "you are not the only one to have come through here this morning."

From church we went to a safe house for a hurried meeting with some of the resistance leaders. Frankly, they, like I, were in a state of total confusion. We had trained for months; we had worked in the Guatemalan and Panamanian jungles, studied all the techniques of guerrilla warfare, and learned our tradecraft. Yet, after everything, it all came down to this one overcast, hot morning, when everything seemed to be going wrong. We spoke for a few minutes, but the conversation seemed fruitless to me, so I left, and we went back to the apartment in El Vedado where I'd been staying.

I tried, unsuccessfully, to raise people on the telephone. Almost none of them answered. Either they had been arrested or they were afraid to pick up the phone—perhaps one of their colleagues already in Castro's hands was on the other end of the line. Some of those who picked up the phone had strange voices; often they would tell me to come over right away. They were security agents, and I hung up immediately.

Outside I could see hundreds of military trucks moving in the streets, and soldiers, armed. It was profoundly depressing. Unable to move, I stayed in the apartment for the next three days, occasionally watching television. I saw TV news pictures of my comrades from the training camps captured and herded into trucks like animals, and I wept when I saw their faces painted with frustration and defeat. I had no idea what had become of my infiltration-team colleagues. Edgar Sopo was at Varadero Beach. Segundo Borges, Javier Souto and José González Castro were in Las Villas Province. But it was impossible to contact them.

In fact, I didn't discover until later what had happened to them.

Sopo made it back to Havana, where he received asylum from the Venezuelan Embassy, but in another building at a different location. I didn't know for some time he was only a short distance from me. Our radio operator, Javier Souto, made it safely, radio in hand, to the Ecuadorian embassy in Havana. In fact, I was able to relay messages to him, which he would in turn transmit back to the U.S. Souto was very security-conscious, and his caution served him well. He'd set up a system in Las Villas Province with one of his relatives, who would place a flower arrangement in her window if everything was all right. When the G-2 came to question her, she managed to send him a signal, and he took off for Havana.

Borges and José González Castro, the remaining two members of my team, hid in Santa Clara, southeast of Havana, until July 21, when they were captured within hours of each other by the G-2.

Borges's story is almost like a spy novel—except that it's true. It is best told in his own words—a report he wrote five days after he made it back to Miami in January 1962.

> I was arrested at 10 AM in a house at Colón 219, in Santa Clara, Las Villas Province, by three members of the G-2. I was kept there for seven hours then moved to Santa Clara G-2, where I was questioned by Second Lieutenant Anibal Velez, the G-2 head for Santa Clara. For six days I maintained that my name was Jorge Gutierrez and that I was from Havana. But on the sixth day the maid from one of our security houses identified me, and G-2 discovered that my documents and the Havana address I had given them were false.
>
> So I told them I was Segundo Borges and that my mission was to open up a guerrilla front in Yaguajay. I denied everything else. I denied that I had any connection or contact with any U.S. government or CIA organization, which they specifically asked. All told, I was at the Santa Clara G-2 for 25 days.
>
> Together with Jose Angel González Castro and Miguel Penton, who had been arrested in the same house a few hours before I, I was taken to Havana, to the G-2 headquarters at Fifth Avenue and 14th Street. There, there was

a fortuitous mix-up. Our papers were lost, and the three of us were placed in the same cell until September 10. But because there were no papers on us, we were not questioned. On Sept. 10 we were moved to an eight-man cell in the old Batista Military Intelligence Service (S.I.M.) building.

We were kept there for three weeks, until we decided to escape. From one of the beds we obtained an iron rod, which we used to poke a hole in the wall of our cell, which adjoined a small storage room filled with auto parts. The hole took six days to complete. We finished our work at 10 P.M. on October 10. But we waited until 4 AM the next day to escape. At 4 we went to the storage room and saw only one guard, who was reading a newspaper outside, his back to us. We were able to escape over the wall in two groups. I took a bus, and a taxi, and made it to an MRR safe house I knew about, and from there, after three days, through the help of the aunt of a friend of mine in the MRR I made it to the Brazilian Embassy. I stayed until 22 December. On that day the Cuban government granted my safe conduct to leave and I flew to Venezuela that same afternoon, and stayed until Jan. 7, 1962, when I flew home to Miami.

On April 20 I was forced to leave the safe house. An old friend of Maria's father who was an officer at the Spanish Embassy, Alejandro Vergara, came to see Maria. He told her that Castro's people were conducting house-to-house searches for infiltrators and resistance people and that she was in danger, as they were currently on the next block. Without a moment to spare I grabbed my jacket and Maria and I left with Alejandro.

We took the elevator down from the fourth floor and went out the front door to the circular driveway where the Spaniard had left his diplomatic car. As we piled in, a truckload of soldiers came up the other side of the driveway and pulled to a stop right behind us. Alejandro never looked back. He put the gray Chevy into gear and slowly drove away. As we turned into the street I craned my neck and saw soldiers setting up a perimeter around the apartment house.

Others, weapons at the ready, were moving through the doors we'd just exited.

We went directly to Alejandro's apartment house, a huge place that took up an entire city block. I gasped as we parked the car—my paternal grandparents lived there, too! We went straight to Alejandro's place, apartment 2-B, where I discovered six more Cubans to whom he'd given refuge.

I didn't know it at the time, but all over Havana, Spanish and other Latin diplomats opened up their homes to fugitives from Castro's secret police, saving hundreds of Cubans from prison or execution. Unfortunately the vast majority of infiltrators and resistance fighters were captured. More than two thousand were executed. Others were sentenced to long prison terms.

So my situation was not unique. On the other hand, I was probably the only Grey team member to have found refuge in the same apartment building where his grandparents lived. Alejandro and I considered my alternatives. Obviously, I couldn't stay in his apartment for more than a few days. Either I could apply for political asylum at an embassy that would accept me, or I could head out alone and find my own way back to the U.S.

My instinct was to run. Asylum seemed like giving up, acknowledging I'd been defeated by Fidel. I went downstairs to see my grandparents, wondering if they could help. Maria accompanied me as I knocked on their front door.

"Grandmother—it's me, Felix."

She cracked the door and peered out. A look of shock came over her face. "Felix?!" Then she saw Maria, and her eyes grew even wider. She invited us in and quickly closed the door behind us. "Whatever are you doing here?"

I told her I'd come from Miami to make sure she was safe, and that Maria was my friend from Havana. She looked at me very strangely. After a few hours I told her the truth—that I was an infiltrator and needed her help in escaping Castro.

Strangely, she looked relieved. Later, she told me, "Felix, you showed up with Maria. She's a nice woman, but you haven't finished your studies, and I thought you'd eloped from Miami with her without your parents' consent, and I didn't know what to say. I was actually delighted when you said you were on the run from Fidel."

She may have been delighted to see me, but, to be honest, she didn't help much. She ran around the apartment closing all the shades and pulling the drapes. I tried to convince her that doing anything out of the ordinary would draw attention to her and could jeopardize me greatly. Even so, she insisted on "taking precautions" as she put it—which increased the chances I might be captured.

So, after about a day and a half of being happy to see my grandparents but nervous about my grandmother's "precautions," I went back to Alejandro's and told him I'd changed my mind and would take the political asylum route.

I decided on the Venezuelan Embassy because Venezuela had a treaty with Cuba that allowed political refugees safe-conduct out of the country. Moreover, my grandparents had a friend in the building who was close to the Venezuelan ambassador. Contact was made, and I was guaranteed refuge.

The next six days at Alejandro's were spent trying to make phone contact with the resistance. Although I'd agreed to asylum, I wasn't happy about it. I phoned everyone I could think of—to no avail. Some phones were never answered. Others picked up, but they'd recognize my voice and say, "Wrong number," or something similar.

The fact is, in botching the invasion, the Americans did the very thing they were out to prevent: they caused Fidel to cement his power structure and crush any rebellion. Before the Bay of Pigs we had no trouble recruiting anti-Castro volunteers in Cuba. Before the Bay of Pigs, the Cuban people joked about Castro openly and talked in public about what would happen when he was thrown out. Afterward there was no talk in public—or anywhere else. Castro used the invasion as the pretext for arresting and executing virtually all of his current and potential political enemies, thus ending a generation's worth of protest. He sent agents provocateurs into the streets and the countryside to kill those who spoke against him. I believe that before April 17 there had been a good chance of overthrowing Castro and returning Cuba to democracy. Afterward, that goal became 100 percent harder to achieve.

(One story I have heard supporting my belief concerns a chance meeting between JFK's assistant Richard Goodwin and Che Guevara at a dinner party in Montevideo, Uruguay, in August 1961. Reportedly, Che told Goodwin to pass on Fidel's gratitude for the Bay of

Pigs invasion to President Kennedy. Prior to the invasion, Che said, Fidel's power was shaky. Afterward, said Che, Castro was transformed into the macho Cuban hero who had stood up to the gringo superpower and won. It was the invasion that made possible Fidel's consolidated hold on the country.)

The Americans never realized the extent of their blunders. Not long after the invasion, some of us infiltrators received a message from the Agency that said, in effect, OK, what you have to do now is survive. Get yourselves jobs. Reestablish yourselves in Cuba. Then, when you've built successful lives, contact us again.

The utter naiveté of those instructions! We were on the run. The Agency had given us documents that couldn't fool even the most uneducated militiaman—let alone the bureaucrats we'd have to face. And yet the Americans expected us to live in the open, as citizens of a communist totalitarian state. I have no idea who thought that scheme up, but whoever it was had no contact with reality. All we could do was laugh—and hope that the next group of CIA people we'd be dealing with would work in some semblance of the real world.

The morning of April 26 was cool and overcast, with the threat of rain in the air and a breeze coming from the ocean a block away. At about 7:30, Alejandro asked me to go downstairs and wait with his nephew while he started the car and pulled up in front of the building. I said goodbye to Maria and wished her well. Ultimately she received political asylum from the ambassador of Paraguay. Today Maria lives happily in Spain. My gratitude to her and respect for her will be with me forever. She took great risks and I owe her my life.

Now, for the first time since April 17, I became nervous about my own safety. The reason, I believe, was that I knew I was about to receive asylum. If you are convinced you're going to be killed or captured, your attitude is "What the hell—I'll go for broke." But when you know that you're going to be safe in ten, or twenty, or twenty-five minutes, you start to freeze up inside and begin to worry about all the things that could go wrong.

I stood at the entrance, therefore, worrying where the hell Alejandro was, worrying about what I'd do if we were stopped by soldiers and they pulled me from the car; worrying whether the G-2 would grab me in the couple of yards between the house and the car. Even standing in the entry had been hard: Alejandro's apartment house was also the residence for many of Castro's high-ranking military officers. As I stood there, I was continually being passed—and given the once-over—by officers and soldiers and who knows who.

Finally Alejandro drove up and I just about dived into his car, happy to be inside a vehicle that had diplomatic plates. We went immediately to the residence of the Spanish ambassador, which was relatively close to the Venezuelan Embassy.

"I want to see just how problematic it's going to be to get you to the Venezuelans," Alejandro told me. While he checked, I sat in the ambassador's huge living room, admiring the dark wood furniture and the grand piano and feeling slightly out of place amidst all the grandeur: I had not shaved in two days or changed my clothes in six days.

Alejandro returned and described the situation to me. "We'll take the ambassador's car," he said. "The chauffeur will take us right up to the Venezuelan Embassy. You'll be sitting in the back with me. Don't look left or right. Don't pay any attention to the Cuban soldiers who are out front. Just act like a diplomat."

I interrupted him. "Oh, sure. Some diplomat! That's bull, Alejandro. Take a look at me—I haven't shaved in two days. I haven't had a haircut in about a month. They're going to know I'm not a diplomat in a second."

"Believe me it won't make any difference," he said. "Take my word for it, Felix. I know what I am saying. I've done this before."

Grudgingly I agreed. Then he explained what we would do. "You won't be safe until you are actually inside the embassy building itself," he said. "It's not enough for you just to be on the grounds. So we'll drive through the Cuban guardhouse, up the driveway, and along the side of the embassy, right next to the kitchen door. I'll get out and go inside. You'll wait for me in the car. As long as you stay in the car you're under the protection of the Spanish Embassy, so don't move—even if the Cuban militia starts pounding on the doors or breaks the windows.

"Then, when I open the kitchen door and signal, you run like hell to me." He looked me in the face. "Got it?"

I nodded.

Alejandro clapped me on the back. "OK," he said. "Let's do it."

We walked outside to the ambassador's car. I looked at Alejandro and despite my predicament I couldn't restrain myself. *"Alll-riiight!"* I said admiringly.

In the driveway sat an incredibly beautiful bright-green vintage Mercedes, with the Spanish flag on a staff mounted on the right fender. I sensed the irony of my situation: I had arrived clandestinely, slogging through the surf. Now, beginning the first leg of my departure, an embassy driver in uniform held the door for me and I climbed in, settling back onto soft leather upholstery.

The ride wasn't long—probably less than two minutes. But it was one of the most stressful rides I have ever taken. I felt naked. I was unarmed. I had no documents. I was on Castro's wanted list. I really didn't know whether Castro's people would just say "To hell with all that diplomatic b.s.," and simply pull me out of the car and shoot me on the spot.

Alejandro was talking, but I wasn't listening. I was trying to think of all the ways I could escape if something went wrong. Take a gun from a militiaman and run. Shoot my way out. Commandeer the car and drive through the roadblocks. Get hold of a machine gun.

"Wait here." Alejandro's voice interrupted my daydreaming. We were already in the Venezuelan Embassy compound. I looked around. Cuban troops stood about ten meters from the car.

Then I heard Alejandro's voice again. "Felix—run!" He was holding the kitchen door open. I bolted from the car like a world-class sprinter, went through the door and sprinted the full length of the kitchen, coming to a stop near a dignified elderly man sitting at the table eating breakfast. I recognized him as I careened past, and managed to blurt out, "Good morning, Mr. President," as he looked at me in shock. I had almost collided with Manuel Urrutia Lleo, the former Cuban president, whom Castro had first installed, then ousted.

I was finally safe. Fidel could not get his hands on me. But I would spend the next five months in this building, waiting to get permission to leave.

• • •

There were more than one hundred of us refugees, fighters and defectors in the Embassy. The bedrooms upstairs were reserved for the women and children. We men slept downstairs on the dining-room floor. Everyone was assigned chores. We did everything in shifts—bathing, shaving, eating, even housework and washing the dishes. Weekly rosters were posted, and we each did our share. The Venezuelans were very generous. They provided all our food (later I learned that Cubans who sought refuge in other embassies had been charged for their meals). Care packages had to pass through the Cuban troops guarding the embassy, and they regularly stole most of the food our families sent us. What remained, we shared as a group.

There was very little to do. I read books from the embassy library, wrote some poetry and short essays, and passed occasional messages to my colleagues in other embassies, using Venezuelan diplomats or staff as couriers. I also divided the few thousand pesos that remained from our operation among the members of my infiltration team, after I discovered where they were. I was able to debrief other refugees—political people, military officers, and the like, getting a lot of gossip and a few hard facts, and I sent the results of my intelligence-gathering back to the Agency.

On June 4, for example, I reported about military developments in the Cuban capital. "In the past few days," I wrote, "the government has mobilized a great deal of heavy weapons around Havana.

"An informer says that more than 10 tanks and a number of light bulletproof trucks mounted with 30-caliber machine guns are stored in an underground garage at J and 25th streets in el Vedado." My report went on to cite other arms caches stored in Havana locations. "Our opinion about this," I wrote, "is that the government knows that sooner or later an invasion is imminent.... They believe we are going to bombard all important military targets, and by storing as many weapons as possible in civilian areas they will save them."

To get my messages out, I would put the information in an envelope, seal it securely, address it to my family, and give it to the Venezuelan consul. My parents would pass the envelope on to the Americans in Miami. Normally, we would have had contingency plans for passing intelligence along. But no one had contemplated a disaster the size of the Bay of Pigs. So I improvised. And it must have worked, because from time to time the Americans used my reports. One, citing Cuban weapons shipments to Central America, was leaked for propaganda purposes—I even saw it in a Venezuelan newspaper almost word for word the way I'd written it.

Since we could receive mail and telegrams, we often got answers to our messages. I got a number of telegrams from "Susy," for example. That was my family's way of telling me they had received my messages and passed them on. I also set up a system that allowed me to stay in contact with the U.S. by radio. In fact, I probably sent more radio traffic while I was in the Venezuelan Embassy than I did during my infiltration.

But the single best piece of intelligence I developed during my five months of sanctuary, the Agency—as far as I know—never acted on. In July, a Cuban army captain who had defected told me that the Soviets were building missile bases in Oriente Province. He had personally worked on the tunnels, he said, and when I provided maps he drew in the location of the tunnels and the direction in which the missiles were pointed—toward the U.S. Navy base at Guantánamo. I got him to describe the weapons as completely as possible: height, weight, color, launch-vehicle type—everything I could think of. As usual, I put the information in an envelope and gave it to the consul.

(I never received anything back. In fact, since no one made a big deal out of my discovery, I felt free to talk publicly about it. In October 1961, I visited my old prep school where I spoke to the assembled students about my experiences in Cuba. I gave a full report on the Soviet missile sites—my words were even reported in local newspapers. But the story was not picked up either by the national media or, as far as I knew, by the U.S. Government.)

It was only much later that I discovered I was not the only one who made such a report. Joaquin Powell, a cousin of mine who was an important agent for the CIA in Miami, maintained regular contact with Victor Rodríguez, a farm owner from Oriente Province. Early in 1962, Victor was able to visit Miami, where he told my cousin a strange story.

"The Russians," he said, "are going crazy."

"Why?" asked my cousin.

"They're trucking big loads of ice to their base," the old man said. "Every day, the Cubans drive truck after truck of ice, and the Russians take over at the gate and drive it into the tunnels they've built."

Victor laughed. "Maybe they're homesick for Siberia!"

My cousin was dubious. Nevertheless, he passed Victor's information on to his case officer, who became quite excited. The Agency verified Victor's story, and the explanation the Agency man gave my cousin was that since missile fuel had to be kept at a constant temperature, the cooling system in the tunnels must have broken down and the Russians used the ice as a substitute.

In September the Cuban government finally granted me safe-conduct. I could be repatriated. I climbed on one of three buses and we drove through the embassy gates on our way to the airport; escorted by Castro's G-2 cars. The ride was an emotional one for me as I drove through Havana, looking at sites I might never see again. I had a camera and took pictures even though we'd been warned not to do so. One photograph would become especially meaningful to me: a picture of my Uncle Toto's house at Fifth Avenue and Twenty-eighth Street in Miramar; the place was filled with memories of my childhood. Later I would learn that the day I snapped the picture, five Soviet families were living there.

I reached Caracas safely on September 13. On October 1, I took a flight for Miami.

I arrived back to find a Miami different from the one I'd left only a few months before. The failure of the invasion, coupled with Castro's capture of so many resistance leaders, had caused turmoil and dissension within the Cuban community and its various anti-Castro movements, as well as within the CIA itself. There were, I would discover later, a lot of recriminations, although not a lot of solutions, offered up by various factions within the U.S. Government.

Indeed, the Bay of Pigs invasion still sparks bitter controversy within the intelligence community. As late as December 1987, a former CIA chief historian named Jack B. Pfeiffer sued the Agency under the Freedom of Information Act to force it to release histories of the Bay of Pigs which he had written. Those accounts reportedly —and accurately—spread the blame for the invasion's failure from the CIA to some in the Kennedy administration, including Secretary of State Dean Rusk, Secretary of Defense Robert S. McNamara, and the national security adviser, McGeorge Bundy. The CIA for reasons of its own opposes the release of Pfeiffer's work.

Despite the name-calling and recriminations, there was still, in the summer of 1961, some optimism that many elements of the Government's anti-Castro activities could be salvaged. A bright young CIA officer named Theodore Shackley was brought back from Berlin to oversee plans for the Agency's Cuban operations. Early in 1962, Shackley came from Washington to head Miami Station. One of his lieutenants, a man with whom I would work closely over the next decade and a half (until we broke our friendship because of his activities with CIA renegade Edwin Wilson), was Tom Clines.

The problems Shackley, Clines, and the other CIA officers based in Miami would face were considerable. The MRR leader Francisco was dead, executed by Castro on April 17. His replacements, hand-picked by the Americans, were Manuel Guillot Castellanos and Rafael Quintero. Their task was to infiltrate and rebuild the shattered MRR organization inside Cuba.

But it would not be easy. First, Castro had almost totally consolidated his grasp on the country. Second, there was resentment toward Guillot and Quintero from many MRR resistance fighters still active. Those resistance fighters operating inside Cuba felt that those who stayed there, not a pair who fled after the Bay of Pigs fiasco, should set the priorities. Still, Guillot and Quintero had Agency money and resources behind them—and the CIA operation based in Miami, code-named JM-WAVE, was huge.

Miami Station was the only full-service CIA operation ever based in the continental United States. The CIA has historically maintained bureaus, called bases, in U.S. cities that have high levels of foreign activity—major ports, border cities, and cosmopolitan centers where foreigners come to visit or work—places like New Orleans, San Francisco, and New York. By law, of course, the CIA is not allowed to run domestic operations. But it does legally maintain the capability for keeping track of foreigners, especially those who might have some intelligence potential back in their native countries. It also coordinates some activities with the FBI and other law-enforcement agencies.

But Miami Station was unique. At its height, in the mid-sixties, it had hundreds of employees working out of offices at the south campus of the University of Miami, and throughout the Homestead area. The reasons for the establishment of Miami Station lay in the geography of the Caribbean itself. It was not cost-effective for the Agency to maintain permanent stations on the scores of islands that were moving from colonial to sovereign status in the fifties and sixties. And yet information from the region was—and still is—crucial to the U.S. national interest. So an exception was made, and Miami had its own Chief of Station, CIA residents, officers, agents, and support staff—just like any Agency station overseas.

But in the sixties, during the buildup prior to the Bay of Pigs invasion, and during the years afterward, JM-WAVE went from being a small-time tropical CIA outpost to a major station. There were scores of safe houses and literally hundreds of Cuban exiles like me who worked as agents for our American case officers.

Organizationally we Cubans were relegated to positions toward the bottom of the charts. In fact, as far as I can determine, there were no Cuban CIA officers whatsoever at Miami Station. All the "chiefs" were Americans. There were, of course, lots of Cuban "Indians"— that is to say, agents. The agents were divided into several groups. There were Cubans who worked primarily as paramilitary, or guerrilla, forces. Others did propaganda work, putting out newsletters and doing radio broadcasts. Still others helped develop intelligence by interviewing refugees, or passing on information they had learned from their families.

I became a principal agent. I acted as a cut-out between my case officer, Tom Clines, and the fellow Cubans with whom I worked. When we went on an infiltration, for example, it was the principal agent, not the case officer, who would accompany the team on its missions. A Cuban would drive to our homes and get us early in the morning. Then we would proceed to a rendezvous where Clines or another American would be waiting with an Agency car. One interesting sidelight of Miami Station, incidentally, had to do with the caste system for automobiles. Bottom-rung CIA officers drove Chevys and Fords. Higher-ups got Pontiacs. And Ted Shackley, the station chief, drove a Cadillac.

Principal agents served as interpreters during meetings with Cubans (only a very few of the Americans spoke fluent Spanish). We also maintained safe houses, making sure there was food, keeping the accounts, and often acting as quartermaster, supply sergeant, and paymaster all in one. When our teams infiltrated Cuba, we went with them on the boats, making sure that they got in—and out—safely.

In fact, those agents who risked their lives going into Cuba probably did so with greater confidence because principal agents like me were on the job alongside them. First of all, we all knew each other. There were family and friendship relationships that went back decades. And our fellow Cubans knew we'd never leave them behind.

Once, for example, a CIA case officer forgot to radio a new recognition signal to a team I had accompanied on their infiltration mission. When the Cuban frogman responsible for bringing the team back from the beach signaled them, they didn't answer with the proper response and the frogmen returned to our boat. It was only after I insisted that we go into the beach regardless that we retrieved them. Needless to say, the team that was almost stranded was not happy with the case officer.

But even with its principal agents, the Agency maintained a high level of internal secrecy. I never knew, for example, where Miami Station actually was located until I found out in 1965—by accident. (It was on the old campus of the University of Miami. I discovered this when I worked as a uniformed guard for a security firm hired by the university, and one night saw my case officer walk into one of the campus buildings.) I never knew the last name of my Agency contacts either. They were addressed by first names, which might have been real or might have been pseudonyms.

Obviously, Miami Station enjoyed a couple of advantages over CIA stations overseas. It was based in friendly territory, and hence enjoyed the tacit support of the local government, as well as all the local law-enforcement agencies. Second, there was little the large number of emigré Cubans in Miami would not do—in fact there was little that they *did not* do—to help the Agency in its secret war against the communist dictator they hated so deeply. For us, the fight against Castro was an all-consuming passion. It was a holy war, a crusade.

And there was much to be done. New refugees were debriefed, intelligence was gathered, and operations against Castro were mounted by the dozens. According to an article published in *Harper's* magazine, Miami Station during its heyday in the sixties had an annual budget "well in excess of $50 million." Yet if that was the case, we Cubans weren't seeing very much of those millions. Principal agents like me made roughly $175 to $225 a month, barely enough to scrape by on. I myself would have worked for free, had the Agency allowed me to do so. All I wanted to do was fight against Castro. But they insisted that we all receive our monthly payments and sign for them.

Indeed, within two weeks of my return from Venezuela I was on my way back to Cuba. My job was to reactivate an infiltration route, which would later serve to move Guillot and Quintero into Cuba. As far as anyone knew, I was the only agent who still had the remnants of his operational infiltration network on the island. I used a man named Tito Ortega, whose father, Quirino, had a fish-and-coal-hauling boat. Quirino had instructions to check a certain key near Key Romano in Camaguey province every week or so for contact. That was where I took Guillot and Quintero. Our first try was unsuccessful—we couldn't rendezvous with Tito's father. But I got them in the second time.

It became increasingly important to know with whom we were dealing, since the domestic situation in Cuba had changed drastically since the Bay of Pigs. By fall 1961, it was hard to convince Cubans to engage in the kinds of anti-Castro activities they'd willingly carried out nine months before.

The main reason behind this was Fidel's aggressive and successful program to eliminate popular support for us in the wake of the Bay of Pigs fiasco. Before the April 17 invasion, Castro's security forces were disorganized and had little success in rooting out internal dissent. Most of their major achievements—like Francisco's capture—

were accidents. Afterward things changed. Castro used the invasion to imprison hundreds, perhaps thousands, of his political enemies. Watch groups, in which people were forced to spy and report on their neighbors on a regular basis, were increased. Soviet advisers began to appear in great numbers.

Before the Bay of Pigs, most Cubans would have resisted Castro's moves. We are an independent people and we love our freedom. But after April 17, a nationwide demoralization set in. In some respects the United States was responsible. It had sent us infiltrators in as the vanguard of a major invasion. We were messengers who told our contacts in the Cuban resistance, "Hey, the Americans are going to support us all the way. The weapons will arrive on time. Our own Free Cuba air force will stage massive strikes, and our brothers to the North are going to help make sure that Cuba will be free."

When the Americans abandoned us during that botched invasion, they caused a number of chain reactions. Among them were Castro's consolidation of his power and his aggressive tactics to deny us support inside Cuba. For example, he sent military units dressed like infiltrators to regions where we'd received a lot of backing. The communist provocateurs usually arrived at night. Some spoke English. They would say to some farmer, "Hey, we just arrived from Miami and we need your help."

If the farmer helped, he was arrested and publicly executed for antirevolutionary activities.

The technique was effective. It got so that people in the country-side didn't know whom to trust. So we had to build our relationships very slowly, going from person to person until we could establish a network that was free of Castro informers. It was sometimes a painstaking process. We would first identify a specific area in which we wanted to operate, then target farmers who might help us. To prove our bona fides we would bring pictures or messages from their relatives in Miami. Nowadays, students at the National War College in Washington, D.C., are taught about such techniques when they study unconventional warfare. We had no such instructions—we were operating by trial and error.

Our efforts paid off: Between the fall of 1961 and the summer of 1962 I personally managed to smuggle some ten *tons* of military equipment into Cuba. As far as I know, most of it is still where I hid it, although God knows whether it's still serviceable.

The Agency was reasonably good about supporting us. We were given weapons that ranged from grease guns and BARs, to 57-mm recoilless rifles and bazookas. As a matter of fact, I still have a couple of photographs, taken in the living room of Uncle Toto's house in Northeast Miami, of me and the Agency-supplied "armory" I used for training teams, which I stored at his home.

We had access to an assortment of boats, from slow, eighty-foot mother ships to RB-12s, rubber boats that had specially silenced gas motors. We even had infrared metascopes, although they were pre-historic compared to what is available now. For example, an infrared balloon was tied to the top of our mother ship's mast so we could see it approach the coast at night to read the signal in the distance. But we didn't have the sort of night-vision goggles available today. In-stead, we used either the battery-powered metascope or, worse, one that had to be crank-operated.

And operations did not always run as smoothly as they might have. The report I wrote following "Operation Triunfo, No. 2" re-flects some of the frustrations we faced:

> *Dec. 29, 1961:* We traveled all day and arrived in the mother boat at the fixed point, where we took off for land-ing at 9 P.M. We were six men altogether, 750 lbs of equip-ment and an RS-1 radio. Renato, Omar, and myself got in the Boston Whaler, and tied behind our boat was the cargo in the RB-12, along with Monty, Tito, and Felipe. We also had two radio communications devices, one GE and a PRC-10.
>
> We did not lose contact with the mother boat at the beginning of the trip. At 10:15 P.M. our boat got its nose underwater and we almost sank completely. Both radios were affected by the water. I had to jump out of the boat (it was not too deep even though we were quite far from the coast) and change some of the equipment we were taking in the RB-12. I contacted the mother boat on the GE, but discovered that I could not both transmit and re-ceive because of the water damage. Still, I managed to transmit to the mother-boat commander that we would

move forward and that he could pick us up the next day as prearranged.

At 10:45 P.M. we bailed ourselves out with an empty water can and proceeded toward Cuba. It was difficult to use the small compass to guide ourselves in.

At 11:45 P.M. we arrived at the place where we'd hidden the first equipment [N.B.: from an earlier mission]. We rowed in and were 15 meters from the coast at midnight. Omar and I made a patrol in the landing zone. The place was deserted. We started to unload the cargo, and after we finished we took the RB-12 and its motor and hid them in a secure place inside the key. After that we went to bed for a while as our feet and legs were sopping.

Dec. 30, 1961 We slept from 1 to 5:30 A.M. Then I woke everyone up. We took the motor off the Boston Whaler then hid them both in some bushes, after which we went back to sleep.

At 8:30 A.M. Renato and Tito went on a patrol to the south coast of Key Romano looking for Quirino's boat. They returned at noon. Nothing was found.

We deliberated a further infiltration in the Whaler but it was impossible to make the trip on the 35 gallons of gas we had in the tank and still have enough to make it back to the mother boat. Also it was probable that Quirino was home in Morón, not at his place near the Cienega River's mouth.

At 2 P.M. Tito went on patrol to the south coast where he saw a sailboat at some distance. He came back to our position and at 3:35 P.M. he and Renato took off in the RB-12 to check the sailboat.

At 5:30 P.M. we took the Boston Whaler from cover and prepared it to return to the mother ship.

At 6 Renato and Tito returned. They said the sailboat was moving toward Nuevitas port, so it could not have been Tito's father.

Our time was running out. Monty and Tito decided to stay on the key and wait for Quirino Ortega. They asked only for salt and food from the mother ship, as Key Romano has drinking water and wild horses they can hunt in an emergency. They can safely stay on the key for 6–10 days in any case, which means they'll be all right until our next Triunfo operation, which should be before 10 January.

We took off for the mother ship, establishing contact through the infrared metascopes at about 8 P.M. in a very rough sea. As we moved toward the mother ship we detected seven other craft, but none was a Cuban Navy gunboat. We arrived at 9 P.M. soaking wet, sent the Whaler back with supplies for Tito and Renato and were finally on our way by 11 P.M.

Dec. 31, 1961: We traveled all day. At 3 P.M. a U.S. Navy hydroplane flew over and inspected us. We arrived at our destination at 9 P.M., rendezvoused with our pick-up boat at 10 because it had had engine troubles, and arrived on the Florida coast at 11 P.M.

Things didn't get any easier on the trip home. We were cold and wet and we wanted very much to get back to Miami as quickly as possible. It was, after all, New Year's Eve. But nothing went right. Our Agency contact was late picking us up. Then, once we were on the road, he drove at a snail's pace. I asked him to let me drive. It was one of the Agency's rented cars, a big black Chevy, and I floored it. I made good time—a nice steady eighty or so—until I was pulled over by a state trooper. The situation was not great—a big car with four unshaven Cuban guys in grungy, damp, green fatigue uniforms, and an Anglo along for the ride.

The trooper was cool, but clearly unsettled. He asked for identification. I told him I had none. He asked my friends for identification. They, too, said they had none.

He looked at me. "Driver's license?"

"I left it at home."

The trooper sighed. The Agency guy took him aside for a couple of minutes' private conversation. Then the cop came back. He fined us one hundred dollars on the spot—fifty dollars for speeding and another fifty for driving without a license—and made me fill out long forms, stating my name and address (I gave fake ones), before driving off.

Later, the CIA man said he'd told the trooper we were refugees and he was a social worker from a humanitarian agency taking us to find work in Key West. The agency part of it was right, but the way we looked I doubt the cop believed the cover story for a minute.

That wasn't the end of it. A couple of weeks later, the CIA man actually asked me to take my driver's license and show up in court, so he'd get fifty dollars back. I refused. After all, I'd given a fake name—which would have cost me more than fifty dollars.

Another time, a group of friends and I were stopped by a sheriff's deputy. He was cruising the highway, and he spotted our station wagon. In the rear was a 57mm recoilless rifle and a bunch of ammo for it—each shell must have been two feet long. We were coming back from some training exercise or other. He pulled us over and I thought his eyes were going to jump out of his head when he saw the big-barreled weapon and tank-stopping ammunition lying in the back of the wagon.

"What the hell are you doing with that?" he asked, pointing at us.

"We are going duck hunting," we told him with a smile.

For some reason, he didn't believe us. He said he was going to have to confiscate the gun and take us in. But we knew better—we knew the law.

At that point in time, the Florida gun law allowed people to own and transport any single-action weapon—no restrictions of caliber were mentioned. So we told the deputy, "Look—what we've got is a single-action rifle. It's not illegal—you can check it out with your people while we wait here."

He called it in while we waited by the side of the road. Finally he came back to us and said, "Jesus Christ, this is unbelievable, but you're right. You can go!"

We left him scratching his head and muttering to himself about having to get the damn law changed.

These sorts of stories were not isolated incidents. They were the way of life for those of us in the Cuban resistance working out of South Florida during the sixties—a mixture of heroism and theater of the absurd.

But we had our successes, too. In August 1962, my dear friend

José Basulto sailed into Havana Harbor with half a dozen of his friends and shelled a hotel full of Russian advisers.

I first met Basulto in Guatemala in 1960. He was a radio operator in the 2506 Brigade—one of its earliest members. Basulto's identification number was 2522. We have been like brothers ever since. He has been active for a decade in supporting the Nicaraguan freedom fighters ever since the Sandinistas took power, and is constantly organizing Contra support among Miami's Cuban community. He has even been to Contra camps in Central America, helping to dispense humanitarian aid.

José Basulto had been a freedom fighter and a lover of democracy since his teens. He and his family were first active in anti-Batista activities run by Cuba's Catholic student organizations in the fifties. Then, after Fidel took power, the Basultos worked against the communist dictator. His mother moved radios from place to place for the resistance fighters in Havana. The whole Basulto family was active in getting weapons both in and out of the country before they finally emigrated to Miami. Basulto likes to tell a story about the fact that his family's three-level house in Havana became a weapons warehouse for the MRR. The building had an elevator, and they stored weapons in the shaft. They also managed to set up a radio transmitter in the attic.

Like me, José Basulto became an infiltration-team member. And because he was a radio operator, he got to spend a few weeks at the CIA's "farm" at Fort Peary, Virginia. The Cubans nicknamed it "The Icebox," because they went there in the winter (many saw snow for the first time courtesy of the CIA).

Basulto was one of five men sent to the city of Santiago de Cuba in Oriente province before the invasion. He was an architecture student, and, unlike me, he didn't go in surreptitiously by boat. Instead, he posed as a student from Boston College coming home on vacation, and he flew straight into Havana airport. Later, when things fell apart, Basulto managed to jump the fence at the Guantánamo U.S. Naval Base, and was flown back to Miami immediately. The other members of his team weren't so lucky—all were killed or captured.

In one way, Basulto is responsible for my continuing with the CIA. It was hard to find radio operators for my missions. Still, the

CIA was not willing to remove me from operations for communications training. So I went to Basulto, and he made the effort to teach me Morse code. Morse is hard to learn, but Basulto, who was living at home in the fall of 1961, used an effective carrot-and-stick method with me. Early every morning for two or three hours he would sit with me and watch patiently as I practiced with the keypad. Then his mother would cook us up a big batch of pancakes, which she'd top with chocolate ice cream.

I was happy to be working with the Agency in 1962. Basulto was not. He felt—and still feels—that the CIA was more interested in promoting the U.S. national interest than it was in seeing a free and democratic Cuba. Basulto has always felt that the Agency's dealings with Cubans reflected a dangerous mixture of cynicism and naiveté.

As he said one day recently, "The problem with the Agency was that it was only interested in East-West—U.S.–Soviet conflicts. Not democracy in Cuba, or getting rid of a dictator. We Cubans were not important to the CIA. If it had not been Cuba—if it had been Mexico—they would have been recruiting Mexicans; if it had been Brazil it would have been Brazilians."

So Basulto quit working with the CIA and decided to strike out on his own. Like many Cubans in Miami, he was outraged by what he perceived as the Kennedy administration's public softness on Fidel. During the first half of 1962, Kennedy's tone on Cuba was indeed much less strident than it had been prior to the Bay of Pigs. The Agency was pushing fewer paramilitary operations and more straight intelligence gathering.

In March, for example, they tasked Rafael Quintero, to find out the number of checkpoints between Morón and Havana; to evaluate the efficiency of neighborhood defense committees; to report on any changes in documents and identity cards; and to look closely at military security operations in the Keys. He was asked to "give us the general psychological situation of the people in respect to the communist government," and was also queried about Castro's success in indoctrinating the Cuban people.

It seemed to many of us a period of inaction—which was something we didn't want. We didn't know at the time about JFK's behind-the-scenes efforts to repatriate the 2506 Brigade members in Cuban jails, the administration's intelligence-gathering operations regarding Soviet missile sites in Oriente province, and the increasing sentiment at the NSC that such actions as mining Cuba's harbors would be necessary to contain and ultimately overthrow Castro.

Basulto, of course, had no idea what the U.S. Government was up to. He wanted action. So he and a friend named Carlos Hernández pooled three hundred dollars of their own money to buy a Lathi semiautomatic 20mm cannon, one hundred rounds of ammunition, and half a dozen magazines. It may sound bizarre now, but in 1962 you could buy arms like that on the streets of Miami, or through the mail. Next, they borrowed one of their friends' father's boats, a thirty-one-foot Bertram power cruiser with a top speed of about thirty knots, outfitted it with extra fuel tanks, and added a deck mount for the cannon.

On August 24, 1962, Basulto and half a dozen of his friends, all of them in their early twenties, sailed from Miami into Havana harbor and staged a raid on the waterfront Hotel Rosita de Hornedo, where scores of Soviet advisers lived. Nobody was killed, although Basulto and company shelled the front of the place with the cannon and raked it with small-arms fire. Somehow they managed to make it back to Miami without taking a single hit from either the Cuban army and navy or the Soviets.

Basulto thought of the mission as a way to make a strong personal statement to Fidel. He also knew that if he and his friends were successful they would become front-page news in Miami. They did better than that: they became front-page news all over the world. Basulto and his pals also created a hell of an international incident. Castro accused President Kennedy and the CIA of staging the raid. The U.S. Government, which didn't know anything about it, was embarrassed. And a firestorm broke out at Miami Station as the Agency tried to discover how a bunch of Cuban kids with no formal operational support could run such a successful mission.

I would have liked to have gone with Basulto, but I had other things on my mind. On August 25, 1962, Rosa Nodal and I got married. We'd known each other since 1955, but things didn't get serious until about six months before our wedding. Still, somehow, I'd always had a subconscious feeling that I'd marry her. In the Dominican Republic, for example, I reported in my journal about several relationships I had with women in Ciudad Trujillo. But then, prophetically, I wrote, "Maybe I'll marry Rosa. Of course, she will be hard to conquer." I'd even risked my life to visit her home in Cuba, only to show up and have her father tell me that she was on vacation at the beach!

Rosa emigrated to the U.S. in December 1961. She was able to leave Cuba before her parents because she had a student visa— she'd studied in 1958 and 1959 at a Baptist college in Bristol, Virginia. She arrived shortly after I got back from my five months' sanctuary at the Venezuelan Embassy. When I discovered that she'd come to Miami and was living with her aunt and uncle, Aurelia and Luis Carbonell, we started dating almost immediately.

Naturally, getting married brought new responsibilities. In July, I told my CIA case officer that I was going to have to stop working with the Agency and find a regular job. In truth, I had no official, certified relationship with the CIA—nor would I have one until the late sixties, when I went to Peru and Ecuador at the CIA's behest, and in 1969, just before I left for Vietnam on an Agency contract. In 1962 my relationship with the CIA was based on an oral understanding. No papers had been signed, no contract had been offered. For its part, the CIA never acknowledged its own operations. Everyone knew who was who and what was going on, but no one ever came out and said, "I am a CIA official." I guess if we had demanded to become full-time Agency employees, a decision would have been made. However, neither we nor the CIA raised the subject.

As a result I, like many of my friends, drifted into a sort of free-lance relationship with the Agency, without any formal connections and, I might add, benefits. In some ways, things were better that way. I could come and go as I pleased. On the other hand, it didn't have much of a future for a man just starting out in marriage.

We had a simple wedding—Rosa didn't even wear a long dress— in a church in a shopping center at Northwest Twenty-seventh Avenue and Seventy-ninth Street. There were no wedding pictures except for Polaroids and other snapshots. Our tiny reception was given to us by our cousins Aurora and Omar Vaillant. To put it bluntly, funds were tight. My savings totaled $700. Of that, $250 went for an engagement ring, and another $200 for our honeymoon —a couple of days in Fort Lauderdale and then a week's trip to Florida's West Coast. We'd both been living with our families, and our first home together was a motel room across the street from Rosa's aunt.

We both worked. Every morning I'd drop Rosa at her job as a secretary at a radio station, and I'd continue to the ACE Letter Service, which printed folders and brochures for Miami hotels. They paid me a dollar an hour to stack and carry brochures. Then, in September, with help from my Uncle Raul I found a job that paid $1.55 per hour at a meat-packing plant. There I took hams out of the freezers and carried them into the preparation area. I made more money, but the working conditions were horrible—going from freezer to hundred-degree heat dozens of times a day.

Fate intervened before I contracted pneumonia. Early in October I got a call from my old case officer, Tom Clines, who asked me in urgent tones to meet him right away at a Howard Johnson's near the University of Miami. I walked off my job without a word to anyone and drove to see what he wanted.

"Felix," he said after a cursory greeting, "I am speaking to you as a representative of the United States Government's intelligence community."

His bluntness shocked the hell out of me. While I knew very well Tom worked for the CIA, he had never once admitted any connection with it.

"U.S. Marines are going to invade Cuba," he told me. "And we need your help."

I said, "All right, what do you need?"

Clines explained. He wanted me to parachute with a handpicked team of Cubans into Las Villas Province. The objective was to set up a radio beacon pointing toward a Soviet missile base, so that U.S. planes could attack the installation. He added that we would probably have to defend the beacon for a few hours from Cuban and Soviet troops. We would be dropped in at night and the planes would attack the missile sites the following morning.

I agreed to lead the mission even though I had never worn a parachute in my life, much less trained to jump out of a plane at night. We went directly from the Howard Johnson's to an Agency safe house. I never called Rosa or anyone else. At the safe house I gave Tom a list of prospective team members, and he left with the names in hand.

I sat in the house by myself. Meanwhile, Rosa finished at the radio station and waited—and waited—for me to pick her up. She finally took the bus back to our motel room, wondering all the while whether I was in a hospital somewhere. About midnight, after calling a number of our friends, she realized something was up and that I had probably gone on some mission or other. Word was already circulating among the Cuban community about what would come to be known as the Cuban missile crisis.

Tom Clines showed up seventy-two hours later. He was apologetic. "Felix," he said, "I'm sorry—we seem to have forgotten about you, but other things were going on."

He explained the mission had been scrubbed, thanked me for volunteering, and drove off. That concluded my small role in the 1962 Cuban missile crisis—except for the not-so-minor inconvenience that I was now out of a job and my wife had been half crazy with worry for three days and was mad as hell at me. Why is it that such things never happen in James Bond novels?

8 The first prisoners from 2506 Brigade flew into Homestead Air Force Base on Sunday, December 23, 1962. They had been ransomed from Castro by the U.S. for $53 million in food and drugs—an indication of the state of the Cuban economy under communist dictatorship. Six days later, I watched President John Kennedy stand only a few feet away from me in Miami's Orange Bowl, holding high the 2506 flag that had flown for a few hours over Cuba. "I can assure you," the President told the cheering crowd, "that this flag will be returned to this Brigade in a free Havana."

Another, less publicized vow was made by the President that day.

It gave 2506 Brigade officers the opportunity to become commissioned as regular U.S. Army officers, even though we were not citizens; indeed, even though most of us didn't even hold a permanent resident's green card. It seemed like a good opportunity at the time. Rosa and I talked it over. We decided the army might make a steady career. No more craziness like disappearing without a word and not coming back for hours, days—even months. So I accepted President Kennedy's offer, was commissioned as a second lieutenant, and in March 1963 I reported for my basic training at the infantry school in Fort Benning, Georgia.

But even before the basic course was completed, I had a visit from Manuel Artime and Rafael "Chi Chi" Quintero, which changed the direction of my life once again.

"We're going to overthrow Castro—this time we're really going to do it," they said, explaining that the President of the United States himself was sponsoring a liberation movement. Even better, this force would be entirely Cuban-run and Cuban-led. Unlike our previous efforts, we would not have to endure the whims of U.S. advisers and bureaucrats that we'd had to endure prior to the Bay of Pigs. This time, Artime promised me, we would stand or fail on our own.

The operation would be run out of Central America, utilizing hit-and-run tactics against Castro, stinging him like a boxer with repeated jabs until he became weak and could mount a major military attack.

They guaranteed the U.S. Government was behind the plan; that it was sponsored by Robert Kennedy and the President himself. They asked me to become a high-ranking officer in the endeavor, heading up the communications division. The only hitch was that I'd have to resign my army commission. The operation was to be covert.

I told them I liked the army, and that I'd been selected for intelligence training after my basic course was over. Also, I had doubts. The U.S. had left us in the lurch before—would that happen again? Moreover, I wasn't sure that Artime and Chi Chi Quintero spoke for the U.S. authorities. Resigning my commission was a serious matter.

Still, I'd known them both for a while. I'd met Chi Chi Quintero in 1956. There were three good-looking sisters from Camaguey who were spending the summer at Varadero Beach that year. I dated the eldest, Chi Chi the youngest, and his brother dated the middle sister. I hadn't seen him since then until just before the Bay of Pigs, although I knew from mutual friends that he had become close to the political leadership of the Cuban resistance movement. After Francisco's death, Chi Chi was one of the resistance leaders I infiltrated back inside Cuba—there is a picture taken of us together on one of those missions.

Now he was Artime's deputy. Manuel Artime was one of those charismatic people you get to meet only once or twice in a lifetime. I'd known him since 1960, when he was the political leader of the MRR. During one of our first meetings he asked Edgar Sopo and me to help him set up anti-Castro training camps. Right on the spot we donated the Diaz Lanz organization's Rolodex so he could contact potential sponsors and soldiers. He engendered that kind of trust in people. Artime was a doctor—a psychiatrist—and he knew how to play mind games to get what he wanted. But he was also a good soldier. He was the political officer of the 2506 Brigade—in fact, he was captured on the beach at the Bay of Pigs. Twice Castro threatened him with execution. Once one of Castro's men even put a pistol in his mouth and pulled the trigger. The hammer fell on an empty chamber. It was a mind game they played on him.

Artime was in his early thirties, with dark wavy hair and a husky voice that served him well as a public speaker. He was one of those people who, if he showed up at your home, would give your mother a kiss and within five minutes she'd be cooking his favorite dish for him.

"What assurance do you have it's a U.S. operation?" I asked Artime.

"What assurance do you need?" he answered.

I thought for a minute. "All right," I said. "You say you want to give me special communications training. Give it to me here, in U.S. Army uniform."

"If that's what you want, OK."

A short time afterward, two civilians who said their names were Mr. Moose and Mr. Flannigan showed up at Fort Benning to give me and two others communications training, on the base and in uniform. That convinced me that Artime was planning a bona fide U.S. Government-sponsored operation, and I took steps to resign my commission.

I finished basic training in early October, and on October 9, 1963, I received an honorable discharge from the U.S. Army.

Rosa was not pleased. She had hoped I'd settle into an army career, with the stability—not to mention the benefits—that it promised. She was pregnant with Rosemarie, our daughter, and she didn't want me out of the country.

But the possibility of helping to bring about a decisive victory against Castro was something I couldn't pass up. As I told her, "I stopped working for the Agency when we got married and I promised you I'd settle down. But I also said that if something for Cuba arose, I'd volunteer. I left my parents to fight for Cuba—and I'd have to leave you, too."

The fact of the matter was that the fight for Cuba was and remains the central focus of my life. Such is the case for many of my generation.

The summer of 1963, for example, marked the end of an era for many Americans—although they didn't realize it at the time. In retrospect, it was a summer of unabashed optimism, during which Martin Luther King made his historic "I have a dream" speech on the steps of the Lincoln Memorial in Washington, D.C.

The summer of 1963 was the last of America's innocent summers: the summer before JFK was assassinated in Dallas; the last summer before the name Vietnam insinuated itself into our national consciousness.

For us, veterans of Castro's prisons, fighters since our teens (I was still only twenty-two that summer), virtually none of these things mattered or existed. We lived outside the mainstream of American culture—societal orphans, whose one goal was Castro's overthrow and the reestablishment of a democratic republic in our homeland.

For me, the summer of 1963 was infantry training at Fort Benning, followed by Mr. Moose and Mr. Flannigan's tutorials in the fine art of clandestine communications.

It was not the happiest of times domestically. Rosa had believed she could change me. She could—but not where the freedom of

Cuba was concerned. I made my plans, and just around the time President Kennedy was assassinated, I left for Central America.

I spent almost two years in Nicaragua, running the communications network for Artime. The scope of the operation was considerable—more than three hundred people in all, based in Nicaragua, Costa Rica, and Miami. Our three main bases were in Nicaragua: the operational headquarters, my communications base, and the commandos' base. Artime was in Miami, and our arms cache was in Costa Rica. The funding for the project came from the CIA, but the money's origin was hidden through the use of a cover corporation, a company called Maritima BAM, which are Artime's initials spelled backwards. Periodically, deposits of hundreds of thousands of dollars would be made in Maritima BAM's accounts, and disbursed by Cuban corporation officers. The U.S. Government had the deniability it wanted; we got the money we needed.

The funds were spent well. We had two mother ships, each 250 feet long; two 50-foot aluminum-frame Swift boats for our commando forces, plus assorted smaller craft for silent landings and special operations. There was one C-47 aircraft plus a couple of Cessnas and a small Beaver aircraft that was capable of water landings. Our weapons came from Germany on a huge barge that we hid up a Costa Rican river. There were more then 200 tons of arms—all American-made—including a pair of 20mm anti-aircraft cannons in case Castro decided to stage an air raid on the communications headquarters, which was under my command. In all, the operation ended up costing the Americans somewhere in the area of $6 million over two and a half years.

We staged fourteen missions in that time, of which four achieved their objectives. While that success rate may seem low, it was not. The first year and a half was spent getting the project organized. We were running an entirely self-sufficient operation, put together from scratch. In fact, what we did in Nicaragua twenty-five years ago has some pretty close parallels to the Contra operation today. The lessons we learned back in the sixties are ones I believe might benefit those who look critically at the Contras today.

For example, patience is an essential requirement. Resistance operations take time and do not become successful overnight. Each element must be built slowly to insure success. My area of responsibility was communications. I held the rank of major and commanded ninety men. The problems I faced were not insurmountable, but they required time to solve. I had to come up with methods that allowed us to communicate securely with infiltration teams and commando units many hundreds of miles from their home base. I had to rig communications systems between each of our bases and our political headquarters in Miami, and mobile systems for our boats. These are tremendously complicated procedures because radio frequencies vary greatly according to the time of the day, atmospheric conditions, and weather, as anybody who is a ham radio operator knows.

I had to train operators to work with high-frequency radios, telegraphy devices, encoders, decoders, one-time cipher pads and the like—the whole tradecraft of communications—and have them ready to go operational within a few months. I had to design and oversee the construction of our communications sheds. In the tropics, especially in the days before microswitches and transistorized communications, not only was selecting the location of the equipment important, but protecting it from moisture, heat, and insects was top priority.

The most vital thing I had to do was create a signal plan for the operation, something that took me weeks to complete. The signal plan is the centerpiece of all secure communications operations. It tells you what frequencies to use and when to use them; what call signs to use and when to use them. We, for example, transmitted and received on two frequencies to make enemy interception more difficult. The signal plan also tells you in what sequence the frequencies are used, when they change—and how often. In addition, it determines what ciphers will be employed. We used an Agency five-letter cipher code that is even today almost impossible to break because it is based on random groupings of letters, each of which is used only once.

This was just my own area of responsibility; there was much more involved in the total operational scheme. Boat captains and crews had to be hired and trained. Commando units had to learn to work together as teams. Intelligence networks had to be set up and intelligence gathered, evaluated, and passed on. Up-to-date documents, everything from identity cards and drivers' licenses to the sorts of detritus normally found in old coat and trouser pockets, had to be designed and fabricated. Forward operational bases had to be scoped out and our long supply lines designed. Each of these elements takes time. Each takes planning. And once they are complete, they must be blended into the whole operational plan, becoming part of a coordinated system.

It is impossible, despite what many in Congress currently seem to believe, to create a large, efficient and successful freedom-fighting operation without money, and, just as important, without adequate time and sufficient patience.

We learned back in 1963 that it takes sustained effort to equip and train a sharp fighting force, no matter how good its motivation may be (and ours was very, very high).

Like the Democratic Nicaraguan Resistance, the Contras, we were just getting proficient and our success rate was beginning to climb just as our funds were cut and our operation scrapped. As a matter of fact, the Nicaraguan resistance is in a better position than we were militarily, because they are based in camps bordering their own country, or actually within their homeland. We were hundreds of miles away. Our troops had to spend days at sea before they could even see the coast of the country they were fighting for.

Another problem we faced was security. Castro's intelligence services targeted us immediately. It took a while, but we finally discovered one infiltrator, Gabriel Albuerne, in our midst. Albuerne tried to sign on with me as a communicator, but he didn't have the right stuff and was disqualified. So he joined our force as an electrician. As soon as he arrived at our base at Monkey Point, Nicaragua, things started to go wrong.

The generators on our boats began to malfunction. Soon after that, our power plant developed trouble. I had my friend Papo Reyes check the electrical lines, and we discovered that Albuerne had overloaded one of the three-phase lines, running a hot wire into the warehouse where we stored all our explosives. We confronted him and he admitted he was a Castro agent. We kept him under lock and key for a while, then turned him over to the Somoza government, which threw him in jail. Albuerne managed to escape during the

1973 Managua earthquake. He was given refuge by the Chilean Embassy then made his way back to Cuba, where he's still with the DGI, as far as we know. (Years later, I was contacted by the FBI's Miami office, which inquired whether I knew anything about a Cuban named Gabriel Albuerne, who they said had come to the U.S. illegally from Canada. I told the agent what I knew, and Albuerne was deported to Canada.)

The sorts of operations we ran against Castro combined economic warfare with guerrilla tactics. Although of limited success militarily (only four complete operations took place before our effort was shut down), they were still valuable propaganda tools.

One case in point is the May 1964 mission we called Zenon Viera 2. Its target was the Cabo Cruz sugar refinery on the south coast of Oriente province. The mission required ten guerrillas: two frogmen, two scout commandos, two support commandos, three assault commandos and an RB-12 crewman. The commandos blew up the refinery's water-cooling pipes and pumphouse, while a fast boat, the *Monty*, armed with 50mm machine guns and .75 and .57 caliber recoilless rifles, shelled the warehouse, molasses and alcohol tanks, and smokestack.

It may sound simple. But this was no war movie or TV show, where commando missions are undertaken without much preparation, and where the sentries are always looking the other direction when Rambo or Clint Eastwood come over the wall. We mounted a complicated, coordinated military operation that involved sending ships and men more than a thousand miles from their base into hostile waters, hitting a target with precision, withdrawing without sustaining any casualties, and returning safely to our home base. We even had refueling facilities in the Dominican Republic—my old friend Rafael García Toledo was Artime's liaison with the Dominicans.

Unlike war in Hollywood scripts, war in real life, I have found, almost always follows what the great military theorist Clausewitz called *La Friction*, which is a fancy way of stating Murphy's Law: What can go wrong, will go wrong. Radios usually do not work, ammunition gets wet, boats inexplicably sink from under you and the sentries stare right down your throats. So when my radio picked up the message, "Refinery burned various explosions," sent from the commandos to the mother ship, my sense of accomplishment and pride was overwhelming. Our men had succeeded—on their own, with no American advisers, no CIA trainers, and no overt U.S. assistance.

I was not the only one who felt that way. Artime's message to the commandos, while filled with hyperbole, was also bursting with pride.

> It is [he wrote] the hardest blow Cuban communism has received since the Bay of Pigs. Damages are calculated at five and a half million dollars. . . . The international press gave it equal space with a statement by [Secretary of Defense] McNamara. The brother of a president cheered in spite of being recently operated for ulcers. . . . The same day as the operation Brazil broke relations with Cuba and people think we have guided the Brazilian government. The shot is of Olympic proportions in Cuba. Fidel had to issue a war bulletin. . . . By this message I inform you that all those participating in the operation will be decorated with Trident medals. . . . Viva MRR. Viva free Cuba. Viva God. Cuba or nothing.—Artime.

Still, by the end of 1964 our operations were being slowly shut down despite our success. Money wasn't coming in as readily as it had. The intelligence we received from the Agency wasn't as current, or as valuable. Our operation had been conceived and planned by the Kennedys. But in 1964 JFK was dead and Robert no longer had the power that he once had. Lyndon Johnson had different priorities—Vietnam, for one—and we Cubans did not figure into his administration's goals.

We were also hurt because one of our operations badly embarrassed the U.S. Government. Toward the end of 1964 we launched a commando raid against Cuba's north coast. For forty-five days our men traveled on the open seas in very bad weather. When they arrived on site in Cuba, having refueled and restocked provisions in the Dominican Republic, they discovered that the intelligence they'd been given by the CIA was outdated: the landing zone that had been chosen was now bathed in light and their target was unapproachable.

They were frustrated. But as they bobbed in the current off the coast, they saw a huge ship pass in the distance. The first thing that came to the commander's mind was that it was the *Sierra Maestra*, the flagship of the Cuban merchant marine. Immediately, he radioed me with this on-site information and asked permission to stage an attack on the ship.

I tried to locate Artime, as our rules of engagement forbade any attack without permission from the top. I signaled Miami with an urgent message, but Artime was not to be found. All the while, messages were arriving from our forces saying that they'd lose the target if they had to wait much longer.

In retrospect, I suppose I shared the commandos' frustration over the fact that we hadn't been able to hit our primary target. I signaled back: "Cannot locate Artime. If you are sure target is *Sierra Maestra*, you have approval to attack."

Shortly afterward I received word that they had hit the boat. It was on fire and there were explosions. I radioed the information to Miami on a frequency I knew the Agency monitored, giving the coordinates of the attack so that rescue teams could be dispatched, and letting Artime know that we had attacked the *Sierra Maestra*.

A little bit later the same morning I got a message back from Miami: "Please tell us where the hell you are operating—Atlantic or Pacific oceans? *Sierra Maestra* passed through Panama Canal two weeks ago enroute Red China."

I was worried sick. If we had attacked a U.S. vessel, the damage to our cause could have been of immeasurable proportions. Only afterward did I discover what had happened. The commandos had come up on the stern of the freighter from the rear starboard quarter and shined their spotlight on it. They saw the word *Sierra*. Overjoyed at the prospect of hitting such an important target, he said they didn't bother to sail around the stern to check the lettering on the other side. If they had, they would have seen that the rest of the name read *Aranzazu*, not *Maestra*. What they'd done was attack an innocent Spanish freighter with their .57mm recoilless rifle and 50-caliber machine guns. They killed the captain, injured many of the crew, set the ship on fire, and disabled it.

We subsequently discovered that the ship was carrying a boiler for a Cuban sugarcane facility as well as some Christmas foodstuffs. We felt terrible. Soon after the incident, our operations were rolled up. Our fast boats were taken by the Agency and sent to Africa, where they saw service in the Congo. Some of the people who served with me in Nicaragua volunteered to fight in Africa too.

I went back to Miami, where I once again found part-time work as a principal agent. I spent time getting to know to my baby daughter, Rosemarie. I had not been in the U.S. for her birth—something Rosa resented deeply. And I held down two jobs in addition to my CIA work to be able to pay the bills. We had a second baby, Felix, Jr., on April 26, 1966, and I rejoiced in having both a son and a daughter.

I accepted one short overseas assignment during this time, in Venezuela. There, I worked with two Americans—I'll call them Bert and Joe—and had a pleasant and remarkably quiet, hassle-free three-month stay in Caracas. The only real excitement came when I returned to Miami. Somewhere along the line my documentation had gotten misplaced, and I flew from Venezuela without a single piece of paper saying who I was. When my plane arrived, my CIA control agent had been alerted to my predicament and was waiting for me. He handed me a packet—everything from driver's license to a Puerto Rican identity card—and had me sign for it all right there under the nose of U.S. Customs. They must have known what was going on, because I had no trouble passing through immigration.

So for almost two years life was pretty normal for Rosa and the kids and me. Then one day in June of 1967 I received a phone call from a CIA officer. The ramifications of that conversation haven't ended, even today.

9

The CIA man's name was Larry S. I didn't know him. I was told that he came from Washington and was a high-ranking individual. My case officer, whom I'll call Earl, arranged a meeting, telling me that Larry had a proposal he thought I'd find interesting. We arranged to rendezvous at a safe house in the Homestead area. There, Larry, described a special assignment for which the Agency believed I'd be particularly well suited.

He said that I might be in South America for some length of time, that the assignment would put to use my skills in unconventional warfare, antiguerrilla operations and communications. I told him I was interested.

"Good," Larry said. Then he continued, "There's a good possibility," he said, "that Che Guevara is engaged in guerrilla activities in Bolivia. Your assignment would be to help the Bolivians track him down and capture him." He paused. "If I were to select you for this mission, tell me, Felix, how long would it be before you could leave?"

I tried—somewhat unsuccessfully—to keep my excitement under wraps. "It depends," I said. "If you want me to leave tonight, I will go home and pack a few things and let Rosa know I'll be gone for a while. If you tell me we've only got a couple of hours, I will call her from the airport to say I'll be away for a couple of months. And if you say 'Right now,' then let's leave, and on the way to the airport I'll give you my phone number and you can call Rosa for me."

I didn't leave that day. But shortly after our interview, Earl called to say that of the sixteen agents Larry had interviewed, I was one of two who had been selected for the mission. I packed a bag, told Rosa I'd see her as soon as I could, and flew to Washington to begin my pre-mission briefings.

I arrived at National Airport and went directly to an Agency-rented apartment in downtown Washington. It was a bright, nicely decorated place within easy walking distance of the memorials. A CIA man contacted me there. He asked if I'd have any problems working with a man I'll call Eduardo. I said no—I'd met Eduardo during infantry training at Fort Benning back in 1963. We weren't close friends, but I had no objections.

"Fine," the Agency guy said. "Why not take a walk for a while. Come back in a couple of hours."

I wandered down to the Mall where I marveled at the Lincoln and Jefferson memorials and the Washington Monument, and peered down the Mall at the U.S. Capitol, majestic even in the summer heat. Americans sometimes take these places for granted. As a refugee from communist dictatorship, I never have done so. It was good to see them up close, and to think about where I might be going, and about the prospect of meeting one of my greatest enemies face to face.

When I returned to the apartment, Eduardo was there. We shook

1

The parlor of our home in Sancti Spiritus, looking toward the dining room. This is the way my father remembers it; today, the house has been confiscated by Fidel.

2

My parents, Rosa and Felix, at their wedding in 1938.

This is me, sitting in the hallway of our house in Sancti Spiritus at age eight or nine—about the same time I tied up the tutor.

3

4

Fidel Castro. I believe that his days are numbered.

My Grey team posing in front of Sopo's house the weekend before we infiltrated Cuba on February 28, 1961. The team, left to right: myself, Segundo Borges, Jr., Javier Souto, a friend, Edgar I. Sopo, Rafael Garcia-Rubio, who was a member of a different infiltration team, and José González-Castro.

This was taken during the 1961 infiltration mission to Cuba.

Rosa and me at our wedding, August 25, 1962.

At Fort Benning, Georgia, in 1963. Rosa thought at the time that my future would be as an Army officer, not a CIA agent.

During my time with Artime: working at a radio in San José, Costa Rica, in 1964.

10

The Zenon Viera naval base compound at Monkey Point, Nicaragua, where I worked from the end of 1963 until operations were closed down in 1965 after our commandos mistakenly attacked the *Sierra Aranzazu*, a Spanish vessel, thinking it was a Cuban ship.

11

The *Joanne*. This was the mother ship used by our forces to carry Cuban commandos during our guerrilla war against Castro from 1963 to 1965.

Che Guevara and me on October 9, 1967. This is the only picture of Che alive the day he was executed. It was taken with my Pentax by Major Jaime Nino de Guzmán outside the schoolhouse in La Higuera. Seconds before this was taken, I'd said to Che, "Watch the little birdie," and he smiled. But his expression became serious—perhaps even grim—at the instant Nino de Guzmán pressed the shutter.

With my beautiful
daughter,
Rosemarie, soon
after I'd returned
from Bolivia in
1967.

13

About to embark on
a parachute jump
during my stay in
Peru, 1968. It's
probably not my
first jump since I am
smiling.

14

April 1971. This was one of the PRU chiefs with whom I worked most closely—Mr. Ai. The picture was taken in Hau Nghia province after capturing a Vietcong intelligence infrastructure organization, utilizing information from a captured VC.

15

16

With Don Gregg atop the U.S. Embassy in Saigon, circa 1972.

17

With General Sánchez de Bustamante and some of his officers in Argentina, 1973.

18

At a Contra camp near the Honduran border in 1984. L–R: Chinto, myself, Enrique Bermudez, military commander of the Nicaraguan Democratic Resistance (the Contras), Jose Basulto, my old friend from the 2506 Brigade, and Dr. Roberto González, who uses his medical skills to help the Contras.

September 20, 1985

Dear Felix:

AFTER READING THIS LETTER PLEASE DESTROY IT. You may keep the
photographs.

Within the next 15 days, the Unified Nicaraguan **Opposition** (UNO)/
Nicaraguan Democratic Force (FDN) air arm will commence
operations with two new types of aircraft: the C-7, CARIBOU and
the M-740, MAULE STOL (see enclosures). These aircraft will be
used for air drop/aerial resupply to units inside Nicaragua.

Two contract C-7s are scheduled to arrive in Honduras on or about
October 10. Initially the aircraft will be flown by U.S.
citizens who are employees of the firm contracted to provide
delivery services for the FDN. It is intended that these
aircraft will operate primarily at night, performing paradrops to
units deep inside. Nicaraguan aircrews will be trained to fly
these missions as soon as possible.

The resistance has also purchased a number of new MAULE aircraft
shown in the enclosed photograph. These STOL a/c will be used
for day and night short-haul missions to include MEDEVAC and
aerial resupply. Each aircraft comes with a spare parts package
and a maintenance line has been established. Two aircraft have
already been delivered. More will follow. All will be flown by
Nicaraguan pilots or other Latin Americans -- not U.S. citizens.

Eventually both types of aircraft will also operate in support of
the southern front from fields in Costa Rica. Neither Costa Rica
or Honduras have adequate sites for maintaining these aircraft.
The only location which provides sufficient OPSEC, ramp space and
occasional hangar time for servicing these aircraft is at Ilopongo.

Since this is a completely compartmented operation, being handled
by the resistance, you are the only person in the area who can
set-up the servicing of these aircraft with General Vides
Casanova and General Bustillo, both have a high regard for you
and you may use my name privately with either of them but no
others. You must not advise the Station Chief; you must also
keep knowledge of this project from del Amico, who is not working
with our people.

Would you, therefore, approach Generals Vides and Bustillo with
the following proposal:

--   Service space for one C-7 on a one day a week basis. A
     representative of the C-7 contractor will ensure that all
     parts and maintenance items are delivered to FDN service
     technicians (three) as needed. No Salvadoran parts or
     maintenance will be required.

--   Service space for occassional MAULE maintenance with parts
     and supplies handled the same as above. Again, no
     Salvadoran parts or labor will be required.

--   This plan requires only discrete use of the ESAF/FAS space
     and no use of FMS; MAP; and/or Agency funds, equipment,
     and/or personnel. The contractor will guarantee discretion.

Please advise soonest as to Salvadoran acceptance of this
proposal. If Bustillo and Vides agree, a representative of the
maintenance contractor will arrive and seek you out. He will
identify himself as coming from Mr. Green.

Warm regards, hope all is well with you. We hear nothing but
good reports about your work. Keep it up. Vaya con Dios!

19

This is the letter Oliver North sent me, asking me to help him in the Contra
resupply effort. When I used his name privately with General Vides Casanova,
the Salvadoran defense minister, and General Juan Bustillo, the Air Force Chief
of Staff, they had no idea who North was.

20

21

Oliver North.

Richard Secord.

During my
testimony at the
Iran/Contra hearings
in Congress, May
27-28, 1987.

22

23

Shortly after my Hughes-500 chopper went down in El Salvador, in 1985. We retrieved it the same day.

24

At Ilopango air base, 1986. L–R: myself, General Juan Bustillo, Rep. Claude Pepper, and Colonel James Steele, the U.S. MilGroup commander in El Salvador.

Sen. John Kerry, who put me and my family through hell when someone close to his subcommittee leaked the lie that I had solicited millions in drug money for the Contras. After eleven months of silence, Kerry finally apologized to me in public.

25

To Felix Rodriguez –
with high esteem and admiration
Geo Bush

26

With then Vice President Bush in his office, May 1, 1986. A highlight in my life. I admire the President for his truthfulness, integrity, and statesmanship.

Dec-23, 1988
Merry Christmas

Dear Felix,

Thanks for your note of Dec-18th. Yes, the Truth is powerful. You have told the truth faithfully — and have won a lot of respect in the process. Good Luck. May

1989 be calmer than 1988. And may it be full of great happiness for you.

With admiration and respect

G. Bush

A note to me from the President-elect. I treasure it.

28

El Salvador, 1988: El Viejo Soldado.

hands. Then the Agency man laid out the basic operational plan. Eduardo and I would travel to Bolivia, where we would work under the direction of a CIA case officer. He was named Jim—and he operated under official cover, that is, he carried an official red-covered passport. Eduardo and I used documents showing us to be Cuban nationals who were U.S. residents. He would use the pseudonym Eduardo Gonzalez. My cover name was Felix Ramos Medina, which I requested because it used my real initials.

The fact that Eduardo and I weren't citizens was important. One of the primary reasons for selecting us, I discovered, was that, as directed by the White House, the U.S. ambassador to Bolivia had issued standing orders that no U.S. citizen could participate in combat activities in areas where the guerrillas were operating.

Our cover was commercial—we would be a couple of Cuban businessmen, U.S. residents, who were coming to explore business opportunities in Bolivia. The Bolivian government, of course, knew precisely who we were. But our cover stories would shield us from undue attention by the press—there was already some speculation about Che's presence—and from any Castro agents who might happen to be in the area. Our cover wasn't designed to hold up forever, but was respectable enough to allow us to get in, do our jobs, and leave without too much risk.

With the team selection process over, we began roughly two weeks of Agency briefings on everything from the Bolivian political situation to the backgrounds of the people with whom we'd be working. As usual, for security reasons the sessions were held in our apartment, not at CIA headquarters. In addition to our political and military briefings on Bolivia, I also had to review and learn a signal plan for communicating with CIA headquarters both by voice transmission and Morse code. We had cipher books and frequencies arranged. Because of the high mountains in Bolivia, transmissions would often be difficult. In fact, it would be easier to transmit to a neighboring communications relay station from some sections of the country than to try to reach the embassy at La Paz. The messages would be relayed to Washington and finally back to La Paz.

Once on site, we would spend much of our time working separately. Eduardo would concentrate on training an elite group of roughly ten Bolivian soldiers in basic intelligence-gathering operations, enabling them to become the eyes and ears of their battalion. The plan was that, after training, they would operate in civilian clothes in guerrilla territory. Simultaneously I would work at the division level, coordinating activities with two intelligence officers, Major Arnaldo Saucedo and his boss, Colonel Joaquin Zenteno Anaya, both of whom I would become very close to. My job would be to look at the overall scheme of things and help the Bolivians react quickly to the raw intelligence information they received.

The most important element of successful unconventional-warfare operations is intelligence. The ability to react swiftly to new information becomes crucial when dealing with guerrillas and guerrilla operations. Like citizens of many third world countries, the Bolivians had not given much thought to dealing with prisoners. Brutality was commonplace in the army, and harsh treatment from officers was standard. Often, troops were ordered not to take prisoners; summary executions, while largely uncommon, were not unknown.

We had been making some progress in demonstrating to the Bolivians that force was not the only answer. A U.S. Special Forces major, Pappy Shelton, showed the Bolivian army that with tough but nonbrutal training, the Quechua Indian *soldados*—enlisted men— could be turned from peasant kids into a determined, brave fighting force. He was, in fact, doing just that with a group of about six hundred Bolivian Army Rangers in the area in which I would be working.

Shelton was one of the finest individuals with whom I would ever have the honor to work. The lanky Tennessee native had been an enlisted man for ten years before he went to Officer Candidate School. He was a sky diver and had undergone Ranger training before he received his Green Beret. He had his work cut out for him, as most of the Bolivian officers treated their own men with varying degrees of callousness.

Still, those Bolivian officers who had received training in the U.S. were taught that brutality—both toward their own troops and to prisoners—was not effective in the long run. For my part, I hoped to be able to convince the intelligence people with whom I would work that the way prisoners are treated does make a difference. A man who believes you are in his corner will tell you more things than a man who believes you want him dead. He will give you details he may consider unimportant, but which, to you, are essential to your entire battle plan.

In addition to helping those officers to refine interrogation techniques, I hoped to be able to show them how to use captured documents. As I told the Bolivians more than two decades ago, and just as I have tried to convince my friends in the Salvadoran armed forces today, the papers in a guerrilla's knapsack are often more valuable than gold. They provide valuable intelligence about how and where he operated, who his colleagues and collaborators are, and what he is thinking. They also give you detailed clues to his personality and to the strategy he plans to use against you. His wallet often contains pictures and notes that allow you to learn about his personal life— elements you can put into play during interrogation.

I have also discovered that guerrillas tend to be pack rats. On the move all the time, they often carry with them papers, books, diaries, communications codes, and account books that allow us to examine their operations in detail. Too often these relics are overlooked, either by the soldiers who come upon them on the battlefield or by the officers in charge. They should not be; indeed, they should be pored over immediately for on-the-spot tactical exploitation. By reacting swiftly to newly captured information, you may be able to launch a successful operation against a guerrilla unit that only hours before seemingly could not be located. By teaching these basic truths to the Bolivians, I believed we would be able to find, isolate, and capture our great enemy, Che Guevara.

During this briefing period in Washington I also received good news about my salary. It was being more than doubled for the assignment. Previously I had been receiving about three hundred dollars a month as a principal agent, which meant having to take supplemental jobs to support my family. Now I would be paid eight hundred dollars a month—after taxes—plus expenses.

But money was not the reason for volunteering. It was the prospect of capturing Che Guevara that drew me like a magnet to Bolivia.

He was born Ernesto Guevara de la Serna on June 14, 1928, in the city of Rosario, about 180 miles northwest of Buenos Aires. Soon afterward, the well-to-do Guevara family moved to the Argentine capital. But when Ernesto was about four, they moved again: the youngster developed terrible asthma and the doctors told his parents that the climate in Córdoba, a city in the country's central highlands, would be better for him. Despite both his infirmity and his small size, young Ernesto excelled at sports, reportedly even playing such physical-contact sports as rugby.

He was also a gifted student, earning a medical degree in 1952 from the University of Buenos Aires. And he was an inveterate traveler. Even before finishing college he had visited most of South America and made his first trip to the United States, spending some time in Miami. After he graduated, Guevara continued his travels. Somewhere in this period of time—I have never been clear about precisely when or where—the young, impressionable Guevara became a Marxist. During subsequent stays in Costa Rica and Guatemala the idealistic physician became involved in revolutionary and subversive circles.

Che—which was a nickname derived from an Argentine expression similar to "hey, buddy"—first met Fidel Castro in Mexico in 1955. They were introduced, some say, by Hilda Gadea, a Peruvian Marxist who would become Che's first wife (others say Fidel's half brother, Raúl Castro, made the initial introduction). Whichever version is true, it is indisputable that almost immediately Guevara was drawn in by Fidel's aspirations. He became an integral part of Fidel's revolutionary plans. On November 25, 1956, Che was one of the eighty-two guerrillas who sailed on the yacht *Granma* to invade Cuba and overthrow Fulgencio Batista.

All but a dozen were killed or captured by Batista's army shortly after their landing on December 2. Che was among the twelve who survived and fled to the Sierra Maestra. And it was there that Che's legend as a guerrilla began to grow. Fidel gave him command of the Las Villas region—the same area where I had been born and raised. Che even assumed Cuban citizenship. And after Castro's ascent to power, Che took on a number of leadership positions in the communist government.

He was appointed Minister of Industry. He became the head of the Cuban National Bank, where he signed Castro's currency with one word—Che. He attended the Alliance for Progress meeting in Montevideo, Uruguay, in August 1961. It was there at a secret meeting with JFK's adviser Richard Goodwin that he sarcastically "thanked" Kennedy for helping Fidel secure Cuba for communism by holding back crucial support during the Bay of Pigs invasion.

As a Cuban minister of state, Che traveled widely, and his reputation as a spokesman for violent revolution increased, especially after a fiery outburst on the floor of the United Nations General Assembly, where he attacked the concepts of coexistence and democracy. He was received in Moscow in the fall of 1964. Later the same year he made his first visit to Africa.

Then, in April 1965, Guevara dropped from sight altogether. Rumors circulated at the time that he had been executed by Fidel for political reasons. A romanticized soft-eyed, wiry, beret-sporting guerrilla (an image he cultivated assiduously, incidentally), Che was always more of an idealist than the pragmatic, flamboyant cigar-puffing dictator Fidel—qualities which made him all the more dangerous.

Che's communism was of the tough, austere "Long March" variety personified by Mao Zedong and Ho Chi Minh—not the more permissive and corrupt version of Soviet-styled Marxist Leninism favored by Fidel and Raúl Castro.

But Che had not been killed. Instead, he was exporting his communist revolution to Africa. Using the *nom de guerre* "Comandante Tatu" and commanding just over a hundred hard-line Cuban guerrillas—including one, Pombo, who later accompanied him to Bolivia as his bodyguard—Che recruited Africans and fought a guerrilla war in the Congo against the Western-backed president, Moïse Tshombe. (And, incidentally, where the fifty-foot aluminum fast boats we'd used in the Artime operations were taken by the CIA and used against communist expansionism again.)

In many ways, the hard goals that Che forced upon himself were examples serving both to crystallize his own beliefs and to illustrate through vivid exploits his particular brand of communist revolution to others. In a letter written to his parents in the mid-sixties, he said:

> My Marxism is firmly rooted and purified. I believe in armed struggle as the only solution for the peoples who are struggling for their freedom and I am acting in accordance with my beliefs. Many would call me an adven-

turer, and I am one; only of a different sort, one of those that risks his skin to demonstrate what he believes is true.

For reasons of his own, Che decided to "risk his skin" by organizing and leading a communist guerrilla movement in Bolivia. By October of 1966 the thirty-eight-year-old revolutionary, having renounced his Cuban citizenship, had arrived in Bolivia on one of two forged Uruguayan passports. Both had been issued in Montevideo. Number 130220 had been issued to Ramón Benítez Fernández on December 2, 1965. Number 130748 was issued on December 22, 1965, to Adolfo Mena Gonzáles. Soon after Che entered the country he left La Paz and assumed command of a small force of communists in the countryside. It was to be a fatal decision.

Unfortunately for him, Che had chosen to lead this abortive insurrection in a country that was not only inhospitable geographically, but also a place where his revolutionary exhortations fell for the most part on deaf ears.

Bolivia is one of two landlocked nations in South America (Paraguay is the other). It is surrounded by Brazil, Paraguay, Argentina, Chile, and Peru. And while it may appear on the map to be an ideal hub from which to export revolution and communism, the fact is that because of its mountains and rough terrain, moving from one portion of the country to another without air transport was, back in the late sixties, virtually impossible.

Moreover, I learned during my Washington briefings that the Bolivian people, most of whom were rural "Indio" farmers belonging to two major groups, the Quechuas and the Aymaras, were in no great hurry to overthrow their government. In November 1964, a former air force general named René Barrientos Ortuno assumed power during a coup staged by the Bolivian armed forces. In August 1966, Barrientos became president.

Although it had experienced its share of domestic difficulties, Bolivia, unlike some of the other countries in the region, was not fertile ground for communist expansionism. The Cubans had figured that, as was the case elsewhere in South America, Bolivia was run by a few large landowners who exploited the peasants. That supposition turned out to be untrue. For the most part, the peasants were stable. There was a lot of land available to them, which they could cultivate as they wished. Furthermore, economic and agrarian reform were already under way at the time Che and his communist allies tried to undermine the government.

There were additional elements that compounded the guerrillas' problems. Some might appear on the surface to be minor—but they were not. Bolivian Indians, for example, do not customarily affect facial hair. So when they saw the Cuban guerrillas and their Peruvian and local Bolivian allies, all with beards and long hair, they were instinctively afraid and mistrustful of the outsiders. This oversight on the part of the guerrillas accomplished two things: it made it harder for the Cubans to obtain supplies as they went from place to place, and it made them easier targets for the army, as the peasants were quite willing to let the Bolivian authorities know about the "strangers" in their midst.

Ultimately, it became virtually impossible for Che's group to operate under Mao Zedong's dictum: "Guerrillas should be able to move among the masses like fish in water." The communists had their own internal problems as well: they were plagued by factional infighting that left them splintered and angry.

It was into this confused situation that Che had inserted himself and his idealistic proletariat revolution. Altogether, his guerrilla band would finally number fifty-three. Of these, thirty were Bolivians, seventeen Cubans, three Peruvians, one Argentine, one East German, and one—whose *nom de guerre* was Danton—was the French communist writer Regis Debray.

On April 20, 1967, Debray was captured. In the first hours he suffered some rough treatment at the hands of the army. But after the appearance of a Cuban-born CIA agent then known as Gabriel García García (actually, his real name is Julio, and he is an old friend of mine), who was the intelligence adviser to the Bolivian Minister of the Interior and Public Security, Debray was treated with humanity and respect. In fact, in an article published in the *Evergreen Review* of February 1968, Debray admitted the CIA may well have saved his life.

García and the Bolivians debriefed the Frenchman exhaustively. Some published reports later indicated Debray insisted to his interrogators that he had never seen Che; that he was strictly a journalistic observer of the guerrilla movement, and that the Bolivians believed his cover story. The truth is precisely the opposite. In the end, Debray willingly told the Bolivians and the CIA everything he knew about Che's operations. It was Debray's testimony, in fact, that helped convince the Agency to lay on a concentrated effort to capture the elusive revolutionary. The Frenchman could have been sentenced to death. Instead, because he cooperated, he was given only thirty years, and ultimately was pardoned at the end of 1970.

In Washington, we spent a good deal of time studying Debray's transcripts, as well as other interrogations made available by the Bolivians. They became our psychological road maps, giving us valuable clues about the people against whom we would operate.

We also discovered that these guerrillas generated a surprising amount of paperwork—both in the form of so-called "revolutionary communiqués"—propaganda statements issued for public consumption—and in that of diaries, journals, and scribbled notes. (The practice of keeping large amounts of such incriminating documents was not unique to the guerrillas in Bolivia. More recently, in El Salvador, I have seen FMLN (Farabundo Martí Liberación Nacional) backpacks crammed full of papers. These treasure troves are obviously tremendous sources of information when they are captured. They are also terrible guerrilla strategy, and yet the communists persist in packing the papers time and time again.)

Most important, I was told that if we actually captured Che, no resources would be spared by the U.S. to get him back to Panama alive for debriefing. I was told that planes and choppers would be standing ready if the situation presented itself.

I also discovered some interesting information about one of the guerrillas described by the Frenchman, a young man named José Castillo Chávez, whose *nom de guerre* was Paco. Debray, describing Paco to his debriefers, had told them repeatedly that Paco was not shy about saying he had been lied to by the communists. The thirty-year-old Bolivian, an upholsterer by profession, considered himself a theoretician, not a fighter, and had been lured to their side by promises of a revolutionary education in Havana and Moscow.

Instead, Paco complained to Debray, he had been given a gun and sent off into the jungles. I thought at the time that Paco could become a wonderful source of information if he were to be taken alive.

Finally our briefings were concluded, and we returned to Miami. Following tradecraft procedures, on July 21 I bought a Braniff ticket from New York to La Paz for July 31 under the name Felix Ramos. The next day I bought a Miami-New York ticket for the same day under my real name.

On July 31 I flew to New York, where, at a Holiday Inn close to Kennedy airport I received my documentation from the CIA. Then Eduardo and I boarded our flight. It was scheduled to make a short stop in Miami before continuing straight to La Paz, and we were warned not to deplane. But as luck would have it, the plane's radar failed, and we spent the night at the Miami Airport Hotel, hoping no one we knew would see us by chance. On the night of August 1 we flew at last to Bolivia.

10 It was early morning when Eduardo and I arrived in La Paz. We were met by our case officer, Jim, another Agency employee and a Bolivian immigration officer. The CIA man took our documents and luggage chits, saying he would get everything stamped, pick up our suitcases, then meet us at our hotel. I was excited and wanted to go to work immediately. But there were formalities that had to be dealt with before work could start. Our first obligation was a visit to the home of the Bolivian president, René Barrientos Ortuño.

The former air force general greeted us warmly in his frigid residence. (That the president's house was cold must have been pretty common knowledge because the CIA's La Paz station chief, who accompanied us, brought an electric blanket as a present for the Bolivian head of state!) Barrientos had already been briefed about our backgrounds. Nevertheless we told him about some of our operations against Castro and our fight against communism. He seemed pleased to hear our stories.

After our talk, the president presented Eduardo, Jim, and me with small cards, addressed to all military and civilian personnel. Each bore Barrientos's own signature and requested that we be given all the cooperation we might need. From there it was on to our hotel, the Paz, for a quick wash and shave. We were then taken to meet with General Alfredo Ovando Candia, Commander in Chief of the Bolivian Armed Forces. Ovando's reception was much more official and formal than the greeting we had just received from President Barrientos.

He gave us a perfunctory once-over, then approved Military IDs for us—small booklets with our pictures that accredited us as members of the Bolivian Armed Forces. I was given the rank of captain. We would pick up the processed documents later in the day at the *estado mayor*—general staff headquarters.

Eduardo and I split up our responsibilities soon after our arrival. We left La Paz so as to be closer to where the guerrillas operated. While he concentrated on working with the Ranger battalion, I based myself in the city of Santa Cruz and began to work with a small group of Bolivian officers at the division level, showing them how to improve their intelligence-gathering operations. About half the time I would commute to La Esperanza, where the Rangers had their headquarters (and where Major Pappy Shelton had his Special Forces training camp).

When we began our assignment in La Paz, and during the first few days I spent in Santa Cruz, we carefully followed all of Washington's security instructions, which included wearing civilian clothes, trying to keep our meetings clandestine, and so on. But as we began working more and more closely with the Bolivian military—using one of their two-and-a-quarter-ton trucks to make the commute from Santa Cruz to the Ranger training facility at La Esperanza, for example—well, it was kind of ridiculous to have a couple of civilians driving an army truck or a military Jeep. So we began wearing uniforms most of the time, although they bore no rank insignias. We didn't wear them when we went out to eat, or in public, but I found when I was with the Bolivians that the uniform helped me blend in better, and I felt less like an outsider.

The Bolivians were exceptionally easy to work with, especially the division's intelligence officer, Major Arnaldo Saucedo, with whom I quickly developed a great working relationship. Saucedo readily accepted the fact that I had more experience in antiguerrilla operations than he, and he was consistently open to suggestion.

From the first, one of the most important suggestions I made to Saucedo and his colleagues was to coordinate intelligence activities with other Bolivian units. In planning his guerrilla operations, Che had managed to use a technique that has become common to many insurgency movements. What he did was set up his base camp in an area controlled by one Bolivian unit, but he operated across a river in a nearby area controlled by another. Che's base camp, for example, lay south of the Rio Grande river in the Bolivian Fourth Division's sphere of operation. Most of his sorties, however, took place north of the Rio Grande, in the region patrolled by the Eighth Division.

Che realized that most military commanders, being naturally competitive, will not readily cooperate with one another. (The Viet Cong knew that, and so now do the communists in El Salvador.) Therefore he kept his nose clean south of the Rio Grande, and the Fourth Division commander, when asked, would tell his counterpart at Eighth Division headquarters, "We don't have a guerrilla problem here." My job was to convince the Bolivians that only by coordinated efforts—sharing information, intelligence, and joint operations— would the war against Che be won.

My workdays soon fell into a certain routine. I would leave at about 7 A.M. for the division headquarters, where I met with the chief of intelligence. Usually there would be documents to analyze— papers captured from guerrillas, intelligence reports, or debriefing transcripts. Every scrap of information we received we put into files. It was a labor-intensive process. Today, intelligence officers use computers and there are rational data bases that can index and sort hundreds of thousands of bits of information in a matter of milliseconds.

But we assembled files on each of Che's guerrillas by hand, adding and copying fragments of information as they were received and checked out, all on manual typewriters. Duplication was by carbon paper.

We built files for each guerrilla in Che's band. We tried to include all the basic facts we could get our hands on, of course—name, *nom de guerre*, rank, age, and citizenship. But our files also held insights that helped us try to predict how these people would act. We wanted to know which ones smoked and which did not; which ones carried rifles, which ones machine guns or pistols. Our objective was to learn what they wore, what they ate, and how they spoke; to ascertain their friendships and jealousies; to discover which ones were natural leaders, which ones followers. Without actually seeing them with our own eyes, we had to be able to see what they all looked like. Without having spoken to them we wanted to discover how they moved in the field—how each conducted himself when on patrol. Ultimately we came to know them as well as if we'd spent time slogging through the jungle with them on the run.

Counterinsurgency techniques such as these, common in the U.S. and other developed nations, were not often used in the Third World. In fact, when the Hondurans and Guatemalans had communist guerrilla problems back in the late seventies and early eighties, advisers from AMAN, Israeli military intelligence, and Shin Bet, the Israeli internal security service, instructed a sizable number of Latin American students in the same elements of antiguerrilla warfare that I'd taught a decade before in Bolivia. The Israelis learned these techniques because they'd had to design similar antiterror intelligence operations in the occupied West Bank and Gaza.

Intelligence gathering was not my only assignment. I also designed several communications networks during this period that would allow the Bolivian armed forces to better coordinate their activities. Their air force planes, for example, were unable to talk to troops on the ground, which made rapid-response joint actions virtually impossible. I was determined to fix that, and began work on an improvised antenna system that would enable the pilots to use a battery powered PRC-10 radio to talk directly to the ground forces and coordinate their activities. I also set up the radio on which Jim would make voice contact with La Paz station, and using an RS-48 system—Morse code—commenced regular communications.

It took about four weeks until our first big break. On August 31, after a firefight on the banks of the Rio Grande river at Vado del Yeso, the Bolivians captured a guerrilla named José Castillo Chávez. This was the Paco I'd read about in Regis Debray's debriefing—the one who didn't really want to be a guerrilla fighter.

So, two days later, when my friend in Bolivian army intelligence, Major Arnaldo Saucedo, asked me to fly with him to Vallegrande to help interrogate the prisoner, I accepted immediately.

On September 3 we took a C-47 from Santa Cruz and, on landing, went directly to the Nuestra Señora de Malta Hospital, where Paco was recovering from his wounds under heavy guard. When we arrived at his room we saw an amazing sight: about a dozen soldiers, all pointing their rifles at one poor, bedraggled, wounded prisoner sitting in a chair. He really was a mess: his hair was long and dirty. He had a droopy Fu Manchu mustache and a wispy little beard.

Paco looked frightened out of his wits—and, frankly, he had good reason to be scared. He had not been the only one captured alive at Vado del Yeso. Another guerrilla, known as Ernesto, had also been taken by the army. But Ernesto, Paco later told us, was arrogant. On his first night of captivity he'd shouted at the soldiers and refused to cooperate. They shot him on the spot and added his body to the pile of guerrilla corpses killed during the firefight.

It took me only a few minutes of time with Paco to realize how valuable he could be to our efforts. Saucedo thought so too, so I asked him to help get Paco released onto our custody and he agreed.

Together, we went immediately to the whitewashed colonial house that served as the headquarters for the Third Tactical Command, which had authority over Paco. We went and asked the commander's permission to take Paco back to Santa Cruz with us.

But the reluctant guerrilla's original interrogator, Lieutenant Colonel Andrés Selich, of the Pando Regiment, argued to the officers, including General David Lafuente, who was visiting from La Paz, that any additional interrogation would be fruitless.

"Look," Selich said, "we've already told the press that the prisoner is badly wounded and is not expected to survive. Besides," he added, "I don't think we can get any more out of him."

He paused. "General, just give me the word and I'll execute him."

At that point I nudged Saucedo. "Move in," I whispered. "Ask the general for the prisoner."

Saucedo tried. But he was quickly overridden by Selich. I saw by the look on his face that he'd gone as far as he dared.

I stepped toward Lafuente. *"Mi General,"* I said.

Lieutenant Colonel Selich moved as if to come between us. I took my identification—the card signed by President Barrientos and my papers from General Ovando—out of my pocket and showed them to him. Lafuente looked me over quickly and I thought I saw the briefest wisp of recognition in his eyes. I had met him once before, at a visit he made to La Esperanza, accompanying a U.S. four-star general named Porter who was the commander in chief, or CINC, of the American Southern Command—Southcom—which was based in Panama. My colleague Eduardo had cooked Cuban-style roast pork for the visitors, and Porter's personal physician, a Colonel Bernstein, had even helped to cure a little Bolivian girl who was living nearby the Special Forces training camp. So Lafuente knew, if not precisely who I was, at least that I was somehow attached to the U.S. Government.

"General," I continued, choosing my words with great care, "give Major Saucedo and me an opportunity with this prisoner. I can assure you that the information he will give us will be invaluable for us. And if, afterwards, you don't agree with our assessment, I'll never ask you for another prisoner again. But, sir, please let us have this one!"

Lafuente looked at me again, searching my face. Finally, he turned to the Pando officers in the room. "Give the prisoner to this young man," he ordered.

An order was written quickly—so quickly that the officer who wrote it out did so on the back of a brown paper bag—and handed to Major Saucedo. We had permission to pick up our prisoner.

Actually getting Paco back to Santa Cruz was almost more difficult than getting the OK to take him. The Bolivians didn't really want to hand him over—they tried to arrange things so Saucedo and I couldn't get Paco on the last plane back to Santa Cruz, promising to send him by road the next day. But we knew what would then happen: Paco would be driven in a car full of armed guards, and somewhere between Vallegrande and Santa Cruz he would try to escape—or so they'd tell us later—and the soldiers would be forced to shoot him.

Saucedo and I got Paco out of the hospital by talking our way past the officers in charge, waving our orders—the piece of paper bag signed by the Vallegrande area commander—and exhibiting a fair amount of army bravado. Then we rushed to the airport only to discover that, to stymie our efforts further, our C-47 was purposely filled with Bolivian reporters who the army was now allowing to ride to Santa Cruz. A major standing on the tarmac was adamant: no way could we take our prisoner on that plane.

By now I was really steamed. "Look," I told him, "we have instructions from General Lafuente to bring this guy with us, and that's exactly what we're going to do."

A yielding look in the major's eyes betrayed the realization that it would be very unwise to argue with me right then. Yet, even so, he started to do so.

I didn't wait. I threw Paco's ragged jacket over his head to hide his long hair and beard, took him by his unwounded arm, and pushed him through the C-47's hatchway.

The reporters looked around as Saucedo and I quickly hustled our prisoner up the steeply inclined aisle and into the front compartment without saying a word. I saw the confused looks on their faces as we passed by. But with the jacket over Paco's head and Saucedo and me in uniform they had no idea who we might be— and we certainly weren't going to tell them. When we'd shut the door and Paco had collapsed into one of the seats, I finally breathed a sigh of relief.

We commandeered some Coca-Cola and cookies from the flight crew and gave them to the guerrilla, who by this time was frightened to death and crying.

"You're going to kill me," he kept saying.

"No, I'm not," I answered.

"I never wanted to be a guerrilla," he bawled. "I never wanted to fight. And now you're going to kill me."

Nothing I could say served to convince Paco that I wanted him alive, not dead.

It didn't help matters that, after landing, we had to wait until the press deplaned—about thirty-five minutes—before we could get Paco off. We then took him the long way round Santa Cruz to the Eighth Division's headquarters. He bawled all the way, thinking we were going through the countryside, not the city, so we could shoot him and dump his body in a ditch.

I don't think Paco believed me even when we finally pulled up to the division HQ. I found a small room for him—not a cell—and after we'd cleaned him up, I had the doors and windows barred with wood. But he wasn't chained or handcuffed, and his room was comfortable. I think when he saw that room he finally realized I was being straight with him. And after that he really started to come around.

I spent two weeks with Paco, debriefing him every day for several hours. I hired a nurse to come twice a day to tend his wounds. I bought him antibiotics and clothes, even magazines to read. I got him a haircut and arranged to have his laundry washed. I talked to him man to man.

I talked about Cuba—about my boyhood there, and how things changed after Castro took over. I told him what communism had done to my country, and how it felt to be an exile. I knew that he was already disillusioned with the guerrillas, and I worked hard to make him skeptical of communism, too. I asked him for his family's address. I told him, "Paco, let me get a message to your parents and tell them you are all right."

I promised him that I would try to see to it that after our debriefings were finished the Bolivians would treat him well. (And they did: the last I heard of Paco, he was working for Bolivian army intelligence—a dedicated anticommunist!)

Using these methods, it didn't take too long to gain his confidence. We actually had only one negative experience with Paco: a U.S. Special Forces captain came to interrogate him without my permission. Paco didn't know the guy and was shy with him. The captain accused Paco of lying and physically threatened him, really screwing things up. I set things right the same day, apologizing to Paco, telling him it was a mistake, and it wouldn't ever happen again.

In fact, I made damn sure that no one else would ever mess up my special relationship with the prisoner, because Paco was giving us golden information. His debriefing is a classic example of how kindness and perseverance work better than brutality and threats.

It also illustrates just how to piece together information. The same day Paco was captured, a Cuban guerrilla lieutenant, Israel Reyes Zayas, whose war name was Braulio, was killed by the Bolivians. In Braulio's backpack was a diary, a typed copy of which was given to me by García García, the CIA man who'd interrogated Regis Debray, and who had come from La Paz to interview Paco in Vallegrande shortly after Saucedo and I arrived.

Braulio's diary runs from 25 October, 1966 ("I left my house [in Cuba] at 5:00 P.M.") to 9 August, 1967 ("The Army surrounded us and during our retreat they killed Pedro and captured the .30-caliber machine gun he was carrying.").

It was an incredible cache of raw information about guerrilla life. And, while reading it, written in its rudimentary, often primitive, Spanish—Braulio was not, after all, an educated man—I could see why Paco had quickly become disenchanted with his life as a revolutionary soldier.

26 Feb., '67: We lost the first man at 3 P.M. It was our friend Serafín. He was passing close to the edge of the Rosita River and slipped in. He didn't know how to swim. Others tried to help him but we were weak [from lack of food] and we could not help him.

2 March '67: We have no communication with the vanguard. I started having cramps in my legs and could not walk. Marcos could almost not walk too. The personnel was very, very weak. We were finally authorized to eat the reserve [food in our packs] because there's no hope of finding a farmer...

But it was not only the tough life described by Braulio that I found so fascinating. For me, the diary's most useful information lay in the

Cuban's semi-literate annotations about his comrades and how they operated.

> 25 March '67: Ramón [Che's *nom de guerre*] made a speech. He fired Marcos from his position and gave Miguel the position he had before.
>
> 12 April '67: We buried Rubio and we retreated a bit higher [into the countryside]. On the 14th we returned again to the base, where we stayed for two days, after which we returned again to Ñancaguazu. There, we left the rear guard, while Ramón and the vanguard proceeded toward a little place called Ballipampa. . . .

I proceeded to debrief Paco using what I learned from Braulio's diary (as well as every other piece of guerrilla material I could get hold of). One of the truths I have discovered over my career is that the art of debriefing, or interviewing, is not an easy one. It is closer to psychotherapy than to courtroom interrogation. There are, for example, definite techniques that can lead to a successful debriefing. If followed, most of the time you will obtain the information needed— plus more. But as I've already said, torture or physical abuse of prisoners is totally counterproductive. The goal is to convert them to your point of view, not beat them into submission.

In Vietnam, for example, some of the best men I ever advised were former Viet Cong or North Vietnamese soldiers who, after a mixture of thorough debriefing and gentle philosophical persuasion, were turned into vehement anticommunists. I especially remember one case—a woman Viet Cong officer we captured. She argued political philosophy and Marxism with us until she was blue in the face. We let her rant and rave. Then we took her to a village marketplace and told her, "Go—talk to anybody you want and ask if they are happier free or communist." She did, and ultimately became convinced of our point of view. She turned into a very successful agent who helped us destroy many VC networks.

The most important element of interrogation is the ability to listen. The debriefer must become a sponge, absorbing every molecule of information. Second, he must develop the subject's complete, total trust. The prisoner has to believe that you are honestly interested in helping his case—whether it is interceding with the authorities on his behalf, gaining him a lighter sentence, or, as was the case with Paco, saving his life. It is crucial to follow through on such offers, because others will see that, if they cooperate, they, too, will help themselves.

And you can never fake sincerity. What is wanted in the end is truth. The debriefer must, of course, also develop the instinctive ability to know whether or not the subject will cooperate. There are those individuals who are hard-core fanatics. You cannot waste your time with them, especially (as was the case with Paco) when you are looking for tactical information and time is a crucial factor.

Also, if a subject thinks you are "using" him, he will tell you what he believes you want to hear, which may not come close to what you should be hearing. So interrogations tend to start on a general note —talking about background, or shared experiences—anything that will give you an opening into the subject's trust.

In Paco's case, we first talked about our backgrounds. I discovered that he had been born February 4, 1937, in Challapata, in the Bolivian province of Oruro. Paco explained that he had first gone to communist meetings in La Paz with a friend of an uncle's named Raúl Quispaya back in 1958. Until 1966, his contacts with the communists remained sporadic.

Then, in late October of that year, he met Quispaya again. In turn, Raúl introduced him to a Bolivian communist named Moisés Guevara (who was no relation to Che), and Paco's relationship with the incipient guerrillas became more formal. They asked him to do several favors for them; he obliged. In January, 1967, Raúl and Moisés Guevara made Paco a very special offer: a revolutionary education in the Soviet Union and Cuba. To start on the long trip, however, they told him he'd have to leave Bolivia surreptitiously, going through the Bolivian countryside. That way Paco's Bolivian passport would never indicate that he'd left the country—all his documentation would come later.

Of course, Paco never made it to Moscow or Havana. Instead, he told me, he was taken on February 13, 1967, to a base camp where he was met by a guerrilla named Juan Pablo Chang Navarro—a part-Chinese Peruvian whose *nom de guerre* was El Chino Peruano. Paco joined a number of other Bolivians who had been recruited. He tried to explain that he was not a fighter, but only wanted to receive his revolutionary education. Instead, two guerrillas, Nato (a Bolivian whose real name was José Luis Méndez Conne) and Antonio (the Cuban captain, Orlando Pantojas Tamayo), gave him a backpack, a hammock, a canteen, a Mauser rifle and 120 rounds of ammunition, underwear, and a pack of Derby cigarettes. He was given the war name Paco and they told him that henceforth he was a guerrilla soldier.

The day after he arrived, Paco was told by Antonio that the guerrillas' chief was named Ramón, and that Ramón was the war name of Che Guevara. Antonio had good reason to know Ramón's true identity: the Cuban captain was a veteran of the Sierra Maestra who had worked closely with Che in the Cuban Ministry of Interior. He had volunteered to come to Bolivia to help his old comrade-in-arms, entering the country on December 12, 1966, with an Ecuadoran passport issued to Antonio León Velasco and numbered 49040.

The conditions Paco described to me were pretty rough. His guerrilla training consisted of day-and-a-half or two-day marches with full equipment—resistance marches or performance marches, they were called—in which everyone ran up and down the hills and mountains as fast as possible carrying weapons and hammocks but no backpacks.

Not long after his arrival, Paco met three characters who would become important players in the guerrilla drama. One was Tania, Che's reputed lover. She was East German by birth (her real name was Tamara Bunke Bider). Tania, it also turned out—I discovered this after the fact—was the KGB's agent. She had been assigned by Soviet intelligence to keep watch on Che. Accompanying her were Debray and an Argentine writer named Ciro Roberto Bustos.

Tania told Paco and the others that her companions were newspapermen coming to visit Ramón. As we discovered later, they also served as messengers, carrying secret documents and money to the guerrillas. According to Paco, Debray even carried a rifle during his stay with Che. In one episode he described for me, the French writer killed a wild bear with it.

Paco also filled us in on the gossip. He told us how Tania had a habit of writing all the nasty things people said about her in a notebook and then reporting them to Che. Joaquín, the rear-guard commander, for example, would call her a high-class lady to her face and accuse her of always talking about how she used to have money. The two of them would argue, according to Paco, about who had sacrificed themselves more for the revolution.

Those arguments, Paco said, always ended with Tania in tears, scribbling in her notebook. He also told us that Tania was in poor health—sometimes she had so much trouble keeping up with the guerrillas that the whole group was slowed down waiting for her.

Paco also said Tania served as Che's radio operator, regularly receiving messages from Havana at twelve noon, from Radio Norte de Montero at 1300 hours (1 P.M.) and Radio Altiplano in La Paz at 8 P.M. Paco didn't realize it, but she was also probably getting secret messages from the KGB during some of those broadcasts. It was her assignment, after all, to keep an eye on Che.

Paco told us that on the day he was captured, August 31, Tania had been shot dead in the Rio Grande at Vado del Yeso. He saw where she went down. Tania was dragged underwater and wedged behind a rock by the weight of her backpack. On September 7, four days after we had started debriefing Paco, we sent a group of Bolivian soldiers back to the riverbank and she was discovered right where Paco said she'd be—somewhat decomposed but still identifiable. Bullets might have killed her, but, Paco told me, she had an advanced case of cancer of the uterus and probably would have died soon anyway.

According to Paco, the guerrillas remained in the big central camp until roughly the second week of March, 1967, when Antonio decided to send some patrols out to make contact with Che Guevara, from whom no one had heard in a considerable length of time. It was during those patrols, Paco told me, that the guerrillas experienced their first desertions: two Bolivians, Vicente and Pastor, who were sent to check on traps set to capture game food.

"They took off," Paco said, "and they never returned."

"At about one P.M. that day, Moisés Guevara started having doubts about what had happened to them. And he went to where their backpacks were. And he found a note from Vicente that said, 'I am not leaving because I am a coward but because I am profoundly preoccupied and worried about my little children. As soon as I can take care of my problems at home I am going to return. It is a matter of economics. My children do not have anything to eat.' It was signed 'Vicente.'"

Two to three days after the desertions, said Paco,

> ... It was getting dark in the afternoon when Ramón or Che Guevara arrived. He was accompanied by Pombo, whose real name was Harry Villegas Tamayo, a veteran of the Sierra Maestra who had been Che's bodyguard from the days in the Cuban mountains and also in Africa. . . . When Ramón arrived, Tania was in the camp's kitchen. And as soon as she saw Ramón she came very close to him—very friendly—and kissed him and shook his hand and from that time on she was hanging on Che's left arm most of the time.
>
> Ramón asked El Chino why there were so many people in the central camp, saying that they should be scattered in other camps. El Chino explained to Che what had happened, about the desertions, and also about the fact that Marcos, the commander of the camp, had retreated because he thought that army was getting too close and he didn't want to fight.
>
> That made Che really pissed off. And he made remarks against Marcos and told everyone that the next day they would all go back to the camps Marcos gave up—that camps should not be abandoned to the enemy without a fight.
>
> Then we cooked some beans and rice and made coffee for everyone, and then we all went to sleep. After we finished, Ramón's people took over the kitchen and they cooked for themselves. That night, Ramón sent Julio [a Bolivian guerrilla whose real name was Mario Gutiérrez Ardaya] to find Marcos and order him to return immediately to the central camp. . . .
>
> [When Marcos returned he had a violent argument with] Ramón, who called Marcos a piece of shit and a coward. And Marcos answered, saying, "I am as much a *comandante* as you—we have fought equally in the Sierra Maestra." Then Ramón got close to Marcos—as if he were

going to hit him in the mouth. And Marcos just shut up. . . .

[Later] we received our new orders from Ramón: Victor [killed June 2], Chingolo [who deserted Che in July], Pepe [who deserted in May] and I should reincorporate ourself with the rear guard, which was located about 200 meters from the center of the unit. On Ñato's orders, probably because he didn't trust me, Walter [a Bolivian guerrilla killed on August 31] got my Mauser, although I was allowed to keep the 150 rounds of ammunition I had. When we arrived, Joaquín [a Cuban veteran of the Sierra Maestra whose real name was Comandante Juan Vitalio Acuña Núñez] told Rubio [another Sierra Maestra veteran, Captain Jesús Suárez Gayol] to take care of us. . . .

That night, Ramón called a meeting. He spoke for about an hour. . . . He told us that his group of Cuban fighters had come to help the Bolivian guerrilla movement because they felt it was their duty to help other countries of Latin America to go up in arms against North American imperialism. He emphasized that all the friendly Cubans in Bolivia were volunteers. He told us that it was going to be a long fight—not a war of one or two years but a war that was going to last no less than ten years; a war that would embrace all of Latin America. . . . He told us that the Cubans would be with us until we could walk by ourselves. "After that," he said, "we'll leave and go on to other countries who'll need our help in their fight against American imperialism."

Then Che went on to analyze the situation of the two deserters, and said how Marcos acted inappropriately by letting Vicente and Pastor desert, and he made some overall critical comments about the condition of the base camp.

After mentioning all the mistakes that Marcos had made and being very critical of him, Che demoted Marcos from the grade of *comandante* to a simple soldier, and ordered that Marcos should go to the rear guard with us, and he put him under Joaquin's command. . . . Then

Ramón made the appointment that the head of the vanguard would be Miguel. . . .

Paco didn't realize it but he was giving us vital information. It was
obvious from what he said that the Cubans, for all their talk of revolutionary independence, didn't trust the Bolivian fighters very much
at all. Paco, for example, had had his weapon taken away; he would
also tell me about other desertions—all by Bolivians who, like Vicente, were more worried about putting food in their families'
mouths than they were about international Marxist-Leninist mumbo-
jumbo.

Che, probably sensing the Bolivians' desperation, put Cubans—
and Tania—in charge of virtually every aspect of the operation. She,
for example, not only worked the radio, she also controlled the revolutionaries' purse strings. Paco told me that when he worked in the
camp kitchen, he'd seen her counting out ten thousand dollars in
U.S. currency and five thousand Bolivianos.

We already knew that Marcos and Che had argued, having read a
somewhat different version of the altercation in Braulio's diary. Che's
demotion of Marcos was in itself tremendously significant. Marcos
was, in fact, a high-ranking Cuban *comandante*. His real name was
Antonio Sánchez Díaz. He had commanded the First Revolutionary
Regiment at Havana's most important military base after Castro's
takeover and had held other command-level assignments in Escam-
bray and Camaguey provinces. He was even a member of the Central Committee of the Cuban Communist Party.

He had infiltrated Bolivia with a Panamanian passport, Number
65966, on November 18, 1966, and had immediately become the chief
of Che's vanguard.

We had been told by Paco that Che's guerrilla band operated in
three groups as it moved through the rough Bolivian countryside.
The vanguard led the way roughly one thousand meters ahead of
the main force. A thousand meters in back came the rear guard. That
distance may not sound so great, but given the terrain and the fact
that one group or another often fell behind schedule, it often meant
half a day's travel from one group of Che's guerrillas to another. The
ravines were so steep they almost went straight up and down. In
areas where the vegetation was sparse there were rocks and boulders

that could give way underfoot and send guerrillas tumbling to their deaths. In the jungles, the undergrowth was virtually impenetrable: thick, sharp-thorned vines and bushes that had to be hacked aside or they'd cut through the guerrillas' clothes. Moving even a few dozen meters might take hours, since, in addition to all the natural obstacles they faced, the guerrillas also had to remain perpetually wary of Bolivian troops and aircraft.

As Braulio wrote in his diary, it took the guerrillas three days to cross a river only a few meters wide. First, they had to build a raft to get them and their equipment across. Once built, the raft was carried four kilometers downstream by the current, which, Braulio wrote, "caused [sic] the life of one guerrilla, Carlos, seven weapons and four backpacks."

The nugget of gold Paco gave us was a specific that Braulio's diary had omitted. The diary said only: "March 25—Ramón made a speech. He fired Marcos and gave Miguel the position he had before." We had always found that a somewhat confusing entry. But because of Paco we now realized that Miguel had been made the leader of the vanguard.

That made all the difference in the world.

On September 26, just over three weeks after I had asked General Lafuente to give us Paco to interrogate, the Bolivians killed three guerrillas in the area near the small mountain village of La Higuera. Dead were the Cuban, Miguel, and two Bolivians—Coco, whose real name was Roberto Peredo Leigua, and Julio—Mario Gutiérrez Ardaya. The bodies were brought to the village of Pucara by Lieutenant Galindos, and I rushed from Santa Cruz the same day to fingerprint them so as to make positive identifications.

The dead Cuban was indeed Miguel. His real name was Captain Manuel Hernández. He was a Sierra Maestra veteran who had entered Bolivia using a Spanish passport numbered 40137 and bearing the name Miguel Angel Mattos LaPorta. It was as if a light bulb went off in my head. Miguel was the vanguard commander. Therefore, the main force of guerrillas—including, I prayed, Che Guevara—could not be far behind.

Immediately I went to see Colonel Joaquín Zenteno Anaya and urged him to move his Ranger battalion to the Vallegrande area from its headquarters in La Esperanza.

"But Felix, they have not finished their Ranger training," the Colonel protested. "They have another two weeks to go. I will move them as soon as they complete their cycle."

"Colonel," I said as forcefully as I could, "if we don't move the troops now, all the training in the world won't help them. Everything I've tried to do since I arrived is coming to a head right now. Because of Paco's information, I believe we can, for the first time, predict for sure where Che Guevara will be moving his main guerrilla force. I am certain we can deal the communists a mortal blow—but only if you act decisively and order the Second Ranger Battalion into combat now."

My tone of voice must have been persuasive, because on September 29, Colonel Zenteno moved the Second Ranger Battalion by convoy—which I joined—from La Esperanza to Vallegrande. The six hundred and fifty men that had been so well trained by my friend U.S. Special Forces Major Pappy Shelton, would at last begin a series of search-and-destroy missions that would prove to have historic results.

During the first days of October I remained in Valle-grande to be near the *estado mayor*—the general head-quarters—of the Eighth Division, which had been temporarily reestablished there by Colonel Zenteno. I spent the time getting acquainted with the area and generally help-ing the Bolivians wherever I could.

I also rigged homemade antennas for some PRC-10s—portable battery-powered radios—that I planned to install on the Bolivian Air Force's T-86 planes. The radios would allow pilots to communicate directly with ground forces. On October 8, I'd just finished installing antennas on two aircraft and was beginning on a third when unbelievable news arrived by radio: the message went: *"Papá cansado"*—which, translated, means "Dad [is] tired."

Papá! It was our code name for a top guerrilla commander. *Cansado* meant captured and wounded. An incredible amount of excitement radiated throughout the Vallegrande runway as the word spread from officer to officer: *Papá* had been captured. But which commander? Was it the Bolivian *comandante* "Inti" Peredo, or was it Che Guevara?

Che? Impossible! How could the dedicated combat veteran of the Sierra Maestra and the Congo allow himself to be taken captive in little over a week by green troops, peasant youngsters whose training cycle had not even been completed.

The Eighth Division's head of operations, Major Serrate, and I decided to go and find out. Each of us climbed into the rear seat of a T-86 fighter, both of which I had just equipped with a radio. Serrate's plane took off first. I followed, but within seconds of wheels up, thick white smoke filled the cockpit of my plane. My mike didn't work, so I shouted forward to the pilot, asking what was wrong. He said there was probably a short in some of the plane's electrical systems. The good news was that, after he played with some of the cockpit circuit-breakers, the smoke finally dissipated, and we could fly all right. The bad news was that it would be impossible for him to fire the plane's .50-caliber machine guns or the rockets that were attached to the wings.

Most crucially, because the radio I'd installed was OK—it was battery-operated—he was able to talk to the soldiers on the ground, and so it was while flying above the Bolivian jungles I finally heard repeated to me the words I'd been waiting for so long: *"Papá—el extranjero"*—"Papa is a foreigner."

So *Papá* was in fact Che Guevara. The original message had indicated the Che was captured and wounded. How badly wounded? Talking to the troops on the ground we discovered that he had suffered only a slight wound in the calf of his right leg.

Because our electrical systems were down, we couldn't support the ground troops with firepower. But we could give them moral support. The pilot began a series of bone-shuddering dives over the La Higuera area, pulling up just a short distance above the treetops, as a way of showing our excitement over the Rangers' victory. But even the G-forces of those dives couldn't match my own excitement at what the troops had done.

When we got back to Vallegrande we confirmed the incredible news to Colonel Zenteno. We were also able to tell him that Che was carrying a lot of documents, including a journal.

Zenteno reacted quickly. He sent Lieutenant Colonel Andrés Selich of the Pando Regiment by chopper to La Higuera to interrogate Che, seize all the documents, and await orders from the Bolivian High Command.

It was not a choice that particularly pleased me, as Selich had been Paco's first interrogator. Not only had he gotten very little out of the reluctant guerrilla, but also he'd wanted to execute Paco. Still, Zenteno's decision was a Bolivian army matter and I was not about to question his judgment at the time.

That night we had quite a celebration at the small Vallegrande hotel where Colonel Zenteno was staying. I'd bought a bottle of Ballantine's Scotch on October 2 in the hope we'd be celebrating the communists' defeat soon. Now was the perfect time to crack it open.

I sat with Zenteno and his divisional high command, and we toasted our good fortune. Then, fortified both by the day's unbelievable events, I asked Zenteno formally, *"Mi Coronel,* would you permit me to accompany you tomorrow morning to La Higuera to speak with the prisoner Ernesto Che Guevara?"

Zenteno looked around the table. Every man there wanted to accompany him. But the mountains on the route to La Higuera were high, the air was thin, and the small chopper could accommodate only the pilot and two passengers.

The colonel rose to his feet. "I know that each of you want to go with me," he said. "But Felix has been tremendously helpful to us, and I want to thank him for all the cooperation he has shown us over these past months. I also know how important it is for him to come face to face with one of the very communists who forced him out of his country; how much it will mean to him to see with his own eyes Che Guevara.

"And so, if none of you have an objection, I will take Felix with me tomorrow to La Higuera."

The table was silent. Then someone, I don't remember who,

called out, "Yes—Felix should go!" Immediately the other officers shouted their agreement.

Colonel Zenteno lifted his glass and made a toast: "To Bolivia," he said. "And to the return of peace for our country," he added.

I could hardly sleep that night. A million things ran through my mind as I tossed in bed. Finally I knew why nothing was impossible, why absolutely anything could be achieved: in a few hours I would be face to face with the legendary *comandante* Ernesto Che Guevara. As dawn approached I prepared a long, coded message—over one hundred groups—to send to the Central Intelligence Agency, describing what had happened in the past few days and requesting new instructions about Che Guevara.

My message also suggested to the Chief of Station at our embassy in La Paz that if the Agency wanted to keep Che alive, as our original instructions from Washington had stated, that he should intercede quickly with the Bolivians.

From my very first briefings in Washington, I had been told, "If he is captured, do everything possible to keep him alive—everything!" But the CIA realized with whom it was dealing, too: the Latinos. I had also been told from the very outset the Bolivians were not in the habit of keeping prisoners alive.

Vallegrande. October 9, 1967. Seven A.M. local time. I bid goodbye to the officers at the airport, and Colonel Zenteno and I settled onto the backseat of the small chopper. The pilot, Bolivian Air Force Major Jaime Nino de Guzmán, strapped himself in and we lifted off. I sat on the chopper's left side, Zenteno on the right. The flight took about thirty minutes, most of it in silence, each of us lost in his own thoughts.

For myself, my mind drifted. I was so close to seeing face to face this assassin of so many Cuban patriots. And here, incongruously, what a perfect day! The sun was shining as I'd never seen it before. The Bolivian jungle looked more beautiful and majestic than I'd ever realized. How much history, how many fantastic stories, were hidden by that silent, remote, unknown area below us? I stared down at the trees and greenery as we moved above them, the chopper jogging in the mountain crosswinds and shear.

Was it possible that the history of the Americas and perhaps even the world would be shifted slightly in its course because of what would happen on this clear October day?

It was approaching 7:30 and we were descending. We landed in a fenced-off area right beside a thicket of big trees and a small shack. La Higuera was a tiny place—a few mud-brick houses sat on the single, rutted street. As the chopper came in, a group of soldiers in combat fatigues was waiting for us. As Nino de Guzmán shut down the chopper's rotor we could hear, in the distance, the distinctive sound of mortars and small-arms fire.

Zenteno and I first looked over the musette bag of Che's documents that Lieutenant Colonel Selich had appropriated. His diary was there, as well as some photographs, microfilms, and a list of accommodation addresses in Paris, Mexico, and Uruguay. Accommodation addresses are useful to guerrillas, terrorists, and, for that matter, intelligence operations. For example, they allowed Che to get messages to Fidel Castro without having to resort to clandestine radio communications. All he had to do was send a letter to one of the accommodation addresses and it would be forwarded to the addressee—to Fidel or whomever.

There was also a small booklet with annotations in it—messages, they appeared to be, from someone in Cuba named Ariel. At first we thought that Ariel might be Fidel himself. But that did not turn out to be the case. Ariel was only the dictator's government communicator.

Che also carried two tiny books of one-time numerical codes, ciphers printed on thin tissue paper. Because these codes are used only once they make it almost impossible to decipher messages. Che carried one set of ciphers in black ink, which were for transmitting messages, and another set in red ink, for receiving them.

After we went over Che's possessions, Colonel Zenteno and I walked to the center of the village where Che was being kept prisoner in the schoolhouse. It was a one-story rectangular structure whose tile roof had disintegrated long ago in the fierce Bolivian winters. The schoolhouse had three rough wooden doors and one window set into the front side. Che was being held in the left section of the building as I faced it. Zenteno pushed open the door and entered the dim, earth-floored room. I followed him.

Che was lying on his side on the floor, his arms tied behind his back and his feet bound together. Near Che lay the corpses of two guerrillas. One—Antonio was his *nom de guerre*—was in fact a Cuban officer named Orlando Pantojas who had served with Che going back to the guerrilla days in the Sierra Maestra. The other, Arturo, had been a Cuban army intelligence captain. His real name was René Martínez Tamayo. In the adjoining rooms to our right, similarly bound, was a Bolivian guerrilla named Willy, a former mine-worker's union leader from Paco's hometown of Oruro, whose real name was Simón Cuba Saravia.

Che's leg wound was slightly, but visibly, oozing blood. He was a mess. Hair matted, clothes ragged and torn.

Zenteno spoke. I stood behind him, silent, completely absorbed in the moment. "Why did you choose to come to Bolivia?" he asked Che.

There was no reply.

"How did you enter my country?" the colonel asked.

The only sound was Che's breathing.

"Why do you fight against my government?"

Silence.

Zenteno asked a few more questions, but Che did not answer.

"The least you could do is answer my questions," Zenteno said. "After all, you are a foreigner and you have invaded my country."

Che lay there, not even looking at us, his cheek against the cold earth floor. Finally, sensing the futility of his efforts, Zenteno motioned to me and we went outside.

I had come face to face with one of my greatest enemies. I had expected to be excited, moved, even shaken. But I was none of those things. Instead, I saw before me the immense number of tasks that had to be accomplished in a few short hours. I was not in La Higuera as a member of the Cuban democratic resistance or to seek personal revenge, but as a foreign national, a representative of the American government. Therefore I put aside my personal feelings and requested permission from Zenteno to photograph all the captured material. The colonel granted me my wish. Then he and the other officers left for the forward command post from which the Bolivian Ranger officers were directing their combat operations.

I unpacked my radio equipment, an RS-48 portable communications system, and extended the antenna. I left a soldier guarding my radio and, in front of the house where the army had made its command post (probably because it had the only working telephone in La Higuera) I started laying out Che's materials to be photographed.

Once I put everything in order I moved a table—it was very rickety and of rustic construction—into the sunlight where I could shoot the pictures with my two cameras, a Japanese Pentax 35mm and a tiny German Minox. I worked as quickly as I could, trying to keep everything in focus. Meanwhile, the Bolivians were bringing more guerrillas down from the combat zone. One, Aniceto, had been shot in the face and was obviously enduring considerable pain. Another, the Peruvian known as El Chino Peruano, was already dead. Both of them were set down close to the table.

By 10 A.M. I had established radio contact and was starting to send my cipher groups out. As I was working the keypad, a soldier came to me. There was a phone call from Vallegrande, and they wanted to talk to the highest-ranking officer in La Higuera.

Until Zenteno got back, that was me, as I had been given the Bolivian rank of Captain. I went inside, picked up the receiver and identified myself: "Captain Ramos."

The voice on the other end gave me the following message. "You are authorized by the Superior Command," he said, "to conduct Operation Five Hundred and Six Hundred."

My heartbeat quickened. Five hundred was the Bolivian code for Che. Six hundred was dead. If the Bolivian High Command had wanted Che alive, the message would have been Operation Five Hundred and Seven Hundred. I asked the officer in Vallegrande to repeat the words so I could confirm them. He did, and then I hung up the phone.

I said nothing to anyone, waiting until Colonel Zenteno returned from the command post shortly before 11 A.M. I took him aside and described the phone call and its grave implications. I stressed that my instructions from the United States Government were to try to keep the guerrilla leader alive under any circumstances. I knew that the U.S. had helicopters and airplanes ready to evacuate Che to Panama for interrogation, and that keeping Che alive was of supreme importance to the Agency.

Zenteno shook his head. "Felix, we have worked very closely, and we are grateful for all the help you have given us. But don't ask me to do this. If I don't comply with my orders to execute Che I will be disobeying my own president and I'll risk a dishonorable discharge."

Zenteno checked his watch. "I know how much harm he has done to your country. It is eleven now. I will leave in the helicopter. It will be coming back and forth to Vallegrande several times over the next few hours, evacuating our dead and wounded, and bringing ammunition and C-rations. At two P.M. I will send it back. I would like your word of honor that at that time you will personally bring back the dead body of Che Guevara to Vallegrande.

"The manner in which you deal with Che is up to you. You can even do it yourself if you want, as I know how much harm he has brought to your country."

I looked Zenteno in the face. The man had been generous to me. He hadn't had to bring me here, but had done so because he knew what facing Che meant to me, and what getting Che's information meant to my government.

"Colonel," I said, "please get them to try to change their minds. But if you cannot get the counterorder, I give you my word as a man that at two P.M. I will bring you back the dead body of Che Guevara."

The Bolivian and I embraced, and then he left.

Alone, a thousand thoughts crossed my mind. The Agency wanted Che alive. Could I bring it off? Could I manage to get him to La Paz without the Bolivians knowing? How would I do that?

It wouldn't be too hard. There was only one telephone, and no radio communications. When the chopper arrived at two, I could very easily go to the telephone, then come back and tell the pilot, Nino de Guzmán, that there had been a change of orders—that the U.S. Embassy had convinced President Barrientos to keep Che alive, and that we were to fly him back to Vallegrande immediately. Once there, the Bolivians would not easily be able to kill him—everyone would have seen Che alive.

On the other hand, I also remembered some pertinent Cuban history: Fidel Castro had once been thrown into jail by Batista, only to be subsequently released. "And look at what we have today, in Cuba and in Latin America," I thought to myself.

So while I debated more than once my chances for success in getting Che out alive, the conclusion I reached every time was this: First, I have tried everything I could through normal channels. Second—and most important—it's a Bolivian decision, not a U.S. one.

We are only advisers here. Third, I realized that if I took the extraordinary step of saving Che's life, I might ultimately have to face up to the fact of having made one hell of a mistake.

It was my call. And my call was to leave it in the hands of the Bolivians. It was their war; Che was their prisoner. I was not in Bolivia to command, but to advise.

Still, Zenteno had said I could execute Che in my own way. I thought to myself, "If I have to do it I will put him in front of a firing squad and execute him the same way he assassinated so many of my friends at La Cabaña Fortress."

Gunfire interrupted my deliberations. It came from the schoolhouse. I rushed down the hill from my worktable and threw open the door. Che looked up at me from the floor. I went into the next room and saw a soldier, his weapon still smoking, and the guerrilla Willy collapsing over a small table. I could actually hear the life escape from him.

The soldier turned to me, fear in his eyes, and said, almost apologetically, "*Mi Capitán*, he tried to escape."

Escape was impossible. The room had but one barred window in the rear. There were troops all around the schoolhouse. No, the soldier was only complying with his orders. The Bolivians didn't want any prisoners. They wanted the guerrillas dead. I turned without saying anything and went back into the room where Che lay, his arms and legs trussed together.

The place was small—about eight feet long and ten feet wide with mud walls and earthen floor. The tiny window was the sole source of light. There was a single, narrow door also facing the front. Che lay next to an old wooden bench. In the rear of the room, just across from him were the bodies of Antonio and Arturo.

I examined him more closely than I had before. He was a wreck. His clothes were filthy, ripped in several places and missing most of their buttons. He didn't even have proper shoes, only pieces of leather wrapped around his feet and tied with cord.

I stood above Che, my boots near his head, just as Che had once stood over my dear friend and fellow 2506 Brigade member, Nestor Pino. Captured at the Bay of Pigs, Pino was beaten by Castro's soldiers when he told them that he was not a cook or radio operator but the company commander of a paratroop battalion. His body battered, he lay on the earthen floor of a seaside hut taking the kicks and blows. Suddenly, they stopped.

Pino opened his eyes and saw a pair of polished boots next to his face. He looked up. It was Che Guevara, staring coolly down at him. Che spoke as matter-of-factly as if he was telling a child tomorrow is a school day. "We're going to kill you all," he said to Pino.

Pino had survived his ordeal. Now, the situation was reversed. Che Guevara lay at my feet. He looked like a piece of trash.

I said, "Che Guevara, I want to talk to you."

Even now he played the role of *comandante*. His eyes flashed. "Nobody interrogates me," he replied sarcastically.

"*Comandante*," I said, somewhat amazed that he had chosen to answer me at all, "I didn't come to interrogate you. Our ideals are different. But I admire you. You used to be a minister of state in Cuba. Now look at you—you are like this because you believe in your ideals. I have come to talk to you."

He looked at me for about a minute in silence, then agreed to speak and asked if he could sit up. I ordered a soldier to untie him and got him propped onto the rickety wooden bench. I got him tobacco for his pipe.

He would not discuss tactical matters or technical things. When I asked him about some of his specific operations, he responded by saying only, "You know I cannot answer that."

But to more general questions, like "*Comandante*, of all the possible countries in the region, why did you pick Bolivia to export your revolution?" he answered at length.

He told me he had considered other places—Venezuela, Central America, and the Dominican Republic were three he named. But, he added, experience had shown that when Cuba tried to foment unrest so close to the U.S., the *Yanquis* reacted strongly and the revolutionary activities failed.

So, Che continued, since countries like Venezuela and Nicaragua were "too important to Yankee imperialism, and the Americans hadn't allowed us any success there, we figured that, by picking a country so far from the U.S. it wouldn't appear to present an immediate threat, the *Yanquis* wouldn't concern themselves with what we did. Bolivia fulfills that requirement.

"Second," he added, "we were looking for a poor country—and

Bolivia is poor. And third, Bolivia shares boundaries with five countries. If we are successful in Bolivia, then we can move into other places—Argentina, Chile, Brazil, Peru, Paraguay."

He told me he believed that he'd lost support in Bolivia because the people were too provincial. "They cannot see their revolution in broad terms—as an international guerrilla movement working for the proletariat—but only as a regional issue," he said. "They want a Boliviano *comandante*, not a Cuban, even though I am an expert in these matters."

We talked about Cuba. He admitted to me that the economy was in a shambles, largely because of the economic boycott by the U.S. "But you helped cause that," I told Che. "You—a doctor—were made president of the Cuban National Bank. What does a doctor know about economics?"

"Do you know how I became president of the Cuban National Bank?" he asked me.

"No."

"I'll tell you a joke." He laughed. "We were sitting in a meeting one day, and Fidel came in and he asked for a dedicated *economista*. I misheard him—I thought he was asking for a dedicated *comunista*, so I raised my hand." He shrugged. "And that's why Fidel selected me as head of the Cuban economy."

He refused to talk about what he had done in Africa although, when I said we'd been told he had a ten-thousand-man guerrilla force, but that his African soldiers were a disaster, he laughed sadly and said, "If I'd really had ten thousand guerrillas it would have been different. But you are right, you know—the Africans were very, very bad soldiers."

He refused to speak badly about Fidel, although he damned him with faint praise. Actually, Che was evasive when Fidel's name came up. It became apparent to me that he was bitter over the Cuban dictator's lack of support for the Bolivian incursion. Indeed, that Che admitted how bad the Cuban economy was represented an indictment of Fidel's leadership, even though he did not specifically criticize him.

Che and I talked for about an hour and a half until, shortly before noon, I heard the chopper arrive. I went outside and discovered that Nino de Guzmán, had brought a camera from Major Saucedo, who wanted a picture of the prisoner. That was when I purposely screwed up the Bolivian's camera, but had Nino de Guzmán snap a picture of Che and me using my own Pentax. It is the only photograph of Che alive on the day he died.

Back inside, we resumed our conversation. Che expressed surprise that I knew so much about him, and about Cuba. "You are not a Bolivian," he said.

"No, I am not. Where do you think I am from?"

"You could be a Puerto Rican or a Cuban. Whoever you are, by the sorts of questions you've been asking I believe that you work for the intelligence service of the United States."

"You are right, *Comandante*," I said. "I am a Cuban. I was a member of the 2506 Brigade. In fact, I was a member of the infiltration teams that operated inside Cuba before the invasion at the Bay of Pigs."

"What's your name?"

"Felix. Just Felix, *Comandante*." I wanted to say more, but I didn't dare. There was still a slim possibility that he might get out of this alive, and I didn't want my identity to escape with him.

"Ha," Che answered. Nothing more. I don't know what he was thinking at the moment and I never asked.

We started to talk about the Cuban economy once again when we were interrupted by shots, followed by the sounds of a body falling to the floor. Aniceto had been executed in the adjoining room. Che stopped talking. He did not say anything about the shooting, but his face reflected sadness and he shook his head slowly from left to right several times.

Perhaps it was in that instant that he realized that he, too, was doomed, even though I did not tell him so until just before 1 P.M.

I had been putting off the inevitable, shuttling between Che's room and the table where I was photographing his documents. I was taking pictures of his diary when the village schoolteacher arrived.

"*Mi Capitán?*"

I looked up from my work. "Yes?"

"When are you going to shoot him?"

That caught my attention. "Why are you asking me that?" I asked.

"Because the radio is already reporting that he is dead from combat wounds."

The Bolivians were taking no chances. That radio report sealed Che's fate. I went down the hill, into the schoolhouse and looked Che in the face. *"Comandante,"* I said, "I have done everything in my power, but orders have come from the Supreme Bolivian Command..."

His face turned as white as writing paper. "It is better like this, Felix. I should never have been captured alive."

When I asked him if he had any message for his family, he said, "Tell Fidel that he will soon see a triumphant revolution in America." He said it in a way that, to me, seemed to mock the Cuban dictator for abandoning him here in the Bolivian jungle. Then Che added, "And tell my wife to get remarried and try to be happy."

Then we embraced, and it was a tremendously emotional moment for me. I no longer hated him. His moment of truth had come, and he was conducting himself like a man. He was facing his death with courage and grace.

I looked at my watch. It was one in the afternoon. I walked outside to where Mario Terán and Lieutenant Pérez stood. I looked at Terán, whose face shone as if he had been drinking. I told him not to shoot Che in the face, but from the neck down. Then I walked up the hill and began making notes. When I heard the shots I checked my watch. It was 1:10 P.M.

Che was dead.

I suppose I might have been more emotional at that moment, but frankly there wasn't time. Besides, there were many other things to do. My equipment had to be put in order; the canisters of film I'd shot had to be stored. I didn't want to lose a single thing.

As I was working, Terán, his deed done, came to me and asked for Che's pipe. I thought about it. Che had told Terán he didn't want him to have the pipe. But, I asked myself, why should I comply with the wishes of a man who assassinated so many of my friends?

I pulled the pipe from my pocket and handed it to Terán. I said, "Here—so you will remember your great deed." I don't think the Bolivian sergeant caught the irony in my voice. Still, he lowered his eyes, took the pipe from my hand and left without saying anything.

Another Bolivian soldier had "liberated" Che's Rolex GMT Master from the guerrilla's wrist. I wore a similar watch—I had bought it for one of my infiltration missions to Cuba in December 1961. Now I

ordered the soldier to show me Che's watch. I took it aside and
quickly removed it from the steel bracelet. When I handed the Bolivian back the watch, he may have had a Rolex, but it wasn't Che's.
The guerrilla's watch, on my own band, was now around my wrist.

Perhaps half an hour elapsed before I finally went to examine
Che's body. Two Bolivian officers came down from the forward command post and I went inside the schoolhouse with them. Che's body
was crumpled on the earth floor. His eyes and mouth were open. He
had been shot as I instructed, below the neck.

One of the Bolivians hit Che's face with a stick, opening a small
wound just above his eyebrow. "You son of a bitch," he said. He had
reason to be bitter—he'd suffered casualties at the hands of Che's
guerrilla band.

Still, I saw no reason to desecrate Che's corpse. After they left, I
called a soldier to bring me a pail of water. I took it and with my own
hands cleaned Che's face, closed his eyes, and tried to close the jaw.

The chopper arrived ahead of schedule. Nino de Guzmán, two
soldiers and I carried Che's body out of the schoolhouse on a canvas
stretcher and tied it to the right skid of the chopper. It was a precarious thing to do because we had to balance the corpse carefully—flying a small chopper with weight attached to one side is not easy. In
shifting him, some of Che's blood that had pooled on the canvas
under his back got on my hands, and I wiped them on my fatigues. I
was still tying the body securely when Nino de Guzmán started the
rotors spinning.

I climbed onto the canvas bench and was strapping myself in
when, from out of nowhere, a Catholic priest came bumping up the
rutted street on a mule. He was coming so fast I thought he'd decap-
itate himself on the rotor. But he stopped just short of the spinning
blades, jumped down, made the sign of the Cross, and immediately
gave a benediction over the body of Che. The priest turned out to be
named Father Schiller. I never spoke to him. At the time, I remember
thinking how strange it was that the self-proclaimed atheist Ernesto
Che Guevara should be receiving a last sacrament.

I spent the half-hour flight to Vallegrande in contemplative silence, thinking about Che and how he'd died; about my family, and
also about how the fates had allowed me to come face to face with
one of my greatest enemies. Seconds after we landed at the airfield

with all its chaos I slipped away into the crowd, just another anonymous Bolivian officer.

My CIA colleague Eduardo got Che's body off the chopper and loaded into an old gray ambulance. Unfortunately for him, his picture was taken several times that day. The photographs were subsequently published in newspapers and magazines all around the world. In many of them, he was identified as "CIA Agent Felix Ramos." I, however, was very careful not to show my face. So while my cover name was made public, my identity never was.

Under Eduardo's direction, the corpse was then driven to the Nuestra Señora de Malta hospital, where all the guerrillas' bodies had been taken. It was in the hospital laundry, converted into a temporary morgue, that the famous photograph of Che's body was taken. I was not there.

The crowd of reporters, soldiers, officers, and onlookers followed the ambulance, leaving the airport quickly deserted. In the rapidly thinning crowd I found Major Serrate and Major Saucedo, both of whom had been waiting for me. We embraced and talked excitedly about my conversations with the legendary communist guerrilla. Nino de Guzmán also showed up, and the four of us walked back to his aircraft. I retrieved the communications gear I'd stored in the chopper's tail boom.

Alone, I went back to the quarters that Eduardo and I shared. As I walked in the cool mountain air I realized that I was wheezing and that it was becoming hard to breathe. Che may have been dead, but somehow his asthma—a condition I had never had in my life—had attached itself to me. To this day my chronic shortness of breath is a constant reminder of Che and his last hours alive in the tiny town of La Higuera.

The rest of that day and the days afterward moved so quickly they are a blurred memory. I spent most of the time talking. First, at the hotel where Colonel Zenteno Anaya was staying, I briefed him and also the Bolivian Armed Forces Chief of Staff, General Alfredo Ovando Candia, on my talks with Che.

The most bizarre episode in the chaos that followed Che's death resulted from General Ovando Candia's decision to preserve proof and concrete evidence of Che's death in case Fidel Castro denied the entire episode. The Bolivian Chief of Staff actually wanted to re-move, preserve, and keep Che's head. Fortunately, he was subse-quently convinced that such an act would go beyond propriety, and it was suggested to him that perhaps a surgically removed finger would suffice as proof.

Ovando's response was quick: he ordered Che's hands to be cut off and preserved. Ovando also ordered the disposal of Che's body.

That same evening I drove back to Santa Cruz where my CIA contact Jim was waiting, and told my story again. Then it was on to La Paz, where I finally arrived on October 12, to be interviewed by yet another CIA officer. Later that day, after following what seemed like an endless series of security procedures to keep me from being tailed—by whom I had no idea—I arrived at a safe house, met with a group of CIA people (including the deputy Chief of Station for La Paz) and delivered to them all my films and notes. Three days had not passed since Che's death.

On October 13 I returned to Santa Cruz, where Jim and my fellow Cuban Eduardo waited for me, and picked up my belongings. We lay low in Santa Cruz because there were stories appearing in the press about Agency involvement in the hunt for Che, and reporters were combing the town for foreigners.

On the 14th, a U.S. air force C-130 Hercules arrived in Santa Cruz to pick us up. But when we went to the airport the next morning we discovered that it had mysteriously developed a flat tire—and there was no spare. Immediately, Jim communicated with the embassy in La Paz, which sent a C-54 down to get us. We flew straight to the La Paz airport, where each of us was picked up by a different Agency car and taken to separate houses. Finally, on the 16th, another C-130 came and took us to Panama, where we arrived—exhausted—on the morning of the 17th. After a week of further debriefings and some well-deserved rest I left for the U.S. on October 25.

12 There was almost no time to relax after I returned from Panama. Six weeks or so later, right at the beginning of 1968, Eduardo and I were on our way to Ecuador to help train an elite intelligence unit in antiterror and counterinsurgency techniques. Our services had been requested by the President of that country. This time we traveled under military cover. When we arrived in Quito, the Ecuadoran capital, I was traveling under the pseudonym Frank Garcia.

Some of the officers we were going to work with had been trained in the U.S. But the Ecuadoran military lacked advanced communications and intelligence capabilities—such as the ability to transmit securely from one location to another, or knowledge about how to use mobile radios and phones on secure frequencies (this was before the days when transportable scramblers were commonplace). We also planned to spend a fair amount of time working on interrogation techniques. The Ecuadorans knew about our experience with Che in Bolivia. Actually, our reputations preceded us, which gave us additional credibility. So when I talked about how to elicit information from prisoners, they already knew that I had been responsible for successful operations in the past, and that I was speaking from proven field experience.

I found a willing audience. The men I trained weren't the old generation of Latin American officers who believed in a caste system and were rigid in their ways. These men were young officers in their twenties who had been reassigned from the army, the air force, or the police. Most had had some training in the U.S., either through military programs or with the FBI.

I taught the same principles of interrogation I'd used on Paco in Bolivia. First, I told my students, make the subject identify with you. That's easy most of the time, because in a majority of the cases I have ever come across, the captured guerrilla or terrorist is waiting to get the bejeezus beaten out of him, expecting torture, lack of food, insults—every hardship people usually get in prison in communist countries. Often, the reason for these expectations is that their superiors have warned them about the consequences of being captured alive to keep them from defecting to government forces.

So when they are captured, and they are treated 100 percent differently from what their communist leader described, they start realizing that what they'd been told is not true. In many cases, this unexpected good treatment makes a tremendous impact and creates a positive framework from which to begin work. Rule number one, therefore, is to get close and make the subject identify with you. Tell him about yourself—up to a point. Give him little bits of information, so he becomes dependent on you and learns to trust you.

The second principle that I taught was to use intelligence to elicit intelligence. If you capture an agent, he will first give you the cover story that he has been trained to give. From previously acquired intelligence you probably know a few things about what he has been doing, with whom he has been working, where he has been, and so on.

Use what you know judiciously, I would tell my students. "Catch him in a small lie. Tell him, 'Look, friend, I know that's not the case at all.' Then you give him specific information, correcting what he has just told you, which makes him believe you know much more than you actually do know.

"Then probe another area—an area that you may not know anything about. Chances are that you'll get new information, and that it will check out."

In Latin America, family is an all-important element of life. Use that, I told them. "If the subject has been in custody long enough so that it doesn't create a security-risk situation, tell him you'll contact his family and make sure everything's OK. If he tells you personal stuff—that his mother has financial problems, or his kid brother's in trouble—then you must help him, even if you don't tell him right away what you've done. Let his family tell him. That way he feels you are helping him not because it is your job but because you want to."

Such techniques can be tremendously persuasive for an individual who has been told that you are a brutal animal who will do horrible things to him if he is captured.

We played out scenarios in class, too, my students taking roles as prisoners or interrogators. They learned well and they learned quickly. They also picked up some basics of surveillance: how to use photography and implements such as parabolic microphones and other listening devices, both indoors and outdoors.

The assignment was challenging and rewarding for me. Eduardo and I shared a room at a nice hotel in Quito, where we had registered as visiting businessmen. Each morning, taking precautions against being followed, we would walk to a safe house. There the training sessions would take place. We maintained regular contact with our case officer, a CIA officer I will call Jack. As a matter of fact, we spent a fair amount of time at his home, to which he would invite us for lunch or dinner. On weekends, Jack and his family took us to see the sights in the Quito region.

We had finished most of the instruction program we'd planned when, one day, I received a call from Jack.

"Why don't you and your colleague come over to the house," he said.

I always looked forward to invitations like that. Jack had a lovely chalet-type home in an upper-middle-class but not ostentatious neighborhood. I used to enjoy the time I spent there, talking with Jack and his wife, and playing with their two children. The kids even called me Uncle Frank.

When we showed up, Jack told us, "Probably it's no cause for concern, but we've had an indication from the FBI that there may be the possibility of a Castro-inspired kidnapping of your family, Frank, or your family, Eduardo." Jack said that, as we might want to leave Quito and go back to our families in Miami immediately, he had made such arrangements for us.

That news was enough to rock us in our boots. But Jack was reassuring: he told us that the FBI was watching our families surreptitiously, and there was no indication of a serious threat. He said that the cable he had received was unclear about which one of us was in potential danger—although it had been Eduardo's wife who had initiated the contact with the Agency.

That made sense to me. Eduardo had been photographed in Bolivia the day I flew Che's body to Vallegrande. He had even been identified at the time as an American and a CIA agent. (Interestingly, because he had a prominent forehead, a light complexion and light-colored eyes, Eduardo was probably misidentified by Cuban intelligence from the very first as a gringo.) Moreover, in some of the news photos published both in the U.S. and all over the world he was called Felix Ramos, instead of the pseudonym he used in Bolivia, Eduardo Gonzalez. But neither alias would mean anything to anyone, as we had used them only once.

Shortly after Jack told us about the cable, Eduardo and I returned to Miami to be with our families. When I finally saw Rosa, she assured me that nothing out of the ordinary had happened.

Indeed, after a few weeks at home, I felt certain it was not I who had been compromised. I had been careful not to show my face anywhere around the photographers in Vallegrande. I had never disclosed my full name to Che. The Bolivians had never heard the name Felix Rodriguez.

My colleague had not been so fortunate. It might have been bad luck, or it might have been a certain lack of self-protective tradecraft on his part, but the fact remains that after we returned to Miami from Ecuador, he never, to my knowledge, received another assignment from the CIA.

Even though I had not been compromised, it was prudent for me always to be careful, because Fidel is not one to forget. The man who made it possible for me to go to La Higuera, my friend Colonel Joaquín Zenteno Anaya, for example, was ultimately promoted to the rank of general, and in 1973 was sent to Paris as the Bolivian Ambassador. But on May 11, 1976, Zenteno was shot to death on a Paris street by a previously unknown terrorist group calling itself the "Che Guevara Brigade." News accounts at the time said the general was assassinated by a bearded man about thirty-five years old who shot him twice in the back, killing him instantly. Fidel's fingerprints were all over the murder. I took the killing as a clear warning to all who had taken part in the operation against Che Guevara. Each of us was in jeopardy. Our only protection was in our anonymity.

Actually, the CIA employs an effective way of keeping its agents' identities secret. Since this technique has been made public before, I am not revealing anything by explaining it here. Each agent is assigned from the very first a CIA pseudonym. Habitually, they are East European names. For example, I am not listed in CIA files as Felix Rodriguez, but under a Soviet alias. Let's say I am called Yaakov Smirnov. What a country, right?

No operational aliases are listed on any of my reports. Therefore, should a CIA defector like Philip Agee or a traitor like Edward Howard take any report and copy it, there can by no way he or anyone else could know that Yaakov Smirnov equals Felix Rodriguez. Nor would the traitor be able to discover that I had used the names Ramos or García on my assignments overseas.

The technique works. When Iranian terrorists overran the U.S. Embassy in Tehran in November 1979, they captured some Agency files. But I am sure no agent's real name was in those files, only their CIA pseudonyms—which would not help at all in identifying who actually were the CIA's people in Iran—at least not by name. That technique was a reassurance to me in the weeks and months following Zenteno's assassination in Paris.

• • •

Later in 1968, I was assigned to help teach basic intelligence and long-range patrol skills to a Peruvian paratrooper unit, one of Peru's first antiguerrilla combat units. Initially the assignment was to last two years, and there was some thought of my taking Rosa and the kids with me to the Peruvian capital. But her parents were getting old and could not travel easily, and leaving them behind to fend for themselves was unthinkable. So we finally decided that Rosa and the kids would stay in Miami with both sets of parents and I would go to Peru on my own, making a trip to Miami every six months or so to visit the family.

My boss was my old friend from Bolivia, Jim who was by then working out of Lima. And for the first time I traveled under my own name. According to my documents I was Felix Rodriguez, and attached under contract to the Peruvian Department of Defense.

The training area was in a little village on the other side of the Andes. To get there you could either fly or drive along a series of ever-narrowing mountain roads until you got to a road so narrow that it was a one-way only westward on Mondays, Wednesdays, and Fridays, and one way eastward on Tuesdays, Thursdays, and Saturdays. On Sundays you took your chances.

The unit was not from the army but culled from the civil guard. Officially it was known as "Los Sinchis," from the Benemerita Guardia Civil de Peru, the police unit whose responsibilities had been extended to rural areas, where they functioned much like the Italian national police, the carabinieri.

The unit had been originally established as a joint Peruvian and U.S. Special Forces–CIA project. The Special Forces did the initial paratrooper training—everything from jump exercises to chute rigging. Later, Agency people provided intelligence skills and communications expertise. Jim and I flew up together, and he introduced me to the Peruvian commander, Lieutenant Colonel Danilo Agramonte, a tall, muscular man who wore dark glasses. Jim took him aside, swore the officer to secrecy, and then told him privately about my experiences in Bolivia with Che Guevara. Then he left, never mentioning to me what he'd told Agramonte.

Later that day, at dinner in the officer's mess hall, Colonel Agramonte stood up and introduced me. "This is Felix Rodriguez," he said. "He is the man who captured Che Guevara in Bolivia."

I just about lost it when he said that. I started to say, "Oh, my, I had nothing to do with that!" But it was too late. Ultimately, I lost my initial reticence and at the Peruvian's request even gave a talk on how we captured Che. But at that moment I was worried. I was, after all, traveling under my real name. Of course the Peruvians didn't know that. But I believed that any information at all leaked about Che's capture and execution would find its way back to Fidel. And even though the Peruvians didn't find any significance in the name Felix Rodriguez, Fidel's intelligence service would have done so.

Life was quite basic, to use a euphemism. On one side of the road were the houses of about two hundred or so townspeople. On the other side was our compound. There was a dirt landing strip, long enough to accommodate a C-47, but nothing much larger. We had training fields, barracks, rigging rooms, and classrooms where I taught communications training on much the same kind of radio equipment I'd used in Bolivia and with Artime, back in 1965. There were officers' quarters and mess halls, of course. I was assigned a house a short distance from the base, and although it had been built for twelve I had it all to myself. Each room had its own shower, and even though the weather was somewhat humid during the day, it was quite comfortable, since the place backed up to the river.

On the first weekend after I arrived, the plane came. It was a C-47, flown by the Peruvian air force, and used by the guard unit to make its weekly practice jumps. Shortly before it arrived, Colonel Agramonte and I were talking.

He said, "Of course you are a paratrooper."

That was a logical assumption. I looked him in the eye and said, "Of course I am, *Comandante*."

"How many jumps have you made, Felix?"

I looked at him with a smile. "Oh, I don't know—maybe a hundred."

"Then you'll jump with us today."

"Sure," I said without an instant's hesitation. "No problem."

I thought back to the training camps in Guatemala. I'd jumped from a bench, learning the three-point-landing technique. I'd jumped from a tower on a cable. But I'd never been dropped from an airplane. Still, how bad could it be?

I'd been at the base less than a week but I'd already made one friend, a captain named Javier Devincensi. I sought him out, took him aside, and said, "I need your help."

"Anything you want."

"OK," I said. "How the hell do I put on a parachute?"

He looked at me as if I were crazy. "You mean you've never jumped out of an airplane?"

I shook my head.

"You are loco, you know. You're gonna get yourself killed."

"Bullshit. Besides, even though I've never jumped from a goddam plane, I can't tell that to Colonel Agramonte. Besides, I had some training. All I need is a little practice. You give me a refresher."

So we went to my room, where I jumped from a chair so Javier could critique my landing style. "Not bad at all," he pronounced. Then we went to the rigging area before anyone else got there, and he showed me how to strap the chute on my back.

"I still think you're crazy," he said. "Look, Felix, it's no embarrassment. I can just tell the colonel and he'll understand."

"Forget it," I told him. "I can do it."

He shrugged. "OK."

I also convinced him to let me jump first. Because the region was so mountainous, it would have been dangerous to allow everyone to jump at once. On those training missions, the plane took off and circled the city of Satipo, then came back flying low through the mountain passes. The unit jumped when the C-47 was over the landing strip. But because the strip was surrounded by jungle and bordered by the river, one man, known as the wind dummy, jumped alone on the first pass. He would float down without adjusting his chute, so the pilot could see how the winds were blowing. Then, the plane's course having adapted to the outside wind conditions, the rest of the men—twenty or so—would follow. The technique cut back on jump casualties.

I wanted to be the wind dummy. I had good reason. First, no one would see my mistakes, if I made any. Second, and perhaps more important, I wanted to face this challenge alone.

I climbed into the C-47 with the unit. I can honestly say I lost a lot of weight that day because I was sweating so much—a combination of the heat, the heavy equipment, and the fear. Take my word for it, it is very uncomfortable to jump into the open sky when you've never done it before.

I sank into my seat, which was next to the open hatchway, thinking that I must not freeze in the doorway. We took off, climbing and performing a long, lazy circle above the city. Then, after five or six or seven minutes, we were back above the airfield, flying between the mountain peaks.

The jumpmaster ordered me to the door. *"A la puerta!"*

I stood, hooked my chute release to the guy wire that ran the length of the plane, and moved to the doorway. I positioned myself at the brink, one of my toes over the edge, my hands braced on the outside of the hatch, the slipstream whipping into my face.

The jumpmaster was kneeling beside me. His face, close to the floor, peered outside the hatchway; his right hand held my left ankle. As we came over the drop zone he gauged the plane's path. I could feel his grip tighten.

I tried not to look down, knowing that looking down was the worst thing I could do—that men have frozen in the doorway after looking down at the ground. But I couldn't help myself. What I saw gave me the sensation of ice running through my body. So I looked straight ahead at the mountain range opposite me.

The jumpmaster thwacked me on my lower leg. I closed my eyes and I went out the door without thinking, my arms and legs forcing me into the heavy slipstream.

Gravity. I felt myself tumble, tumble, tumble. Then I was jerked upward. The chute. It was working. Terrific. I opened my eyes and looked up. I was a little tangled in the cables, as I had jumped incorrectly. But I straightened myself out immediately and knew everything was going to be all right.

It was an incredible feeling, as if I was suspended in air, about two thousand feet over the runway. I could see the jungle and the river and the mountains, all beautifully clear in the cool air. Nothing I had ever experienced could have prepared me for this unbelievable sensation of floating silently, feeling as if I were the king of the world. I relaxed my body, secure in the knowledge that my chute was taking me safely to the ground.

The ground! It was coming up fast. Too fast—it was as if I'd fallen off the third floor of a house. I told myself not to tense up or I'd break my legs. Down I went, missing the runway by about eighty feet, landing right next to a farmer and his mule (I almost hit the mule).

I bounced correctly, then regained my feet and started to bundle up my chute. I watched as the plane made its second pass over the airstrip and the others jumped, coming down slowly and right on target.

Afterward, Devincensi came up to me and gave me a big *abrazo*. "Well, you made it," he told me. "Now I know you're nuts!"

After my third jump I told Colonel Agramonte the truth. We were having a drink one evening, and I said, "May I tell you a story? I have never jumped from an airplane in my life before I got here."

He laughed like hell and said, "Felix, you are crazy." Then a wonderful smile came over his face. "In that case," he said, "we'll graduate you. You've made three jumps. You make five more and you'll get your wings from the Peruvian air force and from our police unit."

I made the eight required—and four more after that. Twelve jumps in all, and every time I jumped I must have lost three to four pounds because I sweat so much. But what incredible fun it was.

I worked with the unit about six months, much less time than I had originally agreed to remain. Four months were terrific. The last two were problematic. The reason was that another adviser joined me, an American citizen (although he was Latino by birth) with whom Colonel Agramonte did not get along.

This adviser was an overly critical individual, and by the time I finally packed it in and went back to Lima and then Miami, he had managed to completely alienate the Peruvians. It got to the point that they refused to give him any cooperation or follow any of his advice. There is—all too often, I have noticed—a tendency among those of us from advanced societies like the United States to become arrogant when we go into the third world. We expect everything to be done on our timetable, and done with the same values that we apply back in Washington, or Miami, or New York. Well, the answer is that's not the way it works. Whether you are a CIA agent or a tourist, you have to learn to shed the rigidity that most Americanos carry with them.

Watching this adviser ruin a relationship I'd spent half a year developing taught me some valuable lessons. The message is so simple: if you are an adviser you must *advise*—not arbitrarily order or command. If you start off only talking, never listening, the people you are supposed to be helping will turn against you. If you do not respect them for their values and their strengths, they will never respect you for yours. If you do not fight for them—become an advocate of their causes—they will not fight for you and your causes. Sometimes I believe that we forget these basic things when we ask others to act as our surrogates—and forgetting them can cause problems, as I was to learn on my next assignment: Vietnam.

13 I volunteered for Vietnam. I didn't have to go. In fact, I'd been offered another assignment in Venezuela, a country I knew and liked, where I spoke the language and could fit in without a second thought. But, to be honest, I felt I could probably do the U.S. more good in Vietnam. There were lots of volunteers to go to South America for the Agency; fewer who preferred war-ravaged Southeast Asia.

I was feeling especially patriotic because I had just become a citizen. On February 24, 1969, I'd raised my right hand and taken an oath of loyalty to the United States (after which one of the first things I did was go out and register to vote—Republican!). I felt I owed my adopted country something. Too often, I believe, we Americans take our freedoms and our liberty for granted. I lost the country of my birth to communism, and so I know freedom must be protected. Indeed, when President Bush talks about the American flag and its very special symbolism, his words take on an added meaning for me and for all of us who have lost our native lands to tyranny. And Cuban-Americans, too, were paying a price in Vietnam. My comrades from the 2506 Brigade, Felix Sosa Camejo, Celso Pérez, and Irenaldo Padrón died fighting communism in Southeast Asia.

I left for Saigon on March 13, 1970. My cover was as a civilian working for the U.S. Army, with the equivalent rank of major. The reason for the deception was simple: CIA employees, especially those working in war zones, don't go around carrying ID cards that say they are Agency personnel. I guess there were perhaps five hundred or so Agency people in Vietnam during the time I was there. Some operated out of the new U.S. Embassy in Saigon, others from our old embassy building, a relic of French colonial days that sat on the bank of the Saigon River. And, of course, there were CIA people working at stations, substations, offices, billets, and compounds in each of Vietnam's five military regions. Region I was Da Nang; Region II, Nha Trang; Region III was based in Bien Hoa and included all the provinces around Saigon; Region IV was the Mekong Delta and extended way down south; and Region V was Saigon itself. My assignment was to be a deputy field adviser for Provincial Reconnaissance Units (PRUs) operating out of Region III and based at Bien Hoa.

In 1970, Saigon Station was rumored to be the biggest and most important CIA station in the world. Those sent to run it were supposedly the same ones who would someday rise to lead the U.S. intelligence community. The importance the Agency placed on its Vietnamese operations was reflected in the fact that each of the five Vietnamese military regions was like a sovereign country: each had its own chief of station, with powers, I was told, equal to those of a chief of station in any country in the world. And at the hub of everything—overseeing each program, every operation, every tidbit of intelligence that was gathered by the CIA in Vietnam—was Saigon Station. To those of us in the Agency, the man who ran Saigon Station had more power than a god. And that man was Ted Shackley.

I had no idea who Shackley was until Jim, my old friend from Bolivia and Peru, told me, shortly before I left for Saigon. "He's the guy who ran Miami Station while you were doing your infiltrations inside Cuba," he explained. Jim said Shackley had had a brilliant career in the Agency and would probably become the DCI—the Director of Central Intelligence—a position held when I was in Vietnam by Richard M. Helms.

I met Shackley shortly after my arrival. Roughly forty of us new arrivals were assembled for his orientation talk in a secure plastic-bubble room at the U.S. Embassy. He was in his early forties and wore extremely thick glasses. I thought he looked like a professor. He was very bright and articulate, and sounded sincere when he said that if anyone had a problem they could come and talk to him anytime.

There were lots of stories about Shackley circulating around Saigon in those days. He had a reputation as a tough guy, very result-oriented, very rigid, and ruthless in an intellectual way. He also had a reputation for levying requirements on his subordinates that could be measured or quantified. For example, X number of intelligence reports about X number of penetrations with X number captured and X number killed was how he liked to see things submitted. The figures made it easier for him to deal with the bureaucrats back at Langley.

He also had the habit of looking over people's shoulders. As one Agency guy I knew who worked closely with Shackley told me, "He's always checking up on me." And he had a photographic memory. My friend (and boss in Vietnam) Rudy Enders worked for Shackley both in Miami and in Vietnam. Rudy once said that Ted had skimmed a sixteen-page report he'd written and then started to quote back paragraphs absolutely verbatim. The people who worked for Shackley sometimes compared him to a dog nipping at your heels: if you screwed up he would bite you. But once you won his confidence, Shackley would support you forever. Loyalty meant a lot to him—and still does. I consider him a friend and I am proud of his friendship.

He was gloriously inventive. Once, for example, he was asked by the U.S. Ambassador to help intervene with Nguyen Van Thieu, the Vietnamese president. The U.S. wanted Thieu to authorize an

ARVN (Army of the Republic of Vietnam) operation near the Cambodian border, and the ambassador had repeatedly requested Thieu's cooperation, but Thieu put him off again and again.

Shackley became determined to find out why the Vietnamese chief of state wouldn't commit his troops to the operation.

It took a few days, but Shackley finally dug out the reason: he discovered that the Vietnamese president went to an astrologer for advice about the timing of virtually everything. The astrologer had told Thieu that the stars were all wrong for an operation near the Cambodian border.

Shackley used his considerable charm on the presidential astrologer. God knows how Shackley did it, but right after he met with Shackley the astrologer called President Thieu and told him, "The stars say, 'Go *tomorrow!*'" Thieu never knew that Ted Shackley was the presidential astrologer for one day!

As I would be advising the Provincial Reconnaissance Units in Region III, and based on what I'd heard from my colleagues, I expected to have Shackley looking over my shoulder, too. In fact, my immediate assignment was a Shackley priority: to stop the VC from rocketing Saigon. There were two important reasons for Shackley's desire to stop the rocketing as soon as possible. First, the VC rockets were killing innocent people all over the city. Second, the press was reporting that neither the U.S. nor the South Vietnamese could stop these attacks, which were taking place in their own backyard. The situation was an embarrassment for both governments and bad for the American image.

There were also those irreverent jokesters at Saigon Station who kiddingly said the real reason for Shackley's concern was that he himself lived in Saigon—and didn't want any rocket-firing communist bastards disturbing *his* sleep.

But although I spoke with Shackley many times while I was in Vietnam, I worked more closely with my other bosses during my twenty-five-month tour. I came to know them well and respect them immensely.

My immediate superior was Rudy Enders. Rudy is an energetic guy (he once held the world record in the 400-meter dash for runners aged forty-eight!) who had a solid understanding of the complexities we were facing. He is one of those rare individuals who can grasp not only the operational approaches to resolving tactical problems but also the philosophical and intellectual background that gives rise to the conflict in the first place. It gives him a real edge when it comes to planning. Rudy had already had a distinguished career at the Agency by the time he reached Vietnam. In fact, when I was running infiltrations into Cuba, he had been assigned to Miami Station in charge of obtaining and operating all the necessary maritime assets. I never knew about Rudy back then, just as I didn't know in the sixties that Ted Shackley was Miami's Chief of Station. It was strange to me that we were now all to be working together again— only this time I knew it.

In Vietnam, I was assigned as Rudy's deputy. Although he ultimately participated in several hundred operations, including a stint with I Corps during the 1968 Tet offensive, during his six years in Vietnam, Rudy was the HQ guy during my tour—he spent most of his time in the office in Bien Hoa. He was, and still is, a terrific writer, who wrote up all the after-action reports (which was fine by me). I was the field guy. I don't think I spent a full day in the office during my entire time in Vietnam.

I guess I was closer to Rudy than I was to anybody during my tour. He lived with his wife and family in a nice house in Bien Hoa. I used to visit him there and play with the kids.

I lived in Saigon most of the time. I had a room at the Duc Hotel, which was where a lot of the Agency people stayed. We didn't often mix socially with military types, and we certainly didn't hang out with the press. Agency personnel tended to stick together. I didn't even eat out too often. The food at the Duc's dining room was pretty good. And besides, when I got back after a full day that had started very early in the morning, all I wanted to do was grab something quick to eat and get to sleep.

The two men who ran PRU operations for the entire country were based in the old U.S. Embassy building in Saigon (Ted Shackley had his office in the new embassy compound).

The PRU director was named Tucker Gougelmann. He was a big man, six feet two or so, and a former Marine. He had been wounded on Guadalcanal during World War II, so seriously that the doctors debated amputating his leg. Tucker kept them from doing it, however, and he still had both his legs, although he walked with a bad limp. He was a tough-as-nails curmudgeon of a guy about fifty or so who avoided all the niceties of life. For example, before running the PRU program Tucker had been the Region III station chief based at Bien Hoa. There he slept on a slab bed in an room without air conditioning. Every morning at precisely eight o'clock he would walk down the hallway to his office on the third floor of the CIA compound dressed in wrinkled khakis, a white shirt, sleeves rolled to the elbows, and hunting boots, shouting as he went, "It's eight in the Ay-Em and I don't hear any effing typewriters clicking!"

Indeed, Tucker was a CIA legend. He had been recruited from the OSS in the late forties, and some nights in Bien Hoa he would sit on his patio overlooking the Dong Nai River, his feet propped up on a table, a drink in his massive paw, and he'd tell stories about his adventures in China, India, Laos, and Vietnam.

At one point during his Bien Hoa posting he kept a pet bear named Go-Go in his room. He'd got it as a cub, but after some months of dining-room leftovers and other assorted treats Go-Go grew to about four hundred pounds, and Tucker couldn't keep it inside anymore. So he had a chain-link fence compound built adjoining the CIA compound, strung it with canvas, and kept the bear outdoors.

Rudy Enders remembers the first time he saw Go-Go. He was walking by the fence one day, "And the bear was up on its hind legs peering out through holes in the canvas, because as I walked by all I could see were these two little beady red eyes looking at me."

Finally, the logistics of keeping the bear became impossible. Tucker requisitioned a chopper and coaxed the bear onto it. Go-Go was ferried out into Long Khanh Province in Region III, where Tucker released it into a berry patch.

Although Tucker, as chief of the Provincial Reconnaissance program for Vietnam, held a rank equal to Ted Shackley, he was uncomfortable with both bureaucracy and formality. Rudy Enders says that once, during a stint at CIA headquarters in Langley, Tucker got so mad at having to follow some formalized procedure or other that he opened a window and screamed obscenities. The one time I saw Tucker at Langley, after both of us had left Vietnam, he seemed unhappy at being confined to a desk and he talked about retiring—which he did shortly afterward.

Tucker also detested stuffed shirts. At embassy social functions in Saigon he could become outrageous. Rudy says that once, a few drinks in him, he actually walked up to some senior American official's wife and introduced himself by saying, "Hi, ma'am, I'm Tucker the fucker."

I'm certain that Tucker wasn't trying to offend people with his profanity and his irascible behavior. He was just one of those larger-than-life characters you come across once in a lifetime, whose behavior is accepted because of who he is and what he has done.

Tucker's deputy was as quiet and reserved as his boss was extroverted and outgoing. His name was William Buckley. He was much more a desk man than a field officer. An excellent analyst with a head for details, he was serious, even rigid, in his outlook on life, and he had a dry sense of humor. He was the perfect foil for Tucker. The two of them were Yin and Yang—exact opposites who fit together perfectly, making a great team. They probably could have played a great road-show version of *The Odd Couple*, with Tucker as the gregarious, sloppy Oscar Madison and Buckley as the punctilious, tidy Felix Unger. In fact, Buckley was so compulsively organized that he had his desk cleaned and polished every night. His spare change was always stacked in neat piles. His notebooks were always perfect, his penmanship legible and never a scrawl.

Buckley's hobby was antique collecting. He could probably quote you the value of anything old from a World War II edition of *Life* Magazine to a Daisy BB gun. During his tours back in the U.S. he made a lot of trips to North Carolina and other places where he bought and traded antiques for a store he owned in Virginia.

He was suspicious of many of the Vietnamese with whom we worked—he once told Rudy Enders that he believed Colonel Lang, the Vietnamese officer in charge of the PRUs, was untrustworthy and only in it for the money. On that subject, at least, Buckley was in disagreement with his boss, because Tucker was close to Lang.

Bill Buckley was a guy who lived by paperwork just as Tucker Gougelmann hated it. As someone who generally disliked writing after-action reports myself, I identified more with Tucker the field man than Bill the desk operator. But Buckley had a deep kindness

about him, an empathy for the situation in Vietnam, which I respected a lot. He had served in the divided country a long time and
had seen an awful lot. But he never became cynical or indifferent to
its people, something that couldn't be said for many other Americans.

Buckley was always willing to listen to my problems and offer
advice. I came to know him through my work in photoreconnaissance, one of the key elements of preparing a successful PRU operation. Under normal circumstances it could take a day or so to get my
pictures back from the lab. However, I didn't want to wait that long.
So, often, instead of going through channels—that is, turning my
film over to the region chief to send to be developed, I would bring it
in myself to the old embassy compound. While the lab developed
and printed my pictures, I would go upstairs and visit with Buckley
and Tucker.

It is a bizarre coincidence of destiny that these two men, who had
shared an office together, would share the same cruel fate, ten years
apart. Each was captured and tortured to death.

Tucker Gougelmann retired from the CIA and then returned to
Southeast Asia, the place where he felt most comfortable. He lived in
Bangkok and started a business of some sort. In April 1975, as South
Vietnam was collapsing, Tucker went back to Saigon. The word is
that he wanted to rescue his Vietnamese family—there was a
woman in Saigon with whom it was speculated he'd had a couple of
kids. That much is fairly certain. Afterward, the facts get fuzzy. Evi-
dently, Tucker never checked in with the embassy or with the
Agency. So when Saigon was evacuated, he was left behind. According to one account I heard, he roamed the streets for several days
before the North Vietnamese picked him up.

Why he was never told about the U.S. pullout, no one knows.
Some people say it was carelessness on his part. Some say it was a
tragic oversight. The fact is, no one knows for sure. What we do
know is that the communists kept him for almost two years before
his body was returned to the U.S. From what I was told, it bore the
marks of prolonged and brutal torture.

Tucker was finally buried at Arlington National Cemetery with
full military honors. I went to his funeral. He lies next to Francis

Gary Powers, the U-2 pilot who was shot down by the Soviets and exchanged for the KGB spy Rudolph Abel.

Bill Buckley's story is better known. He was the Beirut Station chief who had been asked by CIA Director Bill Casey to take that hazardous assignment after the previous chief (and many of his staff) were killed in the 1983 car-bomb explosion that destroyed the U.S. Embassy in West Beirut. Bill was kidnapped by pro-Iranian terrorists in 1985 and tortured to death. According to some reports, Casey obtained tapes of some of the torture sessions and was influenced by what he heard to go to any lengths to get Buckley back alive.

It is easy to see why Casey chose Bill Buckley for Beirut. He was one of this nation's greatest experts on terrorism, a walking encyclopedia on the who, what, and where of how these groups operate. And yet, in another sense, Casey sent the wrong man to Beirut. Buckley, the professorial, brilliant, ivory tower analyst—whose head could hold thousands of details—never developed the kinds of primal instincts that keep field agents alive. He was probably brighter than 99.9 percent of the people I have known. But he lacked street smarts.

In Beirut, for example, Buckley lived by himself in a second-floor apartment on a cul-de-sac. He seldom varied his schedule. He even walked to the embassy, making himself an inviting and convenient target. He was warned, but he didn't listen.

Rudy's boss at Bien Hoa was Don Gregg, the Region III Station Chief who succeeded Tucker Gougelmann. Despite all the stories that have been written in the past couple of years about my "old friend from Vietnam Don Gregg," most of which describe us as inseparable during our days there, the truth is that we were not as close as we have been portrayed by the press.

He was a supergrade region chief; I was a GS-11 contract employee. As they say in the military, generals don't hang out with sergeants. Besides, socially, he was closer to Rudy, with whom he enjoyed an occasional game of tennis—a game I do not play. As a boss, Don took a cautious approach to operations. For example, I remember him always asking, "Are you sure you're not going to hit a hospital?" when we went out on a strike. Don wouldn't approve an operation if there was any kind of medical facility in the area.

My work was both tremendously challenging and immensely time-consuming. The PRUs were, for the most part, former Viet Cong guerrillas or North Vietnamese soldiers who had defected or had been captured. When they *chu-hoi*—that is, were captured or turned themselves in, we made sure word about their cooperation got back to the VC. So, the majority of my PRU personnel had been sentenced to death in absentia by their former colleagues. It sounds cold-blooded, but it kept infiltrators to a minimum and it meant that the defectors were brave and loyal troops—preferable in many cases to the ARVN soldiers who, all too often, could not be relied upon when the chips were down. In the unit I worked with most closely, 80 percent of the eighty or so men I advised were former VC or North Vietnamese soldiers.

The idea behind the PRUs was simple and effective: they were designed as small, highly mobile strike forces that relied on top-quality intelligence. They had the ability to deploy rapidly to target and destroy the enemy. In fact, the military was already using a primitive form of rapid-deployment tactics well before I arrived in Vietnam. Called Pink Teams, or sometimes high-low teams, their tactics were to fly a small chopper—usually a Hughes 500 or a Bell Ranger—at tree-top level over hostile territory. When they received ground fire, the crew marked the spot with smoke grenades, and then helicopter gunships would come roaring in to rocket and shoot the hell out of the area. It was a reasonably effective but crude method of dealing with the VC.

At the PRU, we took the Pink Team concept one step farther: We combined rapid deployment with terrific intelligence. Instead of flying blindly over hostile territory, we almost never went after a target we hadn't previously identified. Our hit ratios were very high. I have been told that the Provincial Reconnaissance Units could justifiably claim some of the highest success rates in the whole Vietnamese conflict.

The PRUs were not only supposed to engage the VC and North Vietnamese, but also had the responsibility of capturing prisoners, both to replenish their own ranks and to obtain intelligence. It was a demanding assignment but the potential for success was high. If you look at those elements that make up a good operation—means, motive, and opportunity—the PRUs already had two out of three: motive and opportunity. What they often lacked was the means—access to airborne reconnaissance intelligence data and choppers to deliver PRU units to a target area quickly. One of my first priorities, therefore, was to make sure that when opportunities arose, my units would be able to get where they had to go.

The challenge was made more complex because, at the time I arrived, the PRU's advisers were going through a change in personnel and the units themselves were in a sort of bureaucratic never-never land. Prior to my tour, PRUs were supervised by Agency people and advised by U.S. Army Special Forces and Navy SEAL personnel. But because of America's Vietnamization of the war, the U.S. military was being withdrawn from many operations, including advising the PRUs. Before I arrived, the units had been attached to the military. Now, in 1970, they were a special combat unit of the South Vietnamese National Police. I was one of the first civilian advisers to lead them on a day-to-day basis.

This new status often meant a double whammy when it came to PRU operations: U.S. military choppers would often be denied because of the American phase-out, and Agency assets were nearly impossible to get because of other priorities. Without the ability to react quickly and decisively, the Provincial reconnaissance Units would lose their unique ability to get results.

I understood from the start that I would have to forge some links to the military. There was a Navy commander at Nha Be, south of Saigon, named James Williams III, with whom I became friendly. He had a healthy respect for the PRUs because of their effectiveness against the VC—as he said, they didn't just go chasing the enemy all over the place. From Commander Williams I was able to get choppers both for reconnaissance and operations. On the army side, I received tremendous support from General James Hollingsworth, with whom I've stayed friendly since 1970, Lieutenant Colonel Bill Lumpkins, whose Cobra choppers I was able to use to great advantage, and a number of other military people, like Lieutenant Colonel Jack Rollinger, who were generous to me and my unit.

I probably worked longer and harder in Vietnam than I had anywhere else. I spent a lot of time in choppers, often taking fire as we skimmed above the jungles and paddies on photoreconnaissance, intelligence gathering, or operational runs. As a matter of fact, it was in Vietnam that I learned how to fly a helicopter. It made sense to learn after one of my pilots explained one day, "Felix, there are just the two of us in this thing, and if something happens to me, we're both dead!"

At first I learned by watching. But as time went by and they saw I had a natural talent for it, the pilots with whom I worked would let me take the controls for a short time. When I had mastered the essentials, they began teaching me how to hover, how to take off, and how to land. One of the people with whom I most enjoyed flying was a captain named Charlie Marvin. Now retired from active duty, Charlie lives in New Orleans but still jockeys choppers with the National Guard.

When I wasn't learning to fly or out gathering intelligence, I was in combat. Depending on the quality of the information we brought in, we might run only one combat operation in ten days, or as many as five in a seven-day period.

Our technique was always the same: Start with good intelligence; never strike blindly; always move swiftly. Because of these rules, our casualty rates were lower than average, and our kill and capture rates higher. The same antiguerrilla intelligence-gathering techniques I'd applied in Bolivia had been refined by the time I put them to use in Vietnam. We were also privy to a lot more information and could assemble it much faster. It was later estimated by U.S. officials that during my tour more than 95 percent of our targets were successfully hit.

Sometimes we achieved our goals when we least expected. One day, for example, an Agency operative was driving with a defector through the Binh Duong marketplace when the defector saw a woman shopping. His eyes went wide with amazement and he exclaimed, "That's Colonel Tu Ton's secretary over there."

That was a find! Tu Ton was the North Vietnamese military proselytizing chief of Subregion 23. We wanted him badly because his agents—almost a hundred of them—had the potential of penetrating the South Vietnamese government and ARVN.

The car screeched to a halt and the defector, a former NVA military section chief whom the secretary knew well, jumped out, ran up behind her, tapped her on the shoulder and said, "Come with us." She was so surprised that she actually did what he ordered without a word of protest.

We'll call her Lan. We spent a lot of time going over her ideology and convincing her that she'd be better off with us than back in North Vietnam. It didn't take too long before she agreed to switch sides. In fact, Lan had already been thinking about defecting for personal reasons. She hated Tu Ton and wanted revenge. It turned out that she'd been in love with Tu Ton's son, back in Hau Nghia province. They'd tried to keep their relationship secret, but one day Tu Ton had returned unannounced to the village where his wife and son lived, found the two youngsters in bed and went crazy. The furious colonel shipped his son off to a military unit. Shortly thereafter, the boy was killed during a B-52 raid. Lan held Tu Ton responsible for her lover's death and was willing to help us get him.

Ultimately, because of her help, we were able to run operations against Tu Ton that resulted in the destruction of a 95-agent operation, most of whose members were captured. We also discovered, much to our relief, that the North Vietnamese army had been able to penetrate only two agents into our forces: one into the police, the other as the local province chief's butler. We got both of them.

Another of our major targets was an NVA colonel named Tu Thang. There were a lot of Tus in Vietnam. Tu Thang had been a thorn in our side for a long time as he was the highest ranking NVA commander southeast of Saigon and the officer in charge of rocketing the Vietnamese capital. He'd been at it before I arrived, and Ted Shackley wanted him stopped.

He used Soviet 122mm rockets that were brought down the Ho Chi Minh trial from Cambodia and then hidden in base camps in the paddies across the Saigon River. (Like Che in Bolivia, he followed the pattern of keeping his base camps—where his personnel lived and where they stored their supplies—separate from his operational sites.) Using small groups of guerrillas, Tu Thang had the assignment of moving the rockets across the river into groves of nipa palm trees and firing the weapons blindly into Saigon. The idea wasn't to hit any specific target but to terrorize the city and cause the Americans to lose face by showing that even five hundred thousand U.S. soldiers could not stop a determined VC force. Although he had the rockets, we put so much military pressure on him that he was unable to cross the river and fire them. But we wanted more than this stalemate: we wanted Tu Thang.

An important break came when we captured a North Vietnamese paramedic who worked as Tu Thang's bodyguard. He gave us important details about the number of soldiers in Tu Thang's operation (there were about a hundred in the unit) and even agreed to show us specifics about the camp's location.

I took him up in a chopper and we overflew the general area. He was able to point out places we hadn't been able to locate even after studying photos taken from five hundred meters with a telephoto lens. I had a Polaroid camera with me, and I shot pictures as we flew. While we were still airborne, I showed the instant pictures to the North Vietnamese, who was able to pinpoint all the hidden entrances to Tu Thang's command post, show us where the defenses were, and indicate the camps' weak spots.

We assaulted the communists on December 4, 1970, with thirty-six PRUs ferried in on UH-1H choppers and two gunships. We would have preferred to capture Tu Thang alive, but that didn't happen. We engaged roughly seventy-five NVA soldiers in an hour-long battle, killing thirty-six of them—including, it turned out, the elusive colonel.

An incredible sideshow took place when I brought Tu Thang's former bodyguard along with me in the command chopper that day. Even though he'd been our prisoner less than seventy-two hours, he completely identified with our side during the firefight. In fact, he was jumping for joy every time our gunships rocketed their targets correctly, screaming "You got it! You got it right on the nose!"

We scored big, destroying a total of five NVA base camps, three sampans, and two hundred kilos of rice. We also captured large amounts of medical instruments and supplies, eight hundred AK-47 automatic rifle rounds and five magazines, plus a pile of NVA documents weighing more than two kilos, which were invaluable for planning future operations. Among the papers I later examined was a copy of a message Tu Thang had sent to his headquarters. It said that he'd been taking a lot of hits, was under tremendous pressure from the Americans, and stressed that he would be unable to remain in the area for much longer. I was proud of that message: it was proof that my unit was doing its job effectively.

But we did not escape unscathed ourselves. I lost two of my men on December 4; three others were seriously wounded. One of our UH-1H pilots, Bruce Bomberger, won the Distinguished Flying Cross for getting our PRU casualties out under extremely heavy enemy fire.

On days when we were going out into the field, I usually rose at four in the morning. I would shower, shave, climb into my uniform and take my flying helmet, M-16 and other gear, then drive half an hour at breakneck speed down to Nha Be, where I would meet my PRU unit, brief them and the chopper pilots, and take off. Our operations ran all day, but we would always quit two or so hours before sunset. The reason was not that we fought a nine-to-five war; we needed to allow time for rescues if one of our choppers was shot down late in the day or if we had to extricate dead and wounded from a hostile area. It happened more than once.

These hours also helped my troops' morale. Unlike regular ARVN forces, who regularly went out on five-day patrols, my PRUs knew that, except during special operations, they'd return every night to eat hot food, watch TV, and sleep in comfortable beds. But they also knew that to earn those luxuries they would have to give 110 percent when they were out in the field.

At first I thought the Vietnamese I worked with were somewhat distant and standoffish—inscrutable, to use the cliché. Before I left the States I'd had briefings, of course, about Vietnamese politics, society, and culture, along with the customary warnings about the local food and water. But nothing I had been told prepared me adequately for working in an environment totally different from anything I had ever known. I couldn't even speak the language—for the first time in my life I needed an interpreter. And I had virtually no background in the subtleties of Vietnam's history, its traditions, and the dynamics that lay below the surface—all things I knew instinctively about Latin America.

Then, not so long after I arrived, I had a heart-to-heart talk with one of my interpreters. "Felix," he said, "we've been at war as long as I've been alive—longer, even. And whenever foreign advisers come, it seems to us that each one wants to do things his way, and only his way. Sure, they want to help us. But, rightly or wrongly, we Vietnamese have come to believe that what our advisers want most is to do something that looks good for their careers."

"That's not the way I operate," I said, hoping I could make him understand what made me different from the others.

I told him—told all my PRU people—how I felt about losing my country to communism. I told them I didn't have to come to Vietnam, but that I had volunteered. I also told them that I didn't give a damn about career track, or promotions, or anything like that. I wasn't in Vietnam to get promoted, but to fight.

"I already lost my country," I said. "But you haven't lost yours yet, and that's worth fighting for."

Unlike previous PRU advisers, who came and went after a few months, I stayed with my units throughout my twenty-five months in Vietnam. We developed a great working relationship. They respected me because I always accompanied them into the field. In fact, I sometimes even led them into combat. That was a violation of the rules, since CIA advisers were not supposed to accompany combat troops on the ground. The Agency was very careful in that respect—it didn't want any of its people captured. I never told Rudy or Don Gregg at the time, but now I can let them know that I hit the ground with my men between thirty and thirty-five times during their raids. The PRUs respected me for that. And I respected them for their bravery under fire.

One of my strongest personal beliefs—in fact, it is a code by which I have tried to live my entire professional life—is that to be effective as an adviser you have to assimilate. That is, you have to learn to understand and appreciate others' societies. You can't demand that they operate the same way we do back in the U.S.

So my men and I reached some accommodations. I told them from the very beginning: "If you capture any money, it's yours to divide among yourselves." One result of this agreement was that my PRU unit probably had better intelligence about North Vietnamese finance officers than any in Vietnam. They were *always* trying to hit

NVAs coming from Cambodia with cash. Not only did it provide an incentive to the men, but, from a fatalistic point of view, it was a way of making sure that their families received death benefits, something the South Vietnamese government was often very lax about.

I also made sure that they received the best of everything, from supplies to medical attention. Since our casualty rates were so low (we averaged half a dozen men killed and less than a dozen wounded per month) I was able to wangle a deal with the medical commander to allow them to be taken to a U.S. facility rather than to the Vietnamese hospital where all other ARVN casualties went. The medical officer in charge, General Bernstein, was a man I'd met in Bolivia when he was a colonel.

With General Bernstein's permission, Rudy Enders and I created an ID card for each man in the PRU. In English and Vietnamese, it said: "This member of a special unit is authorized to be treated at the U.S. 24th Evac Hospital by U.S. Personnel." Then, as chief adviser for PRU, Region III, Rudy signed them.

Those cards were like talismans for my PRU guys. They meant that any one of them who got wounded was guaranteed first-class medical treatment. But they had greater value than that: they showed that we Americans cared about what happened to these Vietnamese who were laying their lives on the line in our mutual fight against communism.

The lesson of Vietnam isn't just that we shouldn't fight wars we're not willing to win. It goes deeper than that. Vietnam taught me once and for all that as a nation, our word must be our bond. If we pledge to help, then we must carry through and not abandon those who fight and die alongside us.

In fact, I wanted to stay on in Vietnam longer than I did, but it became impossible for medical reasons. In all I flew between two hundred and fifty and three hundred missions. On more than a few, my chopper was hit. On a couple, it came down hard. Once, for example, near Cu Chi, we took a hit through the hydraulic system. Neither the pilot nor I felt anything, but a red warning light told us that if we didn't land quickly, we'd lose control of the chopper. We headed for friendly territory and, just in the nick of time, landed right by a minefield at the edge of an ARVN compound. But it was a rough landing—it really hurt. The problem was compounded because I wasn't wearing my shoulder straps as tightly as I should have been, and I was slammed up and down pretty badly when we bounced.

The hard landing at Cu Chi was only one of the times I got slammed around in a chopper. Eventually, my back got so bad that I walked completely bent over and had to sleep on the floor to straighten myself out. I got to the bathroom by crawling. Still, I refused to take pain medication because I didn't want to dull my senses in the field.

Finally, in February 1972, I went to see one of my doctor friends, a captain at the 24 Medevac. He looked me over, took an X ray, peered at it and declared, "Hey, my friend, you should have been sent home months ago—your back is *destroyed*. You have no business even walking."

I took my medical report to Don Gregg, who wanted me shipped home right away. I told him that I didn't want to leave yet—there were still things I felt I could do. So I stayed on through April, working a somewhat reduced flying schedule.

It was hard to leave the Vietnamese with whom I'd worked so closely and grown to respect so deeply. Yet I was consoled by the thought that America would always support them in their fight against communism.

During Christmas 1972, I received a card from Huynh Kim Hoa, the PRU chief from Bien Hoa. It was a moving experience to get that card, which made me realize they still remembered me with fondness. It was handmade and hand-lettered, and along with holiday greetings to me and my family, it posed a question.

Felix, Hoa asked, do you think the United States will ever abandon us?

I wrote him back and answered truthfully, I thought. No, I replied. We will stand by you.

Well, we did not stand by our Vietnamese friends, and when I think of Hoa's card—which I treasure to this day—and I think of my reply, I weep both for him and for us. I vowed that, unlike my country, I would never abandon freedom fighters.

14 I should have retired after I got home from Vietnam. I didn't. Instead, Rosa and the kids and I moved to Argentina. The assignment was fate. In Vietnam, I had worked as an interpreter and guide to General Sánchez de Bustamante, the commanding general of the Argentinian First Army, during Sánchez de Bustamante's visit to Vietnam. We spent no more than four or five hours together but hit it off immediately. Later, I learned that when he visited the U.S. Ambassador in Saigon, Sánchez de Bustamante requested that after I finished my tour in Vietnam, I be assigned to Buenos Aires as his special adviser on counterterror and low-intensity warfare.

Despite my bad back I received a medical waiver. No Argentine of Sánchez de Bustamante's rank had ever before requested a personal adviser from the U.S. Government. I was happy about this new challenge. I wish I could say that Rosa and the kids were equally enthusiastic about the move. They joined me, but not enthusiastically. Rosemarie was eight; Felix, Jr., was six. They'd been raised American style and were not comfortable speaking Spanish. They didn't want to leave Miami and their friends.

Still, I was firm. It was time we all lived together as a family. So in the autumn of 1972 we left for Buenos Aires. My cover was created by the Argentines. I was supposedly an executive at a company that made shaving gear. (My sharp-eyed six-year-old son Felix once asked me why, if I worked for a company that made blades, I used an electric razor. I told him that I had to use it to keep up with the competition.)

We lived in a middle-class suburb of the Argentine capital, and I took the train back and forth to work every day, or so my neighbors thought. As far as they were concerned, I was just an American businessman working for an Argentine company downtown. In reality, I took the commuter train to Buenos Aires, then walked to a penthouse in Calle Florida, in the heart of the city. There, I rumpled the bed and messed up the kitchen, crumpled newspapers and dropped laundry into the hamper—all to create the impression for the maid that someone actually lived in the place.

I was then picked up by an army car, and I proceeded to First Army headquarters. In the evenings, the entire process was reversed. I was dropped off by the army, messed up the apartment again, changed clothes, walked back to the train station and arrived home exhausted—clutching my attaché case. It was a grueling twelve-to-fourteen hour schedule five days a week.

General Sánchez de Bustamante, of course, knew my whole background—everything from my adventures in hunting Che to my childhood in Cuba. But his staff was told only that I was a Nicaraguan colonel.

Sánchez de Bustamante held a critically important political position as well as a military one. The First Army was headquartered in Buenos Aires and was therefore the country's most crucial unit when it came to Argentine politics. No coup could be staged—or prevented—without the First Army. Indeed, its forces controlled the Argentine capital. It had its own armor—tanks and armored personnel carriers. Because of its strategic position, the First Army commander had to have the complete trust of the president. This was, in fact, the case with Sánchez de Bustamante and the man who appointed him, Alejandro Agustín Lanusse, a general himself.

Sánchez de Bustamante had been imprisoned under Perón in the sixties, and after his release and his ascent to power, the general had his old jail cell door brought to his office, and later, after he retired, to his home, where he kept it as a reminder of what can happen in a dictatorship. Unlike many Latin generals, Sánchez de Bustamante wanted to listen to a wide range of opinions, and almost daily he would invite a broad spectrum of people to lunch at his office. There would be ministers from the government, opposition leaders, Argentine ambassadors on home leave, and military officers.

He would start the discussion—he really liked to bring up controversial subjects to see how his guests reacted—then let the give-and-take roll on for hours, while he absorbed everything. I, too, learned a lot by listening, as I was almost always invited to sit in on these freewheeling luncheon salons.

After I'd become a familiar face around First Army HQ, General Sánchez de Bustamante himself told some of his officers my true story. It was all right with me, as the general and I had developed a close personal relationship, and, as time passed and more of his officers learned about my real identity, he asked me to tell them about the dangers of communism, using my personal experiences to explain what can happen when Marxists take over. He was tremendously open with me, taking me to meetings and briefings. In return, he seemed genuinely interested in my advice and listened carefully to what I had to say. Our relationship still continues to this day. He is a fascinating man whose friendship I value.

I liked Argentina. My family did too—after a while. The kids went to the American Lincoln school, where the courses were given perhaps half in English and half in Spanish. The man whose company was giving me my cover, an Argentine of English extraction, became a good and close friend. His wife was more than helpful to Rosa, treating her just like a daughter.

Unfortunately it took a couple of months before we finally got settled in. There were problems with our rented house, and worst of all, our furniture didn't arrive from Miami until mid-spring of 1973. Still, Rosa and the kids soon grew to appreciate the unique experience of living overseas. We took weekend trips to the countryside near Buenos Aires, marveling in the green forests and the landscape, which looked more European than Latin.

Our stay, which we'd expected to last at least two years, was brought to an abrupt end in July 1973. Despite President Lanusse's policies, a new government came to power—the Peronistas again. General Sánchez de Bustamante was retired from office. Worse, the Perón government moved swiftly to improve its relations with Cuba. Just as the new ambassador from Havana arrived, Rosa and I left for the U.S.

I didn't do too much for the Agency during the rest of 1973 and 1974. There were some trips through the Caribbean, a sort of island-hopping intelligence-gathering assignment, which lasted only a few months. Late in 1974, or early in 1975, it seemed that I might work on an antinarcotics program in Southeast Asia. But, to be frank, my back was in terrible shape. And, more crucially, once Vietnam fell in April 1975, it became clear to me and many of my colleagues that a large portion of the Agency's paramilitary assets, of which I was one, would be looking for work in the near future. The Agency was under siege. In Congress, Senator Frank Church and his committee had uncovered Agency illegalities. But they were not content with undoing the bad—they painted the CIA with a broad brush, destroying morale, causing some of the CIA's oldest allies abroad to grow mistrustful of the Agency's ability to keep its secrets—and its friends— safe.

Other serious events took place in the spring of 1975 as well. On May 11 my old friend Joaquín Zenteno Anaya, the Bolivian general who had been appointed ambassador to France, was assassinated on a Paris street. The murder was most likely committed by agents of Fidel Castro in revenge for Zenteno's role in Che Guevara's capture and execution. Soon after that, I received a phone call in Miami. The person on the other end asked for Felix Ramos (my pseudonym in Bolivia), said "You're next," then hung up. When I told one of my

Agency contacts about it he became concerned.

I was told that it might be best for me to retire. As one officer said to me, "Your back is bad. We have more paramilitary people than we know what to do with. And now you're getting death threats."

The retirement process took just about a year, but at the end of it I was given a disability pension, which I still receive today. It was also a year during which the Agency installed a security system at my home (they took a $25,000 lien on some property I own to do it. Nothing is free.) And they armored my car as part of the package, too. I saw no evidence of any overt threat, but I guess the CIA didn't want anything to happen and was going to take no chances. The Agency has always been conscientious about taking care of my security.

During the year of medical exams and paperwork, however, one real adventure took place. Some of my friends think that when it comes to business, I am a naive person. They are probably right. I have, after all, spent my whole life fighting communism. Unlike many of my colleagues from both the 2506 Brigade and the Agency, I never went into business. I never went to college either, although I had been accepted by the University of Miami back in 1960. My retirement pay would allow Rosa and me to live modestly, but I wanted to work at something after I left the Agency. The terms of my pending separation from the Agency, however, made it clear that I would not be allowed to draw a regular salary. The reason was security. A regular job meant regular hours, and the Agency was concerned that, as a potential target, I should remain as flexible in my day-to-day life as possible.

So I was immediately interested when my old Miami Station control officer Tom Clines called me from Washington one day and told me that he wanted me to fly to Washington in order to talk over the possibility of an advisory job in Lebanon. Tom was still at the CIA, working as the Cuban desk officer, as I recall, and we'd spoken a few times after I'd returned from Vietnam.

I went to Washington. Tom picked me up at the airport, then the two of us drove to the downtown Washington office of a man named Ed Wilson. I had no idea who Wilson was, but Tom told me he was an influential man, especially with the Democrats, and that he was working on a special project for Naval Intelligence.

At the office I was introduced to Wilson, a tall, powerful-looking man who appeared to me, at least on the surface, to be friendly and easygoing. I was also introduced to a Lebanese arms dealer named Sarkis Soghanalian, and another man who was introduced as a Lebanese army captain.

Soghanalian gave me a thumbnail sketch of the Lebanese political situation. He said that the PLO had in effect created a state within a state in Lebanon. He described the armed Palestinian camps that ringed Beirut and sat on the outskirts of other Lebanese cities such as Sidon and Tyre. He said that for security reasons the Lebanese military was interested in setting up special infiltration teams in order to penetrate these Palestinian camps and get intelligence on PLO political and military plans.

I believed the goal was attainable and said so, adding that if they were interested, I'd be willing to take a look and see what I could do. On that note the meeting ended. Tom Clines drove me back to the airport and I caught the afternoon flight for Miami.

Later in the year I got another call from Clines. He got right to the point. "You remember that friend you met in Ed Wilson's office? Well, he's ready for the trip. He wants you to go to Lebanon and meet with the chief of intelligence."

I knew the CIA would not approve of my going overseas while I was technically still a contract employee. But I rationalized that since my paperwork was in the pipeline, it wouldn't make much difference what I did. So I told my Agency contact that I was going to Key West for a couple of weeks to try to find some work, packed a bag, and left for Lebanon.

I traveled through Washington, where I picked up a bulletproof vest—a present from Ed Wilson for Sarkis—and on to New York, where I met Sarkis and we flew by commercial airline to Lisbon. There we climbed aboard Sarkis's private plane, a 707 he had recently bought through Ed Wilson that still bore its Pan Am tail markings, N711PA. Once aboard, I was surprised to discover that the plane was loaded with Eastern Bloc arms. Then Sarkis's American crew took off and we flew to Beirut.

We ran into trouble the moment we touched down in Beirut. The airport officials were all Moslems. The arms were destined for the Christian militias. Obviously the Moslems didn't want the plane unloaded, and they ringed the 707 with trucks and their own armed fighters. Our best option was to keep the doors bolted and sit at the military ramp, waiting for Sarkis's Christian allies to rescue us. It was absolutely absurd: here I was, in the middle of the Lebanese civil war, with the Agency thinking I was in Key West looking for work. Finally, a Lebanese military convoy arrived. They got the Moslems off our backs and got the 707 unloaded.

I spent about a month in Lebanon, in Beirut and the Maronite Christian enclaves near Jūniyah. Sarkis and his friends were generous hosts. And, as planned, I did consult with the chief of intelligence from the Lebanese army about infiltrating agents into the PLO camps. I explained the basics of communications, recommended various kinds of equipment that could be used successfully, and suggested methods for constructing secure radio networks and signal plans. I also described some methods that could be used to recruit and train Palestinian agents, as Palestinians would be more easily able to infiltrate the PLO camps than Maronites. I would have stayed in Lebanon longer, but the civil war started to heat up and Sarkis and his friends thought it would be prudent to send me home— which they did through London, my first trip to Britain.

When I finally got back to Miami, my Agency contact was furious. "I've been calling Rosa for a month now," he told me, "and she keeps saying that you're in Key West, and I know very well you're not, and that you're probably going to turn up in some place like Ecuador or Bolivia and embarrass the hell out of us all."

I looked at him with a smile and said, "I can guarantee you that it wasn't Ecuador." Then I gave him a small metal ashtray with three camels on it that I'd bought in Beirut. "Here," I said. "This is a present for you from Key West."

The Agency guy could only shake his head. He said, "Felix, I don't wanna know."

Unlike many of the people with whom I worked, I retired overtly from the CIA. One reason for this was that, unlike those agents whose careers were spent under deep cover, my Agency affiliation was always known by the host countries in which I worked. Another reason was pride at having worked for fifteen years at the Agency.

So as the retirement papers proceeded through the bureaucratic maze, I asked Ted Shackley to help me retire openly. He was successful, and my resumé now includes a one-page summary of my CIA career, along with an Agency phone number so that the references I list can be checked.

Actual retirement was scheduled for April 20, 1976. A couple of weeks before the date, I was told that I had been awarded the Intelligence Star for Valor. The Miami Station chief called with the news. He told me to make arrangements to go to Washington to receive the medal from the hands of the new CIA director, George Bush.

But I refused to go to Washington and accept the medal from Mr. Bush. It was nothing personal. It was simply that Mr. Bush was President Gerald R. Ford's political appointee, and I wanted to receive my medal from a career Agency professional.

My decision was easily reached. The Intelligence Star is not a medal lightly awarded. A number have only received the honor posthumously. It seemed to me at the time that the medal should be bestowed only by someone who had experienced a lifetime career at the Agency and was familiar with the hardships it represented.

Indeed, when I walked out of CIA headquarters early in 1976 for what I believed was the last time, I had tears in my eyes. I'd just been to farewell meetings with Ted Shackley, then to see people in the Latin American Bureau. It was a day crammed with emotion and memories. After all, the institution and its values held—and still hold—great meaning for me.

So, instead of receiving the medal at Langley, on the appointed day the deputy chief of Miami Station and his assistant appeared at my home along with a tall, white-haired man from Washington who I was told had spent thirty-five years with the CIA, and who would represent Mr. Bush. They sat on one side of my Florida room, and Rosa and I sat on the other side.

They gave me the medal, a citation to go with it, and a letter from Director Bush. They also presented me with a certificate of retirement, which I have framed.

It was, as I look back on it now, absolutely correct for the ceremony to take place in my home, in the Florida room filled with mementos from my assignments and adventures. That day, as the CIA officer read the citation, I looked around me and saw the evidence of my career mounted on the walls. Each plaque, each shoulder patch, each certificate filled me with new emotion: my diploma from jump school in Peru; a Viet Cong flag that had been captured by my PRU unit and given to me; nine Crosses for Gallantry presented to me by the South Vietnamese government; my inscribed photographs from commanders such as General Hollingsworth, with whom I worked in Vietnam, and General Sánchez de Bustamante, men whom I greatly respect; the insignia of my beloved 2506 Brigade.

When it was over, we all shook hands and the Agency officers left Rosa and me to our thoughts and our memories. I had no idea then that the wall of my Florida room would within a short time hold a lot more relics—not all of them pleasant.

15 During the last few years of the seventies I felt that my life was proceeding without direction. I watched in frustraton as one after another of my friends at the Agency lost their jobs or resigned in disgust at what Jimmy Carter and his incompetent CIA director, Admiral Stansfield Turner, were doing to the U.S. intelligence community. In my opinion, Turner's tenure at the CIA did the intelligence community more harm than the Soviets were able to do. I fell out of touch with many of the CIA officers with whom I'd worked. In fact, I don't think I spoke to my old boss from Vietnam, Don Gregg, more than three or four times between 1976 and 1981. It was tough looking on from the sidelines as the naive Carter, a neophyte at dealing with communists, was ricocheted between his advisers like a pinball and ended up without any effective policy when it came to dealing with the Soviet Union.

I also watched as Carter stood by and allowed Fidel Castro's Marxist influence in Latin America to expand virtually uncontrolled. It was obvious to us Cubans that Castro had allied himself with the anti-Somoza forces in Nicaragua. The Sandinistas were, to those of us who had lost our homeland to communism, simply another Marxist Trojan horse. They "talked democracy" but their actions paralleled Castro's own totalitarian tendencies. Nicaragua was not the only country in which the Cuban dictator was active, either. He was aiding and abetting antidemocratic insurgencies in Guatemala, Honduras, and El Salvador as well. But Carter and his people remained oblivious to Castro's fingerprints until it was too late, and communist expansionism became a reality throughout the region. In turn, Latin American governments, pushed to the edge by Cuban-supported insurgencies, often adopted dangerously repressive short-term policies. It was frustrating for me to sit by and watch as the prospect of communist domination over the region got stronger and stronger, while democratic principles grew weaker.

Still, I stayed away from direct involvement. For a while I worked, without receiving any pay, for my old friend Nick Navarro, as an intelligence analyst for the Broward County sheriff's department, where he ran the Organized Crime Bureau. Our friendship went back to my school days at Perkiomen. He'd been working near Pennsburg, Pennsylvania, at the same time I was going to prep school. And, being the only two Cubans in the small town, we naturally gravitated toward each other.

In the sixties, after he moved to Miami, Nick worked on some Agency operations in which I, too, played a part. Always aggressive, and with a long-standing record of antidrug activities (he once worked undercover for the Drug Enforcement Agency), Nick was elected Broward County sheriff in 1986 and won reelection in 1988. Currently he employs more than two thousand people, and heads one of the nation's most aggressive narcotics-interdiction programs.

Those years were also a time when I reached some unhappy realizations about people I had worked with for many years: I saw that they had come to value money more than they did freedom and democratic principles. I watched, for example, as my friend Tom Clines and my fellow infiltrator Rafael (Chi Chi) Quintero became more and more allied with Edwin Wilson, who had become a renegade CIA agent.

By late 1979, while I didn't know the whole picture—like the fact that Wilson had sold Qaddafi tons of C-4 plastic explosive, which would be used against Americans and other Western nations by radical and communist guerrilla movements—it was becoming clear to me that this man who flaunted his CIA connections so overtly was not operating in America's best interests, rather his own selfish ones. It was about that time that I first met General Richard Secord one day at Tom Clines's apartment. Clines mentioned to me that he and Secord were partners in some unspecified business venture.

I decided not to have anything more to do with Wilson or any of his associates. I cooled my friendships with Clines and Chi Chi Quintero.

In the early eighties, with the Sandinistas holding power in Nicaragua and Marxism on the rise throughout Central America, I felt compelled once again to become an active participant in the fight against communism. The election of Ronald Reagan had reinvigorated anticommunist movements that had languished during the Carter years, and in the early eighties we experienced a real resurgence in Miami. I'd been involved in the Cuban community's anti-Sandinista activities, for example, since 1979. We were among the first American groups to support the Nicaraguan Democratic Resistance with food, clothing, educational materials, and other humanitarian aid. But as it became evident to us that Cuban-sponsored insurgencies could destabilize the entire region, I decided that more direct action was necessary.

In 1981, I spent a fair amount of time traveling through Guatemala, Honduras, and Costa Rica. I also had made a number of friends in El Salvador, both in military and civilian life. So later that year I contacted a Cuban pilot who had flown Agency missions in the Congo back in the sixties. I did further research, and by early 1982 I began to create a counterinsurgency plan that I believed combined the best elements of what I'd learned in Vietnam with a new level of anticommunist cooperation between all the Central American nations. Indeed, the key element of my concept was that it was an indigenous plan that used few foreign—which would mean naturalized Cuban—advisers.

It took me several months but I finally crystallized my ideas into a proposal. Basically, the plan used B-26K bombers and helicopters against insurgents in Guatemala, Honduras, and El Salvador in much the same way we had deployed PRU units and choppers in Vietnam's Region III. The B-26K is capable of carrying a lot of ordnance, flying slowly, and staying airborne for a long time. These qualities would allow it to substitute for the UH-1M or Cobra gunships we'd used in Vietnam, but which were not available at the time in Central America.

The plan was simple: choppers—Hughes 500s or similar high-speed, maneuverable small aircraft—would fly treetop level and draw fire. Then, the B-26K gunships would come in and destroy the guerrillas. "After the B-26 run," I wrote, "the OH [Hughes 500] will check the area for results and a small PM Unit will be on standby to be airlifted into the area of operations by the UH-1H troop transport helicopters in order to assess enemy damage, seize enemy documents and equipment, and capture, when possible, wounded guerrillas."

I received commitments from my Cuban pilot friends, who confirmed they'd be willing to sign on. I talked to the Guatemalan military, who agreed to allow the B-26Ks to be based on their territory. Initial reaction from the Hondurans was also positive. Yet, when the plan was first discussed with the U.S. military, they were—I later learned—immediately doubtful about its potential.

But I have never been deterred by adversity. Early in 1983 I submitted a five-page draft of my plan (another, longer version included the credentials of the Cuban pilots who had committed themselves to flying), which I called TTF, or Tactical Task Force, to the Hondurans for formal evaluation. The Honduran air force commander, Walter López Reyes, who would in 1984 become that country's chief of staff, recommended it highly to the then-Honduran chief of staff, Brigadier General Gustavo Adolfo Alvarez Martínez.

TTF, López wrote in his May 6, 1983, report, "would be of great benefit to the Honduran air force.... It would be a rapid reaction force, which we believe feasible and with sufficient firepower to neutralize and destroy guerrillas appearing in our territory."

I also went to Washington, where I was introduced to former Senator Richard Stone, the U.S special envoy to Central America by Jorge Mas Canosa, the head of the Cuban American National Foundation. Stone looked my plan over and liked it.

Don Gregg was, by this point, working as National Security Adviser for Vice President George Bush. I hadn't seen much of Don in recent years, but I felt my TTF plan was important enough to impose on our old friendship. Don liked it. For another opinion, he showed it to my old boss from Vietnam, Rudy Enders. Rudy was in charge of the CIA's paramilitary operations; he had visited Central America and was familiar with the problems any counterinsurgency program would face. Enders, too, agreed with my assessments. He believed that TTF was a workable concept. Then Don sent the TTF proposal to the National Security Council chairman, Robert McFarlane, for evaluation. "I believe the plan can work," he wrote to McFarlane. "Senator Stone is equally impressed and asked me to forward Rodriguez's plan to you with my comments."

McFarlane, always the bureaucrat, in turn passed it on to a staffer, a Marine lieutenant colonel named Oliver North. It lay in North's safe, probably unread, for months. TTF was found in North's safe by the FBI in November 1986. It has been referred to in the press as my blueprint for attacking Nicaragua.

TTF is *not* a blueprint for attacking Nicaragua. That is obvious to anyone who has read it, such as Senator Stone, Don Gregg, Assistant Secretary of Defense Nestor Sánchez, and the military officers in Salvador, Guatemala, and Honduras who supported the concept. (Don Gregg's memo to Bud McFarlane is even specific about the location of the TTF's targets: "Honduras and El Salvador." Significantly, the Iran/Contra committee staffs, when redacting—that is, censoring—the documents, deleted the two lines from Don's memo that spelled out the TTF targets. I can only surmise that this was deliberately done for political reasons.)

Unfortunately, reporters often write exactly what their sources want them to write—and in the case of the TTF, it was convenient for news sources to spread the word that my plan called for an attack on Nicaragua, as it placed me squarely, although falsely, in the middle of some covert cabal to destabilize the Sandinistas.

If the press had been on its toes, it might have discovered a real story in TTF—which was the military's skepticism about it when I first showed the plan around.

What reporters would have discovered is that counterinsurgency programs and SOLIC—Special Operations and Low-Intensity Conflict—have always held a low priority in the U.S. military. Historically, the easiest way to stall your career was to go into Special Ops. One reason behind this is that, unlike the traditional battlefield—where tactics from Thucydides to Napoleon to Patton can be studied and analyzed—unconventional warfare is harder to analyze. There are no rules. The situation changes country to country, theater to theater. In Vietnam the VC built tunnel cities; in Salvador, the guerrillas now move in small groups. There is virtually no "book learning" for unconventional warfare because its dynamics change on an almost day-to-day basis. And because it is difficult to grasp and requires seat-of-the-pants, instinctive responses, today's American military officers, who tend more and more to resemble accountants and bureaucrats rather than battlefield leaders, avoid it. Today's generals need rules by which to fight. Yet the unfortunate truth about most of today's wars is that they have no rules.

The unhappy result is that we Americans are no more prepared to fight against insurgencies than were the British Redcoats who decried the American colonial "guerrilla" tactic of firing their flintlocks from behind stone walls instead of marching in formation to confront the better-disciplined and more conventional British.

Current Pentagon thinking is not so dissimilar from those Redcoat officers of more than two centuries ago. We look for complicated, overpriced solutions to problems that can be solved simply. We try to find the best, most sophisticated weapons, when often simpler ones would do just as well. Instead of instinctive crisis management, our Pentagon bureaucrats now turn over their dilemmas to some high-priced consultant, an academic with a Ph.D. but no real-life experience. I find it interesting that in Israel, a country that has consistently won on the battlefield in innovative ways, most of the top military leaders come from a special-operations background, including Moshe Dayan, Ariel Sharon and the current Israeli chief of staff, Dan Shomron, who commanded the commandos at Entebbe.

It was perhaps the frustration of watching from the sidelines that led me in December of 1984 and early January 1985 to a series of fateful meetings in Washington. On December 21 I was visiting the State Department, talking to Bill Bode, a friend I'd met through my old 2506 Brigade comrade, Colonel Nestor Pino. Bill was Special Assistant to the Under Secretary of State for Security Assistance, Science and Technology. I told him that I was on my way to see Don Gregg and that I planned to ask Don's advice about how best to go to El Salvador. I still firmly believed my TTF concept could be adapted to help the Salvadorans win the guerrilla war against the communist-supplied FMLN insurgents who had been bleeding the country dry for half a decade.

I also believed that by employing tactics we'd battle-tested in Vietnam, the Salvadorans would be able to boost the effectiveness of the war, moving against defined targets as opposed to random search-and-destroy missions that all too often ended with many civilian casualties. And civilian casualties were a sore point with the U.S. Congress when it came time to vote on aid to El Salvador.

Bode responded, "If you want to go to Salvador, you should talk to Ollie North."

"Who's Ollie North?" I asked.

"He's the guy at the NSC who deals with the part of the world you want to go to," he explained. Bill called North's secretary, Fawn Hall, and arranged the meeting.

So, after I met with Don Gregg, I walked up to North's paper-strewn office and had a short meeting with him. We talked in general terms about the problems in Central America. I showed North my album of photographs from Bolivia and Vietnam. As I recall, I asked for North's assistance in making my plans known to General Paul Gorman, the Southcom commander, who was responsible for all military operations in Latin America. Gorman was based in Panama and it was in his backyard that I wanted to operate. I don't remember whether North said he'd do something specific, but I do recall that he had a positive attitude about my ideas. As for myself, I felt that at least I had one foot in the door.

Later I checked with Don and discovered that after our meeting he'd called Assistant Secretary of State Langhorne Motley and Deputy Assistant Secretary of Defense Nestor Sánchez. He recommended to all of them that I be encouraged to try my concept in El Salvador. I was tremendously moved by Don's efforts. Until he acted, I'd been met mostly with skepticism. Don understood my commitment to fighting communist insurgency—and was willing to go out of his way to help me achieve my goals.

I mentioned to Don that I'd like to meet the Vice President, and Don said he'd try to find an opportunity for me to do so. Which subsequently he did—in late January of 1985.

From Washington I went back to Miami to spend a happy Christmas 1984 with Rosa and the kids. Prospects for my getting to El Salvador looked pretty good. Then, early in January, I received a phone call from a former Dade County sheriff's lieutenant turned private investigator named Raúl Díaz. I had met Díaz many times at the office of our family doctor, Jacinto Baralt, and we had become friends. Díaz told me he had a client who could compromise the Nicaraguan Sandinista government for drug-money laundering. The client, he said, was a former accountant named Ramón Milian Rodríguez. Milian Rodríguez was a forty-one-year-old money launderer for the Colombian cocaine cartel. He had been arrested by federal agents in May 1983, aboard a Panama City-bound Lear jet with almost five and a half million dollars in cash.

Now, Díaz told me, Milian wanted to save his skin by cooperating with the U.S. Government, and he wanted to speak with someone "clean" who could get his message through to the right people—either at the CIA or the Task Force on Drugs. Díaz told me Milian didn't want to talk to anyone from the local FBI or DEA offices because he was afraid they had been penetrated by the cartel. He asked whether I'd be willing to help. I told him that although I had other things on my mind—like getting myself to El Salvador—I would see what I could do.

I finally met Milian at 10 A.M. on January 18, in Raúl Díaz's office. We spoke for much less than an hour—somewhere between twenty and thirty minutes at the most. I know that because I had a noon meeting to attend for which I couldn't be late, and the meeting was an hour's drive away, perhaps more, depending on the traffic.

Milian said he wanted to cooperate because he didn't want to do any time in prison. He thought he'd be facing five years or so (actually he was later sentenced to forty-three years). He told me about huge amounts of money—in the billions—that were being smuggled into Panama, and that he had proof that Manuel Noriega was heavily involved in drug trafficking. He added that in the last decade the Colombian cartel had given Noriega $800 million. He claimed that he could compromise the Sandinista government in the area of drugs.

I listened to Milian's tales but said nothing. Then I went on to my meeting. Later, I called Carlos Duran, a friend of mine who is an agent with the Miami office of the FBI to tell him about Milian's offers. Carlos was nowhere to be found. By the time I finally got hold of him it was early Sunday morning, and I was about to leave for Washington for my appointment with Mr. Bush. On the way to the airport I stopped at Carlos's home and recounted the meeting with Milian to him. He carefully took notes, which he said he would pass along to the Bureau. When I arrived in Washington on January 23, I went to CIA headquarters and told Rudy Enders about my meeting with Milian. Rudy immediately passed me on to one of his CIA colleagues who had an interest in following international narcotics trafficking, and I told my story again. But I really didn't concentrate on Milian Rodríguez's outrageous claims very much at all. There were more important things to think of.

On the morning of January 22, 1985, I arrived at the old Executive Office Building, my photo album packed carefully in my briefcase. I was truly excited at the prospect of meeting the Vice President of the United States.

Don later explained his rationale for setting up the meeting to the Iran/Contra counsel: "The Vice President has said, up to being Vice President the job he enjoyed most had been the year he was Director of CIA. Felix is one of the really extraordinary human beings I know, and I knew how interested the Vice President was in El Salvador because of his trip there in December 1983, where he had spoken against the use of death squads, and I wanted to introduce Felix. . . ."

I spent about forty wonderful minutes with Mr. Bush, from 8:30 to

9:10, much of the time watching television with him, as his family was being profiled on one of the morning TV news shows. But I did have the opportunity to tell him about my experiences in the CIA and show him some of the photos from my album. The honor of being with the Vice President of the United States was overwhelming. Mr. Bush was easy to talk to, and he appeared to be interested in my stories. One story I did not tell Mr. Bush, however, was that I'd declined to accept the Intelligence Star from his hands nine years previously!

Two days later, on January 24, I had a friendly lunch with General Adolfo Blandon, the Salvadoran Chief of Staff, at the Crystal City Marriott just outside Washington, D.C. Blandon was in the U.S. for a one-week trip touring military facilities. Our meeting had been arranged by my old friend and fellow 2506 Brigade veteran, U.S. Army Colonel Nestor Pino.

I gave Blandon a rundown of my history: Cuba, Bolivia, Vietnam. I showed him pictures of our successful operations in Vietnam. I told him about the terrific possibilities I saw if he would permit me to advise a rapid-response force in his country. I also added that I did not want to get paid—I was already receiving a pension from the CIA—but would simply need a place to stay and some food to eat.

He seemed impressed. He said, "Just let me know when you're coming to El Salvador and we'll try it."

Blandon's response was gratifying, but it did not guarantee anything. Even though he was Chief of Staff, it was not his support I would ultimately need to implement my strategy, but the backing of General Juan Rafael Bustillo, the Salvadoran air force commander. In Salvador, it is the air force that controls the choppers, the paratroopers, and the commandos. So it would be Bustillo who would make the final determination as to whether I would get to use any choppers, and also how I would be able to deploy them.

I called Assistant Secretary of Defense Nestor Sánchez, who had been supportive of my TTF concept, to see if he could arrange a meeting with Bustillo, who was coming to Washington the very next week. Sanchez arranged for General Bustillo to meet with me on January 30th at Bolling Air Force Base.

When I told Don Gregg about the progress I was making, he was delighted. But, ever cautious, Don advised me to see someone from the State Department before any of my plans became finalized.

"Look, Felix," he said. "You don't want to get down there and have the ambassador asking, 'Who is this guy and what the hell is he doing on my turf?'"

He had a point. It took some juggling, but Don arranged a meeting for me with Langhorne Motley, the Assistant Secretary of State for Inter-American Affairs. The meeting was scheduled to take place on January 30th immediately after I'd met with General Bustillo, the air force commander.

Bustillo, like Blandon, was amenable to my plan. He told me I could stay at Ilopango Military Air Base and that he'd be willing to set up conferences with his officers to see whether they believed my plans were achievable.

Motley, a tall, aristocratic man, was diplomatically cautious. He asked, "Have you checked with a lawyer, Mr. Rodriguez?"

"Why?" I asked.

"I'm not sure it is legal for you to fly combat missions as a U.S. citizen," he said.

"Look, Mr. Secretary, I believe strongly in this concept. I also have given my word that I will fly it myself. So, if necessary, I will give up my U.S. citizenship to do that. But I'm not going to check with any lawyer, because I believe what I am going to do is legal."

Motley blinked. "I didn't mean to imply anything," he said. "I was just making sure you knew there might be implications."

Then Motley strongly advised me to contact General Gorman. El Salvador is his area of responsibility, said Motley, explaining that the U.S. military had been given the overall responsibility of advising the Salvadorans in counterinsurgency matters and it was important that I brief him. The Assistant Secretary added that I should also visit the U.S. Ambassador in San Salvador, Tom Pickering, to explain my plan. "I will let Pickering know you are coming. But you should contact Gorman."

Shortly after I returned to Miami I got a call from Don Gregg. "General Gorman wants to talk to you," he said.

It took some time—and more of Don's help—but I finally got through to Gorman's aide, who told me, "It is the general's directive that you come to Panama and speak to him."

Directive? I didn't have to be asked twice. I left the next day.

What I didn't realize at the time was the considerable influence that a call from Don could have, coming as it did from the White House. Bureaucrats are impressed by White House messages. A confidential telex from Ambassador Pickering to Paul Gorman cautioned the general, in diplomatic terms, to be nice to me:

> Rodriguez has high-level contacts at the White House, DOS and DOD, some of whom are strongly supporting his use in El Salvador.
> It would be in our best interests that Mr. Rodriguez confer with you personally prior to coming to El Salvador.
> I have some obvious concerns about this arrangement. . . ."

I also had no idea that Oliver North had called Gorman on my behalf. But this was obviously the case, based on Gorman's response to Pickering on February 8, 1985:

"Subject [that was me] has been put into play by Ollie North. And, while well-acquainted, does not have higher backing. . . . I will arrange for Rodriguez come to Southcom for discussions. . . . Ollie assures me it was his intention to focus Rodriguez on forces operating elsewhere in CENTAM and that nothing more than consulting with the government of El Salvador was contemplated."

Ambassador Pickering's telex, while obviously a diplomatic CYA (or protect your rear-end) document, was a correct evaluation of the situation. General Gorman's reply, on the other hand, was sadly misguided.

I was not "put into play" by North—or anyone else. As I mentioned, I'd just met Oliver North, and he certainly hadn't tried in our few short meetings the previous December to "focus" my attention anywhere in CENTAM—Central America. I knew exactly where I wanted to go: El Salvador. And I knew exactly what I wanted to do: teach my helicopter concept to the Salvadoran armed forces.

Regardless of what Gorman wrote, the general and I had a warm, even congenial, meeting. I showed him my album of photos from Cuba, Bolivia, and Vietnam and he was visibly impressed. In fact, he looked me in the eye and told me, "Let me thank you for what you have done for my country." It occurred to me that our meeting was being held on Valentine's Day, and that this four-star commander couldn't have given me a finer bouquet of compliments than that one.

Then he briefed me in detail on the military and political situation in El Salvador and told me he approved of my ideas for helping the Salvadorans.

He asked when I planned to start, and I told him that I first had a commitment to the Contras—getting them some supplies that I had accumulated in Miami. But as soon as I finished delivering those supplies to Honduras, I'd want to start in Salvador. I explained to Gorman that, like many of my friends in Miami, I'd been actively helping the Contras since the early eighties. I told him I'd acquired equipment to help them make supply drops at night (infrared lights that a friend of mine built from Radio Shack parts), that I'd advised them on radio-telegraphy equipment, bought them a photocopying machine and other office supplies—and had even sent them several sets of dominoes so the fighters could entertain themselves at their camps.

All in all, it was a warm and friendly discussion that lasted for about two hours. Unfortunately, when General Gorman was deposed by the Iran Contra committee counsel, his memory of our meeting failed him completely. Somehow, the trust and approval he had displayed in February 1985 had, by July of 1987, turned to disapproval and skepticism.

"My general notion," he told the committee investigator, was, "Let him have his meetings and then get him out of the country."

"[Rodriguez] was going to become an influence over the Salvadorans and I didn't want that to happen," he testified.

One never likes to dispute generals, but the fact is that Gorman welcomed me with open arms, gave me his private plane to fly on, PX privileges, and flattered me with extravagant praise. If that's "discouragement," then I'd like to see how he signifies his approval.

The day after our meeting General Gorman sent me on his personal plane—a C-12—to El Salvador, where I held very satisfactory meetings with Ambassador Pickering and with the U.S. Military Advisory Group (or MilGroup) commander, Colonel James Steele. What

I didn't know was that after our discussion, General Gorman cabled El Salvador with a "Confidential—Eyes Only" telex filled with misinformation about me and my goals.

He wrote that my "acquaintanceship with the VP is real enough, going back to latter's days as DCI [Director of Central Intelligence]." That was a completely false assumption on Gorman's part. I told him I'd met with Mr. Bush once in his office, and that I'd served in Vietnam with Don Gregg. But that's as far as my relationship with the Vice President went, and I certainly didn't embroider on it.

He wrote that my "primary commitment to the region is in Honduras where he wants to assist the FDN [the Democratic Nicaraguan Forces]." That, too was false. I had explained myself to him in detail about what I wanted. My primary commitment, in fact, was to help the Salvadoran air force win the war against the communist insurgents.

He wrote Pickering and Steele that my desire to fly with the Salvadoran air force was a "bit of machismo [that] seems both unnecessary and unwise." This sentence betrays Gorman's lack of understanding of the Latin mentality—and, perhaps, more deeply, is symbolic of the rigid thinking that keeps Americans from winning the respect (or, as we used to say in Vietnam, the hearts and minds) of those who receive American aid.

For the record, General Gorman, we Latins don't respect people who just talk; we respect people who *act*. Flying choppers with the Salvadorans was the only way I would be able to win both their trust and their support.

The day I arrived in El Salvador for my sessions with Pickering and Steele was also the day that I received the *nom de guerre* by which many people would come to know me. I stayed that night with my old friend and fellow 2506 Brigade veteran Lou Rodriguez a U.S. Army lieutenant colonel who served until 1988 with the MilGroup in El Salvador.

We were standing at the bar at his beautiful home when I said to him, "You know, I should have a name for security reasons if I'm going to come down here."

"That sounds like a good idea," Lou said.

"What do you suggest?" I asked.

"How about Máximo Gómez?"

I liked it. Generalísimo Máximo Gómez was a famous freedom fighter—a Dominican who'd laid his life on the line for Cuba's freedom—and one of my boyhood idols.

Lou and I embraced. "Max Gómez," I said. "I'll use it!"

I flew back to Miami on February 16, then, on the 19th, went up to Washington to see Don Gregg in his office at the old Executive Office Building and bring him up-to-date on my meetings with Gorman, Pickering, and Steele. I explained that things had gone well, and that I'd received everyone's support. I told him that Gorman had treated me like a real VIP—little did I know that the general had tried to sink me behind my back. And I told Don once again how grateful I was for his support. He had really gone out on a limb by opening all the doors he had opened for me. If I was to have any success bringing my concept to the Salvadorans, some of that success would be Don's, too.

On March 15 I finished my commitment to the FDN, delivering their supplies to Tegucigalpa, the Honduran capital. Then I flew on to El Salvador's Ilopango Military Air Base. As the plane taxied up the ramp, I felt an immense sensation of anticipation and excitement. A new battle against communism was about to begin.

16 Those first weeks in El Salvador were tough. I moved into the Camino Real hotel in downtown San Salvador, using the name Luis Santiago Robles when I checked in, as I didn't want anyone connecting me to the Max Gómez who could be found at Ilopango Air Base. The U.S. press also used the Camino Real as the center of their operations, and many was the morning I would ride down in the elevator with TV reporters going out on one story or another. I was just another Latin face to them. If they had only known!

Initially I came up against a lot of resistance from the chopper pilots with whom I would have to work, and from their senior officers. To Latins, having an outsider give advice means that you haven't been doing your job adequately. So I wouldn't have been surprised if, the day after I arrived, the chief of the Salvadoran air force chopper squadron had asked himself, "Why the hell is General Bustillo bringing this guy on board? Am I not doing a good job?"

The pilots' attitude was just as negative: "Hey—don't tell us how much we can learn from Vietnam—you guys lost Vietnam," is the way I read their vibes.

It was an uncomfortable period. Some of the pilots regarded me as a spy sent by the U.S. to keep an eye on them. Others resented me either because I was a foreigner or because I was preaching techniques they regarded as crazy. I was asking them to do things they'd never done before, to push their choppers farther than they were accustomed to do and they didn't like it.

Sometimes when I explained the reasons behind coordinated strikes or quick reactions to real-time intelligence, I felt no one was listening. I'd ask them to fly at treetop level and they'd resist, saying that when they flew low—five hundred to six hundred feet was low to them—the guerrillas shot the bejeezus out of them. Well, that's true. I'd explain: "You're vulnerable at five hundred to fifteen hundred feet, where people on the ground can see you and shoot at you. But if you fly treetop level you'll come in too fast for them to get a shot off; above fifteen hundred feet their guns are useless. So either fly higher or lower." But they just remained skeptical about my techniques.

Many nights I'd go back to my room at the Camino Real and talk to myself out loud, asking rhetorically why I'd ever come to El Salvador in the first place, leaving my friends and family behind, to live in a damn hotel room and be considered nothing but a spy by the very people I was trying to help.

But I kept hammering away. We did our exercises and I kept talking, talking, talking. I told them about Cuba, and my experiences fighting for the country I'd lost to communism. "There's nothing I can do about Cuba," I said one day. "But here, where the Cubans are helping the guerrillas to destroy your system, your government, your country, I can fight them—that's why I'm here. But I'm no magician. It's your fight, and you're going to have to win it."

I made a little headway over the first four weeks. But, to be frank, the only thing that would win the Salvadorans over to my thinking was a decisive victory on the battlefield. That alone would establish my bona fides.

I had arranged for our first mission to be scheduled on April 17, 1985, in honor of the anniversary of the Bay of Pigs invasion. As luck would have it, the operation was postponed for twenty-four hours, so we took off on the morning of the 18th. I had developed reliable intelligence about guerrilla activities in the Rio Lempa area, but when we arrived we discovered that a Salvadoran army battalion had been in the area the day before. That screwed everything up. The guerrillas, of course, had moved on, leaving only their empty base camps behind. We returned to Ilopango late in the morning without even so much as sighting an insurgent. I sat silently, suffering gibes and wisecracks about the wisdom of my concept.

Colonel Steele, the U.S. MilGroup commander, happened to be at the base that day. Disconsolate, I went and spoke to him. "Jim," I said, "I'm at the point of giving up. These people don't want to try."

Steele advised me to have patience. Then he talked to the squadron commanders, who—reluctantly and sarcastically—said they'd give my concept one more attempt. I guessed that the only reason they agreed to a second mission was that, when it failed, they could be sure I wouldn't stay around much longer.

That afternoon we flew into the Cerros de San Pedro area, where intelligence suggested we would find guerrillas moving. We found them. Did we ever! I went in at treetop level in my Hughes 500 and marked the targets with colored smoke grenades. The UH-1H gunships with their homemade armaments followed with rockets and door gunners. Within minutes we had killed seven guerrillas, including one whose bright-blue backpack later turned out to be crammed full of invaluable documents.

We went after another group. I saw one individual in a camouflage hat and T-shirt with a backpack and M-16 running from one tree to another. The 500's minigun was out of ammo, so I told my pilot to swivel the chopper and I emptied about six M-16 magazines in the guerrilla's direction. The insurgent fell.

I pointed toward the ground. "Let's go," I told my pilot. "I want to pick up all the backpacks."

Reluctantly, my pilot set down—right beside a bearded guerrilla lying on the ground. Still wearing my flying helmet and mike, I started to unstrap myself and swing out of the chopper. Suddenly the corpse moved. His rifle swung in my direction. I cut loose with my own M-16. The insurgent's body jerked as my slugs hit it.

Above us, the pilot of a hovering UH-1H gunship screamed, "Take off, take off, you're taking fire!" into his radio.

For an instant I thought my pilot would bounce me out of the chopper. "No—it's me," I yelled into my headset. Quickly I strapped myself back in and the pilot soared aloft. Then we radioed for backup: troops to go in and search the area carefully.

It took almost an hour before paratroopers from Ilopango reached the site. They were so sure I was going to fail they hadn't been ready. It was only after they arrived that we discovered the guerrilla I had shot and wounded in the foot was a woman.

All told, the paratroopers recovered seven backpacks filled with documents. We learned later that the guerrillas were switching base camps and therefore carrying all their files with them. I felt pretty good as we flew back to the airbase. Finally, all my work had been justified.

Later in the day I went to the hospital to see the woman we'd captured. She had refused to speak to anyone—hadn't uttered a word since she'd been taken prisoner. Somehow, when I saw her close up, she didn't strike me as the sort of woman guerrilla I'd run across before. Her hands were smooth, not rough. She didn't look like a nurse or a cook. "I'll bet she's a *comandante*," I told one of the Salvadoran officers.

I turned out to be right. The woman guerrilla we'd captured was Nidia Díaz, a female *comandante* in the FMLN, and the leader of one of its fiercest groups, the PRTC (Revolutionary Party of Central American Workers).

The Salvadorans identified Díaz by reading her mail. In her backpack, among other papers, was a note she'd received from another guerrilla, congratulating her on the way she looked in recent *Time* and *Newsweek* photographs taken at La Palma. La Palma was the small town where President José Napoleón Duarte had met with guerrilla leaders during a short ceasefire. Nidia Díaz had been the only woman commander at the meeting.

Bingo!

Díaz's capture couldn't have occurred at a better time. El Salvador's foreign aid package was being debated in the U.S. Congress, and dozens of the documents we'd collected that day were flown north and shown to the American lawmakers. Without a doubt, they helped ensure that Salvador got its assistance. The papers, notebooks, and other evidence convinced even the most skeptical U.S. congressmen that the Soviets, Cubans, and Nicaraguans were not only training Salvadoran insurgents but also sending vast amounts of equipment to keep them in the field.

Even though the Duarte government later exchanged Díaz for the President's kidnapped daughter, her capture did much to disable the PRTC terrorist cell as a functioning organization. From the backpacks we had the PRTC's entire files: names, addresses, passports. It was a tremendous intelligence coup for the Salvadoran air force. And, it convinced them that I had been right: we could wage an effective anti-insurgency campaign through the judicious use of helicopters, rapid response to good intelligence, and small, highly motivated military units. Frankly, I was ecstatic.

Two days after Díaz's capture, I sat down and wrote a long, heartfelt letter to Don Gregg, telling him how hard it had been. "People were reluctant to my intentions here without any '$' gratification. They were looking and trying to find an employer that did not existed. Believe me, Don, it was hard...."

I explained about the fruitless attempt on the morning of April 18. "I prayed hard that we could get some results, and by God, Don, I got a hell of a good response" later in the day.

Then I wrote, "Don, I thank you and the Vice President for supporting me. Without your help I could not have made it here." I knew that the Vice President hadn't actually *supported* me—not the way Don had. Still, he had listened politely as I explained my concept, and he had told me it was a good idea.

It was one of those things you write when your heart is full; when you are proud of what you have done. Unfortunately, the words would come back to haunt not me alone, but Don and George Bush as well, even though none of us has anything to be ashamed of.

After the Nidia Díaz capture, the Salvadorans began to open up toward me. I was accepted by the pilots, and I began to cement a good relationship with General Bustillo. General Juan Rafael Bustillo is a truly remarkable man. He is firmly committed to democratic values. He believes in simple things: honor, truth, justice. He is loyal and he does not spend a lot of time blowing his own horn.

Once I went to Ilopango's carpentry shop to request a few ammo crates to use as shelves in my room. The sergeant in charge told me they didn't have any spares right then. Somehow, the general had learned that a small village school nearby was without desks—the request had stalled within Salvador's bureaucracy. Bustillo had commanded the air force carpenters to use ammo crates to build a desk for every child. Although the publicity would have helped the military's image, the desks were trucked over with no fanfare.

General Bustillo does not believe in publicity. He believes in action. Recently, when a group of his paratroopers were reticent about moving onto a certain hill because of land mines and the danger of attack, he choppered to where they were and led them up that hill personally.

Our relationship was based on two values both General Bustillo and I live by: trust and honesty. He saw that, as opposed to American officials—even the best of them—I was not required by my job to look at everything I did as a reflection of U.S. interests. Unlike Ambassador Edwin Corr, Tom Pickering's successor in El Salvador, who is as good a man as exists in the Foreign Service, or Colonel Jim Steele, a competent and gifted officer, I was a private citizen. I could look at the situation and deal with it, the interests of Salvador uppermost in my mind. Bustillo liked that, because he could use me as a sounding board. I would tell him the truth as I saw it—no strings attached.

I wish U.S.-Salvadoran relations always ran as smoothly as did my friendship with General Bustillo. This was not, however, the case. Congressman David Obey, a powerful member of the House Foreign Relations Committee, for example, decided at one point to deny the Salvadorans four or five additional Hughes 500 choppers. He did this during a fight he was having with the Reagan administration over the Gramm-Rudman deficit bill. Denying the choppers was Obey's way of proving his power. And despite Ambassador Corr's advice to the contrary, as well as efforts by Colonel Steele, Obey decided that he would show the White House who was boss. Single-handedly he made sure that the Salvadorans received no additional Hughes 500s. It took Ambassador Corr months and months to convince anyone to release the desperately needed helicopters. In the end, he was able to get the Salvadorans a few of them—but it took him almost a year.

Unfortunately, the congressman's arrogance cost Salvadoran lives —civilian lives. Without adequate Hughes 500s, to mark the targets, the air force used other aircraft for its antiguerrilla missions, and other aircraft don't have the ability to differentiate targets as carefully as Hughes 500s flying at treetop level.

Few U.S. congressmen, in fact, have taken adequate time to personally examine the problems in El Salvador. It is far more pleasant for them to travel on fact-finding trips to Paris, Rome, and London. And when they do visit this country, they all too often arrive for only a few hours with their minds already made up. They are prepared to support only those issues they've set into their personal agendas.

We Americans also tend not to understand the fundamentals of Latin friendships. Colonel Jim Steele, always eager to do the best possible job, once asked me how to cement a solid relationship with the Salvadoran air force. Jim was liked and respected by the Salvadorans, but he wanted to become closer to them.

When one of my pilots was wounded, I went to Jim and told him to visit the young man in the hospital.

Steele understood what I meant perfectly. But most American officials would not have grasped what I was getting at. My premise was simple: military assistance alone is sometimes resented, as Communist military aid is often more generous than America's. But for Salvadoran officers to see that our officials care about their wounded can mean more than millions. Their respect and friendship cannot be bought with dollars.

Steele took my advice. He and a U.S. military doctor went to see one of the chopper pilots from my squadron who had been wounded during an operation. It took only a day for word to filter through the ranks that the top U.S. MilGroup adviser in Salvador cared enough about the air force to visit a lieutenant in his hospital room. In Latin America, personal contact means a lot. Simply throwing money at the problem, lecturing, or pontificating means nothing. It earns a man scorn.

My life in Salvador had its share of excitement, too. On one mission, the tail rotor of my chopper hit a tree and my pilot and I came crashing down in guerrilla territory at Copapayo, about thirty-five kilometers north-northeast of Ilopango. The hard landing in a rough jungle area was compounded when my smoke grenade went off in the cockpit and the final seconds of our fall were spent in a thick red cloud. In the end, we were shaken up but OK. The choppers right ski was completely destroyed, however, as was the chopper's main rotor blade.

Luckily for us, the squadron's gunships hovered above until we struggled through the rugged terrain to a nearby hilltop. After it cleared the area with rocket and minigun fire to make sure no guerrillas could get close to our position, the UH-1H came down and extracted us.

At the next day's briefing, one of the squadron officers told General Bustillo about the dire consequences had I been captured by the guerrillas.

"Don't worry, General," said the helicopter squadron commander, Captain Trigueros, "I was right above Felix all the time."

Then he added, "And I would have shot him immediately if the *comunistas* were going to capture him."

Between March and September 1985, I flew over one hundred missions in Salvador. All told, my choppers were hit more than fifteen times—I still have the bullet from one M-16 Vietnam vintage round that went right through the fire-extinguisher hanging next to me.

On September 29, a letter arrived. It would change the course of my life. Typed on plain paper, the first words after the greeting were all in capital letters. They read: "AFTER READING THIS LETTER PLEASE DESTROY IT." The letter had been sent to me on September 20 by Oliver North. He'd sent it Federal Express to my home, and Rosa had simply stuck it in another envelope, unopened, and sent it on to me in El Salvador, first-class mail.

What North sent me was a request to become the liaison between the Salvadoran government and his "Enterprise"—a covert Contra resupply operation. In the letter, Ollie wrote that when I asked General Bustillo and General Vides Casanova, the Minister of Defense, for their cooperation and assistance, I should mention his name because it would add credence to my request. "You may use my name privately with them," is how North phrased it. Of course, when I mentioned his name to General Bustillo and General Vides Casanova, all I got were blank stares. They had no idea who the hell Oliver North was.

I never really got to know Oliver North very well, so I cannot speak about him with authority. I did form a few opinions, however. One is that North had grandiose ideas about himself. During one of my visits to his office in the old Executive Office Building, we were talking when his phone rang. He looked at me and said to the other party, "My chief of staff from Central America is here with me." He also had the habit of telling people that I had been "recruited" by him. Indeed, he would make a point of keeping my old friend Don Gregg in the dark when it came to my participation in his covert Contra operations. Why? Perhaps because Don would not have approved of the way he was going about it.

In truth, I was neither North's Central American chief of staff nor was I his recruit. I agreed to help Oliver North because I believed in what he was doing—helping the Democratic Nicaraguan Resistance, something we in the Cuban community had been engaged in since 1979. And I went along with him as long as his interests paralleled my own. When they diverged—which ultimately happened—we came to a parting of the ways.

Another of North's qualities was naiveté. While he prided himself on the ability to manage covert operations, North was, in fact, wet behind the ears in such activities. His heart may have been in the right place, but he was sorely misled by many he mistakenly trusted. Although I didn't know it until almost five months into my affiliation with North's operation, he had selected retired Air Force General Richard Secord, a man who had ties to several shady deals, to run his secret operation. Secord's partner, Albert Hakim, was known as a financial manipulator, a man who knew how to hide money. North was convinced that Secord, Hakim, and the people they hired to help them were patriots.

But there were problems galore. One, for example, was operational security. The long-distance phone lines in El Salvador were all monitored in Nicaragua. Yet North's people, including the chief resupply pilot, Bill Cooper, and Bob Dutton, a retired U.S. air force colonel who worked for Richard Secord, used the phones to relay sensitive information about operations, including air routes and radio frequencies. By the time the resupply effort was closed down, reporters based in Central America were able to discover virtual phone logs showing repeated calls to Oliver North's office from the San Salvador houses where the pilots lived.

In addition, the aircraft the "Enterprise" had bought were in horrible shape. Navigation equipment in one of the C-123s was so bad that it caused the plane to go ten miles off course and graze the top of a mountain—branches jammed into the left jet engine. But repeated requests for good equipment and safety devices were all spurned by Secord and his people.

As John Piowaty, one of the pilots, wrote in a letter of complaint that I gave to North:

> I demand respect for my life, the lives of my fellow crew members, and some respect for those we are supposed to be supporting. I would like to think that we/you are all motivated by respect for life in this endeavor. How, then, can we be pressed into service (and, please, don't deny the pressure) without equipment listed above [radar, LORAN, altimeters, night vision goggles, functional instrumentation] without parachutes, without minimum survival gear, without adequate communications with the DZ [drop zone], with inadequate (even withheld) intelligence, without secure communications?
>
> Is it simply greed that drives some of you to drive the rest of us?

North, upon reading the pilot's letter, asked me, "Is this a joke?" I told him it was not.

I tried to tell North about the dangers posed by the people he was using, basing my concern on their past relationship to renegade CIA officer Edwin Wilson. Indeed, the "Enterprise," as it came to be known, had more than eight million dollars in various banks by the time it finally ceased operations. Yet the American pilots and kickers

—the guys who packed and shoved the loads out—in San Salvador received only a trickle of money.

Later on, at the Iran/Contra hearings, I discovered that Secord was billing the "Enterprise" for two or three times the amount they were actually paying the pilots and others. Those profits ended up in Secord's and Hakim's bank accounts.

In fact, when I was told that Secord and his people were trying to sell the Contras old grenades and ammunition at inflated prices— nine dollars for three-dollar grenades was one of the figures I heard —I passed the information on to North. He did not realize the seriousness of what was happening under his nose. Even after he had been warned, North did nothing to remedy the situation.

A couple of other incidents from the shoddy operation come to mind as well. The first took place on June 7, 1986, when Bob Dutton, who managed the resupply operation from Washington, showed up in El Salvador. One reason he was there was to answer complaints from the pilots about the horrible physical condition of the aircraft they were flying. None of the planes even had the proper radar to defend against Soviet-made, radar-guided Sandinista missiles.

According to John Piowaty, one of the pilots in the room at the time, Dutton showed up "beaming." He carried a plastic shopping bag containing two Fuzz Buster automobile radar detectors, which he instructed an incredulous Piowaty to install in one of the planes, both fore and aft.

That was the level of protection Secord, Dutton, and the rest of them believed sufficient for people laying their lives on the line: car radar detectors to go up against Soviet combat radar!

Despite the fact that I was suspicious of Secord and his people, I liked their pilots and crewmen and tried my best to help them out. Because of my relationship with General Bustillo, I was able to pave the way for North to use the facilities at Ilopango. But because I could not devote much time to their project, I found someone to manage the Salvadoran-based resupply operation on a day-to-day basis. They knew that person as Ramón Medina. I knew him by his real name: Luis Posada Carriles.

I first met Posada in 1963 at Fort Benning, Georgia, where we went through basic training together, having both been commissioned by President Kennedy as U.S. Army second lieutenants. He is older than I, so we didn't see much of each other or have many friends in common. But I knew who he was.

In the sixties, he reportedly went to work for DISIP, the Venezuelan intelligence service, and rose to considerable power within its ranks. It was rumored that he held one of the top half-dozen jobs in the organization. As is the case in many countries, the Venezuelan intelligence structure is subject to political influence. That is to say, when the Social Christians are in power, DISIP takes on a decidedly Social Christian cast. If the government changes, DISIP's politics change along with it. Posada's rise to power came during the reign of President Rafael Caldera, a member of the Social Christian Party. As is also the case with the majority of intelligence services in the second and third world, DISIP has engaged in domestic spying—including surveillance of rival politicians.

In the course of his domestic intelligence work, Posada, so the story goes, managed to obtain some very juicy tapes of a Venezuelan politician from the Democratic Action Party named Carlos Andrés Pérez. The tapes were of Andrés Pérez engaging in an animated, X-rated conversation with his girlfriend.

When Andrés Pérez, who reportedly learned about the tapes, was elected Venezuelan President in 1974, Luis Posada Carriles was not, to say the least, one of his favorite people. Posada was fired from DISIP. Subsequently he formed a successful private security company in Caracas.

But Andrés Pérez was determined to get revenge. After the midair bombing of a Cubana airliner on October 6, 1976, in which seventy-three people were killed, Posada was charged with planning the attack and was thrown in prison by Andrés Pérez, even though the Venezuelan president had no hard evidence in the case.

One indication that Posada's incarceration was framed is that he was never convicted of any crime by the Venezuelan courts. As a matter of fact, he was even acquitted of the original charge of terrorism. Still, Posada was confined for more than nine years as a result of political pressure from Andrés Pérez. After Pérez left office in 1979, the pressure to keep Posada in jail was kept up by Fidel Castro, with whom the Venezuelans were trying to improve relations.

On August 18, 1985, Posada escaped from Venezuela's San Juan de los Morros prison. He did so, I understand, by bribing a prison official. He then simply walked out through the gates wearing a guard's uniform. With the help of a Venezuelan friend, he was smuggled to the Netherlands Antilles. Then, using forged documents identifying him as a Venezuelan named Ramón Medina, Posada flew to Central America.

He was there when I was contacted by an individual who explained Posada's predicament and asked if I would help. My reply was to ask Posada to make his way to San Salvador. When he arrived, I gave him a job.

I never told any of the Salvadorans with whom I worked, or the American resupply crews, or Oliver North, about Ramón Medina's real identity. I certainly didn't mention anything about Posada to Don Gregg. I had been asked to help him and I had agreed. I put him to work as the day-to-day manager of the resupply operation. He ran the four houses (later cut back to three) we used for the American flight crews. He saw to it that they were stocked with food; he hired maids, and drivers to get the crews back and forth from Ilopango Air Base. Occasionally he even accompanied them on their runs when someone who spoke Spanish was required. Once during a mission to Costa Rica, Posada was bitten by a bat and had to receive a series of painful rabies shots.

Shortly after Eugene Hasenfus's C-123 was shot down on October 5, 1986, Posada and I were both identified by the captured American cargo "kicker." No doubt the Sandinistas had been assisted by DGI —Cuban intelligence—who knew Posada was in El Salvador—with photographs from Castro's files. His real identity known, Posada disappeared once again. Rumor has it that he is still somewhere in Central America. I have not seen him in over two years. And with his old antagonist Carlos Andrés Pérez now back in power in Venezuela, there's certainly little chance Posada will return there soon.

In spite of repeated reports that I "ran" North's operations in El Salvador, the truth of the matter is that I worked on the Contra resupply effort as a part-timer. It is difficult to fight a day-in, day-out war against communist guerrillas and find the time to do anything else, especially to coordinate a complicated resupply operation. In fact, between April 18, 1985, when we captured Nidia Díaz, and October 5, 1986, when Hasenfus's C-123 went down, I flew more than one hundred combat missions with the Salvadoran air force.

During those thirteen months we saw the number of guerrillas drop from more than ten thousand to less than four thousand. We also saw the air force's civilian casualties plummet from the hundreds to less than twenty-five.

While I was happy to help North out, my primary commitment was to General Bustillo and his forces. Generally I could be found at Ilopango. After a stay at the Camino, I'd secured a room at the air base's bachelor officers' quarters. It didn't have room service or even hot water. But it was convenient to my squadron, and I enjoyed being close to the pilots and their youthful enthusiasm and energy. My days were spent flying.

If the need arose, I'd drive into San Salvador. Sometimes I'd stop by Ambassador Corr's residence for breakfast and bring him up to speed on the progress I was making with the military. Occasionally he'd ask me to bring General Bustillo. I believed the better a relationship these two men shared, the better Salvador's chances were for survival, so I encouraged their friendship and was gratified to see it grow.

Corr had been skeptical of me when we'd first met—I had the feeling he was holding me at arm's length. But after the capture of Nidia Díaz and the reduction of civilian casualties, he became one of my strong supporters. Among the improvements I had helped institute were new rules of engagement for the chopper pilots. In suspected areas of guerrilla activity, they could not fire unless they had taken enemy fire or had made certain visual contact. Corr liked that. He could cite concrete figures when he wrote the bureaucrats back in Washington.

Also valuable to him was the intelligence we gathered from the backpacks of captured or killed guerrillas, which the Salvadorans made available to the Americans. In fact, the FMLN generated so much paperwork that Ambassador Corr used to joke that the guerrillas were the ultimate bureaucrats. "When they're not fighting, they're writing" is how he described them.

While I openly discussed the progress we were making against the FMLN, I never told Corr about the other activities that were going on at Ilopango. In light of the congressional prohibition against aiding the Contras, he had warned his staff against this kind of activity. A directive issued over his signature insisted that no U.S. official in El Salvador should "direct, administer or in any way materially support" the Nicaraguan Democratic Resistance.

When American visitors came I would make sure they, too, learned about the advances we'd made in fighting the communists. I took great pleasure in giving Don Gregg's deputy, Colonel Sam Watson, a firsthand account of our achievements when Watson came to visit in January 1986. One night, over dinner with General Bustillo, I described to Sam steps we'd taken to improve Salvadoran combat capabilities; I was also proud to be able to report my success in instilling the nation's military with democratic principles.

I hadn't known Watson too well before. But after he visited El Salvador, I had no qualms about calling him—or Don—when I thought they could help run interference with the Pentagon to speed up deliveries of spare chopper parts. I must have made many such calls during the spring of 1986. Without operating Hughes 500s, it was impossible to carry out my strategy against the insurgents—and we were, at that point, further hampered by Representative Obey's prohibition on new choppers.

North's resupply operation geared up through the winter of 1985–86, but overall I couldn't give it very high marks. It was only in February 1986 that I learned Richard Secord was a part of it. I found out only by chance. A mechanic had been sent to join the operation. The guy showed up on February 5, and by the 6th he'd not only drunk sixty beers but bragged that he'd worked on drug-smuggling planes in Belize and Puerto Rico. I wanted him gone, and I called Ollie North to complain. North put me on the phone with someone he referred to as "Dick." That Dick turned out to be Dick Secord.

Knowing what I knew about Secord and his relationship with Ed Wilson, I became worried. I was already uneasy about Rafael "Chi-Chi" Quintero's participation in the resupply effort, especially since he had not bothered to tell me about Secord.

Early in 1986, I complained to my old friend and former Agency colleague Rudy Enders during a trip to Washington. I told him in vague terms about the North operation, described the people involved and said that as far as I could see it, the Secord group was in the resupply business simply to make money.

Rudy's suggestion was that I go to Don Gregg—immediately. "Don will know what to do," he said.

I refused. "It's nothing that anybody connected with the Vice President's office should know about. Believe me, if North wanted Don to be aware of the situation, North would have told him."

I didn't approach Don about my misgivings for months. Rudy was upset that I didn't open my mouth to Don about Secord and his business partners. Rudy could take or leave Secord. But he thought that Clines's participation was an absolute disaster.

By April I was downright skeptical about the way things were proceeding. I wasn't the only one. On April 20, I was present at a meeting in San Salvador when the Contras' top military commander, Enrique Bermúdez, complained to North in person that the aircraft North's people were using were too small and in such bad shape that they were unable to deliver the supplies his troops desperately needed.

Shortly before that April 20 meeting, Rafael Quintero had asked me to impose upon my good relations with the Salvadoran military to obtain "end-user" certificates made out to Lake Resources, which he told me was a Chilean company but which, I discovered after the fact, was really owned by Richard Secord. End-user certificates are as valuable as multimillion-dollar cashier's checks. They are documents issued by governments which allow arms companies to legally traffic in restricted weapons by guaranteeing the identity of the "end user" —in other words the country that will finally receive the goods.

The Salvadoran end-user certificates for Lake were supposedly to be used to obtain Blowpipe ground-to-air missiles for the FDN freedom fighters. The Blowpipes would then be employed against Soviet-supplied HIND choppers flown by Cuban-trained Sandinista pilots in Nicaragua.

The Salvadorans complied with my request, and in turn I supplied the certificates, handing them over personally to Richard Secord at that April 20 meeting. The FDN, however, never got its Blowpipe missiles. And, when I later asked Quintero for the certificates back so I could return them to my Salvadoran friends, I never got a response.

Two days after North and Secord left, I decided it was time to go our separate ways. I was uncomfortable with North and the people he'd associated himself with. I'd been in El Salvador for more than a year; I'd flown more than one hundred missions. So when I arrived in Washington for a visit with Don Gregg (and another appointment with the Vice President), I decided to tell North I was leaving and that he should find someone else to coordinate things in El Salvador. I also planned to tell Don and the Vice President that I felt I had done all I could to help the Salvadorans—it was time for me to come home.

On May 1, 1986, I had a fifteen-minute meeting with Mr. Bush. Don accompanied me to his office. I showed the Vice President my pictures of antiguerrilla operations in El Salvador and believed at the time that Mr. Bush was totally absorbed in what I was telling him about my exploits and the progress we were making against the communists. But another visitor who was with us in the office, Nick Brady, now Treasury Secretary, saw the situation somewhat differently.

"It seems to me the Vice President was being perfunctory with Mr. Rodriguez," is the way Secretary Brady recalled the meeting when he was deposed by the Iran/Contra investigators. Brady explained that my visit interrupted a conversation he'd been having with the Vice President. He went on to say that, in his opinion, Mr. Bush, having seen the pictures I'd brought, "wanted to return to the political matters that we were talking about. . . . We had an unfinished subject and . . . he was anxious to get back to that."

Toward the end of my session with Mr. Bush, before I could tell him and Don that I wanted to leave El Salvador, Ollie North showed up along with Ambassador Ed Corr in tow. Ed was very generous in talking about my contributions in El Salvador and said he hoped I'd be staying on to continue my efforts.

Mr. Bush graciously listened to Ambassador Corr and thanked him for stopping by.

What do you do when an ambassador you respect tells the Vice President of the United States that you're doing a good job and he wants you to stay on?

The answer is, Say thank you, and keep your mouth shut. Which is exactly what I did—for just over a month.

On June 25, I traveled again to Washington, this time for a meeting with North—a most unsatisfactory meeting. With Bob Dutton in the room, North accused me of security violations. This is the same Bob Dutton who used long-distance telephone calls that were routed through Nicaragua to plan which operational frequencies the pilots should use on their missions!

I challenged North to prove that I had violated security in any way whatsoever. Then I told him that he could take his whole operation and shove it. I told him there was stealing going on. He didn't believe me. I warned him—as I later recounted in my public Iran/Contra testimony—"This could be worse than Watergate. It could destroy the President of the United State."

Naive as ever, North called Tom Clines a patriot.

The small TV set in his office was on—there was a Congressional vote that day regarding aid to the Contras.

Ollie North moved from one side of the room to the other, pausing to look at the screen. "Those people want me, but they cannot touch me because the Old Man loves my ass."

Later, during his testimony before the Iran/Contra committees, North told Senator Bill Cohen from Maine that he had "absolutely no recall whatsoever of that conversation."

After June 25, I never met with Oliver North again. I felt sorry for him. Not because he was breaking the law of the land—whether or not Oliver North broke any laws is not for me to say. I pitied North because he was manipulated by people whose motives were dishonest, and he couldn't face reality enough to cope with the situation.

The sorry demise of Ollie North's resupply operation is reflected in the tone of a pair of KL-43 coded messages I sent from El Salvador to Rafael Quintero in Miami during the summer of 1986

7/21/86—Ilopango to Miami. Today last day to pay tel bills. We have responsibility with house owners and no cash has been received. . . . For your info we are closing all activity on this end until a serious approach is taken on your end. . . .

7/21/86—Ilopango to Miami. After we had long meeting, Gen. Bustillo expressed his deep concern and disappointment at the total lack of professionalism, operational capability your organization has displayed. He believes that hundreds of thousands of dollars are being spent with almost no results. . . . A/C [aircraft] are in terrible condition. . . . If this situation is not completely resolved within a week the General will require all personnel from your organization to leave Ilopango.

In fact, during July and August 1986, Ollie North's resupply operation was able to stage only one successful mission—a deplorable record considering the huge amount of money that was going into the pockets of those organizing the "Enterprise."

But actually getting supplies to the Contras seemed to be the least concern of those who ran it. With renewed Contra aid now approved by Congress, I reached the conclusion Secord and his partners were now only interested in turning a quick profit.

Late in July, Rafael Quintero told me that Secord and North were going to close everything down—no further money was available for salaries, fuel, housing, or other expenses, he said. I knew what was happening. Secord and Company didn't want to spend another dime until they sold the whole operation to either the CIA or whoever was going to take over the resupply duties for the U.S. Government. Meanwhile, the Nicaraguan Freedom Fighters were getting screwed. I talked with the pilots and crews, who all volunteered to keep going without being paid. I found someone to make fuel available to us. For the moment, we didn't need Secord's people.

Besides, I didn't think that anything was Secord's to sell. I believed the planes and everything else belonged to the FDN. As North had explained it to me, the money for our resupply efforts had been privately raised. Everything that had been bought, therefore, was a gift to the Contras. Secord and his cronies thought it all belonged to them. I was shocked and outraged when I heard it from Quintero.

On August 8, 1986, I visited Don Gregg. I told Don about Secord, Clines, and Quintero's involvement with Oliver North. As a former Agency officer, I knew Don would understand, and I believed that he could help straighten things out.

Don went ballistic. He called North's office but Ollie wasn't there. Still, in frustration, Don told Bob Earle, North's assistant, that if Tom Clines were part of any operation whatsoever, it was outrageous. Didn't North know about Ed Wilson?

I returned to El Salvador. My relations with the "Enterprise" group got worse than ever. I was forced to ask FDN commander Enrique Bermúdez to put armed Contras aboard resupply flights to prevent anyone from the "Enterprise" from making off with the aircraft. Like me, Bermúdez believed that the resupply operation belonged to the FDN, not to Secord.

It was one of those brave young security guards who lost his life on October 5, when the C-123 piloted by Bill Cooper was hit by a Sandinista soldier's missile, and Eugene Hasenfus was captured. That day the whole operation came crashing down around Ollie North's head, and my anonymity ended forever.

17 I was in Miami when Hasenfus's plane was shot down. I wasn't really on speaking terms with Ollie North, but I still felt that someone in Washington should be told. So I called Don Gregg's assistant, Sam Watson, at his home and gave him the news. Not too long after that, my name started to emerge as one of the resupply-operation players, and camera crews and reporters started arriving on my front lawn, staking me out. It finally got so bad that I surreptitiously left the house altogether and moved into the apartment of my friend Dr. Roberto González, a physician who has been active in fitting Salvadoran soldiers wounded by communist mines with prosthetic limbs, and who has also volunteered his medical services to Contras.

I stayed at Roberto's a couple of weeks, then took Rosa, Felix, Jr., and Rosemarie to the Keys for a few quiet days by ourselves. I knew by the end of 1986 that some of my story was going to come out. I just didn't realize how much of it would be made public.

When it became clear that I would appear as a witness at the Iran/Contra hearings, there was a real question in my mind about whether my testimony should be public or private. At first I considered appearing behind closed doors. But I was dissuaded by a Guatemalan army officer and good friend. He told me, "Felix, you can do ten times better if you go openly. Because that way all the reports will be in your own words—not the media's interpretation of what you say."

My friend made sense. I called the joint committees' intelligence analyst, Tom Polgar, whom I had known when he was the CIA Station Chief in Saigon. When I got Tom on the phone, I explained that I didn't want to appear in executive session or to sit behind a screen to hide my face from the cameras. I explained I'd decided not to testify in private. I told him that everything I had to say I could say in front of the American people.

I had previously refused the offer of a lawyer to accompany me, made by my longtime friend Jorge Mas, the head of the Cuban American National Foundation. My reasoning went this way: If I have to bring a lawyer to help me explain why I've been defending this country for the past twenty-seven years, then I'm in the wrong country.

I was not—and am not—ashamed of anything I've ever done, either as a CIA agent or in my private life. So when I explained to Polgar that I'd be coming without counsel, I added, "I don't want any kind of immunity, either. If I've done something wrong I should go to jail.

"I went to Cuba and I was willing to face death, prison, or torture for what I believed in," I added. "Things are no different now."

So I spoke willingly with every federal investigator who wanted my help and cooperation. John Keker, the lawyer who was trying the Oliver North case for the special prosecutor, even came to El Salvador to see me, accompanied by FBI agents and a second lawyer from the Independent Counsel's office. I cooperated fully—after all, I had nothing to hide.

I spent a lot of time with the Iran/Contra committee staff in Washington, where I was deposed on May 1, 1987. Unlike many of those who testified, I did not devote hours and hours to rehearsing the things I'd say. My preparation consisted of making sure I had the correct dates for important meetings, and that was it.

A friend of mine in Miami who has a lot of experience in law enforcement gave me some solid advice about appearing on the stand. He said, "I always get nervous in court because I'm a field person. You're a field person, too, Felix. So do what I do: make sure you understand the question. Even if you have to ask it five times. If you know the question you can answer it truthfully. And don't go beyond what you know. Don't speculate. Don't guess. Just say what you know."

On May 27 I made my first appearance in front of the joint committees. I was a little nervous as the staff car picked me up at the house in Georgetown where I was staying with friends and drove me to Capitol Hill. I arrived in time to catch some of the performance by Bob Dutton, who testified just prior to me.

Actually, Dutton was in some way responsible for my strong appearance that day. He tried to defend his own shoddy record by attacking me and misrepresenting my position.

• He told the committees that I "had been *sent down* [to El Salvador], I understand, to work with the local military." He understood incorrectly. I had been sent by no one.

• He portrayed me as interested in money and greedy for power. He was wrong. As anyone who knows me will attest, money has never been important to me. And power is something I don't need.

• He hinted that I might have leaked information about the resupply effort to a left-wing group, the Christic Institute. It was inconceivable that I would ever do such a thing.

Back in Miami, Rosa and the kids were watching Dutton's incredible act on TV. Rosa told Rosemarie and Felix, Jr.: "The hair on your father's neck is standing up right now. He's saying, 'That s.o.b. is going to know who *I* am pretty soon.' And he's going to be a little harder on Secord and the rest of them because of the lies this man is telling." She was right—as usual. That is exactly what I said to myself.

I had been taught as a child, "If you don't have anything good to say about someone, then don't say anything."

I planned to tell the truth. But I was not going to say anything nasty about anyone. It has never been my style to do so in public. Besides, I'm convinced that Bob Dutton, Dick Secord, and Ollie North know in their hearts about their mistakes and their lies. That's enough for me.

But after watching Dutton's unbelievable series of prevarications I realized that I had to speak out from my own heart, explaining what these people had done—which was to make huge profits from freedom fighters.

Unlike Dutton, Secord, and the others who spoke about me personally, I cast no aspersions on their character; I tried not to make any personal statements. But I didn't hold back when it came to talking about the shoddy equipment, poor security, unsafe aircraft, huge expenditures, and profiteering. In anyone's book, three-dollar hand grenades being sold for nine dollars is profiteering—and I wanted the American people to know about it. From the positive reaction I was accorded by congressmen and senators from both sides of the political aisle, I believe that my testimony was a success.

I returned to Miami after my appearance to watch the rest of the hearings, and to decompress. By early summer I was back in El Salvador, flying with the air force. On June 30, Rosa called me, tremendously upset: a story in that day's *Miami Herald* said I'd been accused by Ramón Milian Rodríguez, a convicted money launderer for the Colombian cocaine cartel, of soliciting a $10 million donation of drug money for the Contras.

The story, she said, was given to the press by "unnamed congressional sources." Milian Rodríguez's testimony had taken place behind closed doors. It had been heard by Senator John Kerry, a Massachusetts Democrat—a Vietnam War veteran who once, to demonstrate his opposition to the war, threw someone else's medals over the White House fence in protest. Kerry was chairman of the Senate's Subcommittee on Terrorism, Narcotics and International operations. The subcommittee, it turned out, was investigating alleged ties between the Contras and drug smuggling in Central America—a specter raised by a range of left-wing public-interest groups.

I told her, "Rosa, don't worry, it's just another of those dumb stories." But I didn't remember the meeting I'd had at Raúl Díaz's office with the convicted money launderer back in 1985. "This story is nothing," I said.

"No, Felix, it's serious," Rosa insisted. "People are looking at me strangely all of a sudden, because they think my husband has been involved in drugs."

She added that a subpoena from Kerry's subcommittee requesting that I appear and testify about Milian Rodríguez's outrageous claims had been left at our front door that day.

I welcomed the request and made arrangements to leave for Washington. As with the Iran/Contra committees, I wanted neither a lawyer nor any immunity. After all, I had done nothing wrong, and I had nothing to hide.

But I was politically naive. I believed that those elected to the U.S. Congress would put truth and the national good ahead of partisan politics. The eleven-month ordeal I was about to begin would disabuse me of my innocence for good.

There were many things I did not know about Kerry and about the subcommittee's special counsel, Jack Blum, at the time I first appeared before them. If I had been aware of these things I might have been more cautious—and I would certainly have taken the offensive sooner.

• I did not realize that Kerry's subcommittee was politically motivated—that Kerry, a top foreign-policy adviser and political ally of Massachusetts governor Michael Dukakis, wanted to embarrass the Reagan administration and help Dukakis win the Democratic presidential nomination.

• I did not know that the subcommittee's special counsel, Jack Blum, was, when Kerry hired him, a lawyer and board member of the International Center for Development Policy, a left-wing think tank that not only opposed President Reagan's Latin American policies but had actually provided funds for a joint investigation of the Contras with Senator Kerry's staff.

Blum was even predisposed not to believe me. He told a friend that he'd felt I wouldn't be a credible witness because I had been trained by the CIA to hold a false cover story "unto death," as he put it.

• I did not know that for almost a year people with regular access to the subcommittee's closed-door testimony and locked files would, as far as I could determine, engage in a systematic series of leaks to friendly journalists that fueled speculation that I—and by extension, Vice President Bush—was somehow involved with drug trafficking.

So I flew to Washington early in August 1987 with an open mind. I came to tell Senator Kerry the truth. Based on my experience with the Iran/Contra committees and their professional staffs, I believed that I would be treated fairly.

I got a suspicious when Jack Blum insisted on a closed hearing. I had nothing to hide—I would have preferred to tell my story to anyone willing to listen. But Blum claimed sources had to be protected. So my testimony was scheduled to be given behind closed doors.

Kerry himself was not well prepared for me. He apparently hadn't been told that I'd immediately reported my contact with Milian Rodríguez to both the FBI and the CIA. Still, I gave him the facts of my single meeting with Milian Rodríguez. I described how it had come about at Raúl Díaz's suggestion, recounted the money launderer's claims about Panamanian strong man General Manuel Noriega's involvement in drug trafficking, and his claim that he could compromise the Sandinista government. I told Senator Kerry that Milian had never offered me any money for the Contras and denied that I'd ever solicited any.

He went back over my story again and again, as if to find some loopholes in which to catch me. He couldn't—because I was telling the truth.

Kerry spent a lot of time asking about unsubstantiated rumors about me, some of which had been reported in the press—things like my "longtime friendship with Vice President Bush," or the "fact" that I had gone to El Salvador at the behest of the CIA. He also asked ridiculous questions about the international drug trade—matters I had absolutely no knowledge of. Obviously, what he wanted was to connect the Vice President and the top Contra leadership to drugs.

And he seemed upset that I was of no use in helping him achieve his goals.

At one point, Kerry said to me by way of explanation, "Mr. Rodriguez, you have to understand that there are many allegations about the Contras that we have to probe."

I answered, "Senator, you should know there is a disinformation apparatus within the Soviet and Cuban intelligence services; it is in the best interests of the Soviets and the Cubans that the Nicaraguan Freedom Fighters do not prevail."

Kerry then switched the subject. Incredibly, he wanted to talk, not about Nicaragua and the Contras, or General Noriega, or Ramón Milian Rodríguez, but about Che Guevara and my exploits in Bolivia in 1967. He wanted to know all the details of Che's capture. He even asked me somewhat sarcastically why I did not fight harder to save Che's life.

After a while it became apparent that he was speaking simply to hear himself talk—creating a record for his own benefit. I spoke up: "Senator, I think you have called me here to talk about drugs, but we are going on to things that have nothing to do with drugs."

We sparred verbally a few minutes longer. Finally I lost my temper. I said, "Senator, this has been the hardest testimony I ever gave in my life."

He looked up, glasses perched on his nose. "Why?"

"Because, sir, it is extremely difficult to have to answer questions from someone you do not respect."

Things got even more bitter after that. He exploded at me, and I came right back at him. There was a lot of shouting that morning.

I told him outright, "Senator, my name was leaked by your committee as being involved with drugs. I take that very seriously because it affects my family, my reputation, and my friends."

Kerry looked at me sternly and said, "You're making a very serious accusation, because this committee doesn't leak."

"Senator, leaked or not it was in every goddamed newspaper that, at one of your *closed* committee hearings Ramón Milian Rodríguez said I solicited money. That is a damned lie. And if you're sincere, then you will put out a statement about what I told you here today. I don't want to influence what you say, but I want the American people to know about my testimony. And as far as I am concerned, you can make my whole testimony available to the American people."

Kerry and Blum never released my testimony. Nor did the good Senator from Massachusetts ever put out a statement explaining that I had denied the convicted money launderer's lies. I finally called a press conference in Miami on August 11, 1987, to give my side of the story. According to an Associated Press report, Jack Blum's wimpish reaction was to state that Kerry's committee "was very sensitive" to my concerns and hoped to make portions of my testimony public within a month.

It did not happen. For the next *eleven* months I fought in vain either to have Blum release my testimony or allow me to testify in public. My Uncle Fernando Mendigutia, a lawyer, represented me in my endeavors. All his requests fell on deaf ears. Senator Kerry's staff even misrepresented to him—or so the Senator later told me—my availability to testify. Not only did Blum refuse my requests, he even made a number of trips to Miami during this period to talk to people who knew me. I'm sure he was trying to shake my story.

During one such trip he approached Raúl Díaz, the private investigator, and asked him to testify about the meeting I'd had with Milian Rodríguez. Raúl told Blum that if things could be worked out, he'd be happy to testify. Díaz added that his testimony would confirm what I'd said and that Milian was not credible. Raúl says that Jack Blum did not appear happy to hear that my version of things was the correct one.

Whether by design or by coincidence, allegations about me kept seeping out all through 1987, right up to Election Day, 1988, connecting me with various covert activities concocted or overseen by Vice President Bush on behalf of the Contras. None of these allegations was ever proved. None, in fact, could even be substantiated.

If I were paranoid, I might have thought that someone close to Blum and Kerry was out to get me. Here are a few examples of why I thought that:

• Blum's former organization, the International Center for Development Policy, used as a consultant Richard Brenneke, a Kerry subcommittee witness who claimed to have high intelligence connections and tried to link the Contras with drug smuggling.

- Blum's own conspiracy-laden theories about a secret network of Israeli arms dealers, Latin American drug smugglers, and Contra leaders somehow found their way into magazine and newspaper articles, books, and television news stories.

- Kerry and Blum never challenged the May 9, 1988, testimony of Jose Blandon, a former Noriega aide who, under oath, swore that "Felix Rodriguez is a very close friend of Ramon Milian Rodriguez." Blandon's sources for this outrageous lie were, he told the gullible Kerry, Panamanian and Salvadoran intelligence officials. From my experience, only witnesses whose views were ideologically opposed to Kerry's and Blum's anti-Contra philosophy were questioned aggressively.

- One of Kerry's fellow Senators, Kentucky Republican Mitch McConnell, privately wrote the Massachusetts Democrat that the investigation was turning into a "witch hunt." McConnell got no reply.

Finally, McConnell—a supporter of George Bush—became so outraged by Kerry's antics that he called a Washington press conference on June 10, 1988, ten months after I'd appeared behind closed doors. There, standing beside the Kentucky senator, I released the true details of my meeting with Ramón Milian Rodríguez.

Because of Senator McConnell's pressure, I was finally permitted by Kerry to testify in open session—eleven months, eight days, two hours and thirty-four minutes after my initial appearance. But Jack Blum had one more surprise waiting for me: he managed to schedule me as the final witness on a hot, humid Friday afternoon in July— Bastille Day, July 14, 1988, to be precise.

By the time I was sworn in at 4:30 P.M. most of the press had gone home and most of the cameras had been turned off. I was consigned to the same media vacuum I'd suffered since the original leaks appeared.

There were few people in the room to hear Kerry say publicly that, after a year of investigations and millions of taxpayer dollars, he believed the version of events concerning Ramón Milian Rodríguez I'd stated so concisely the previous August.

"I believe what you said, and I want to make that very clear," is how a contrite Senator Kerry put it to the almost-empty chamber.

I was gratified by Kerry's statement. So was Rosa, who had come to Washington with me. In fact, I ended up respecting the Senator at this second hearing much more than I had after our first encounter. I believe that Kerry was misled by his special counsel Jack Blum— who put me and my family through hell. Still, when Kerry finally apologized, he made certain to do it at a time and place when his apology was least likely to be covered by the news media.

Why? Probably because what I said did not fit Kerry's liberal Democrat agenda, or help him try to ensure that George Bush would be defeated. In 1987, I probably wouldn't have thought that way. But these days I've grown up—politically speaking.

18 With my testimony before the Iran/Contra committees and John Kerry's subcommittee, the anonymity
I'd once enjoyed disappeared forever. Whether or
not I wanted it, I became a public figure, my face in
the newspapers and on television screens.

Moreover, what I said was often quoted—accurately in some
stories and incorrectly in others. I learned, sometimes painfully, in
the weeks and months following my initial Capitol Hill testimony,
that people tend to deal not in the truth as it really is but the truth as
they want to see it—and the facts be damned.

I had the misfortune to be linked to the Vice President's office through my longtime friendship with Don Gregg. With Mr. Bush running for President, any damaging connection, no matter how tenuous, that could be cobbled together between me and Mr. Bush, or between me and Don, would serve the Democrats' goal of weakening the Republican front-runner. My relationship with Don and the Vice President was exploited by Mr. Bush's Republican primary opponents as well. By questioning his integrity they would advance their own positions. The press became a willing conduit for all the gossip, rumor, and innuendo. And why not? The temptation to draw Mr. Bush into the Iran/Contra scandal was just too much for many reporters to resist.

There was another element as well. I provided an easy target for journalists. Few got to know me, or discover what values I stand for. It was easier to categorize me as "ex-CIA agent" or "Cuban exile" Felix Rodriguez. Moreover, a common qualifier used in the American press for "Cuban exile" is "right wing," as in "right-wing Miami-based Cuban exiles." It is a clichéd stereotype that is both hard to escape and inaccurate. At the Iran/Contra hearings, for example, Senator Daniel Inouye tried to paint me into the far right-wing corner by trying to get me to admit that I was pro-Batista—in other words a stereotypical fascist, totalitarian-supporting, right-wing Cuban.

With all respect, the Senator was—and is—mistaken. I am none of these things. Further, it is a fact that many anti-Castro Cubans were anti-Batista as well. I have good friends who worked for Batista. I have good friends who did not support him. I can condemn none of them for seeking democracy in their own way, in their own style.

It seems to me that the press takes on a racist edge when it stereotypes Cuban exiles as right-wing fanatics. We are lawyers and architects, doctors, politicians, and, yes, freedom fighters, too. Many of us have achieved the American dream. We cherish American values —and have died defending them. Our appreciation of these things goes too often unreported in the news media.

In my own case I found scores of reportorial errors of fact. Some might be considered minor. But taken as a body of work, they led me to the inescapable conclusion that too many journalists just don't care very much either about the facts or telling the truth. A few examples include:

• An August 1987 *Washington Post* article drew on General Paul Gorman's misleading memo of February 14, 1985, to assert—erroneously—that I'd called the Contras my "primary" commitment. The article led readers to assume that the Vice President helped me go to Central America to resupply the FDN freedom fighters—a false assumption.

• An August 1987 Associated Press wire story referred to me thusly: "Rodriguez—also known by the CIA code name Max Gomez..." The CIA had nothing to do with giving me the pseudonym Max Gomez—it was suggested to me by my old friend Lieutenant Colonel Lou Rodríguez.

• Jack Anderson, the same man who once volunteered to help me set up anti-Castro training camps and who introduced me to my first arms dealer, wrote early in 1988 that Don Gregg allegedly "puffed up" my reputation, "spreading the word that Rodriguez was part of the special team that hunted down Cuban revolutionary Che Guevara" as a way of insinuating me into North's Contra supply enterprise. As readers of this book know, Anderson was completely wrong about Don Gregg's trying to get me into the North operation.

• In *US News & World Report*, writer Steven Emerson reported early in 1988 that it was Don Gregg who had introduced me to Ollie North. Emerson was wrong. That fact had been contradicted during my on-the-record Iran/Contra committee deposition.

Unfortunately this body of misinformation about me will be used by reporters for years to come. These days, journalists researching stories regularly use computerized "clip files" data bases, built from major news sources—wire-service stories, major newspapers and magazines, and even the transcripts of network nightly news shows.

The problem is that, when stories contain inaccuracies, those bits of bad information are used over and over by reporters who pull the information from the data base. Anyone who uses Nexis, the news-source data base, to pull out "facts" about me will discover a *Los Angeles Times* story from October 1986 that says I fought in the Congo. I never fought in the Congo.

• • •

Perhaps the most irresponsible of the print stories was a November 1988 "Special Report" in *Rolling Stone*, alleging that Don Gregg and I ran a secret Contra weapons-smuggling operation called Black Eagle.

It didn't help me to know that the co-author of the piece, Howard Kohn, had been fired by the *Detroit Free Press* in 1973 for lying. From this I could surmise that he had a fertile imagination.

Kohn and his coauthor, Vicki Monks, wove together an exciting tale that combined rumor, innuendo, fact, fiction, and wishful thinking. Aside from the fact that no operation code-named Black Eagle that I'm aware of ever existed—it is wholly a figment of the authors' imaginations—among Kohn's blatant errors of reportorial fact are:

• Kohn implies that I was in El Salvador when Eugene Hasenfus's plane was shot down on October 5, 1986. I was not. I was in Miami.

• Kohn describes Don Gregg as CIA Station Chief in Saigon, a post Don never held.

• He describes me as a helicopter pilot in Vietnam, and, later, a "stunt-level pilot." Neither is true.

• Kohn says that Watergate burglar Eugenio Martínez was a member of my five-man infiltration squad in 1961. He was not.

• Kohn attempts to place me on the so-called Operation Mongoose teams sent by the CIA to assassinate Fidel Castro. He is writing fiction.

A close reading of the *Rolling Stone* article leads me to the conclusion that Kohn and Monks had only four or so major sources. Included, it would appear, are two unsavory characters who have tried for almost three years now to connect George Bush's office with drugs and weapons smuggling. They are José Blandon, a former assistant to Panamanian strongman Manuel Antonio Noriega, and Richard Brenneke, a Portland, Oregon businessman who seems to make a habit of changing his story every time a new fact turns up in the papers. I have never met either of them. But that has not stopped Blandon from telling any gullible journalist within earshot that he knows me and knows a lot about me.

According to a report issued by Senator John Kerry's Subcommittee on Narcotics, Terrorism and International Relations, Richard Brenneke has made all sorts of outrageous claims. He told Kerry's subcommittee that he had worked closely with Israeli agents who smuggled drugs into the U.S. "and he had personally discussed the operations with members of the Vice President's staff." None of Brenneke's claims were ever proved by Kerry's investigation.

Brenneke has also told reporters he was an Israeli agent working for the Mossad, and has alleged that he worked for the CIA, even producing a document to that effect signed by a CIA personnel officer. The Mossad, of course, never comments on anything. (Even the name of its director and top officers are classified.) So anyone claiming to work for Mossad is probably lying. As for Brenneke's alleged CIA connection, investigators discovered that the man whose name was attached to his employment certification had retired a decade before the date shown on Brenneke's "bona fide" letter.

Richard Brenneke is currently under investigation by the FBI for impersonating a federal officer, and by the CIA for impersonating an Agency employee. From what I can tell, Brenneke appears in the *Rolling Stone* article under the pseudonym Aaron Kozen. He is referred to by Kohn and Monks as an Israeli agent.

Blandon was a general factotum for Manuel Noriega. He worked in the intelligence area and ran various errands for the Panamanian military strong man. In thinking about him the word "lapdog" comes to mind.

One small section of the article reads:

"Rodriguez's main job in Black Eagle, according to several operatives, was to organize the logistics for weapons drops to Contra camps in Honduras and northern Nicaragua. His base of operations was El Salvador's Ilopango airfield, commanded by a close friend, Salvadoran general Juan Bustillo. Rodriguez met with Bustillo in December 1983 at Ilopango to discuss Black Eagle, according to two men who were also at the meeting—an Israeli Agent we'll call Aaron Kozen, and José Blandon, the former Panamanian chief of political intelligence."

Kohn's imagination is vivid. But he is a sloppy investigator. I was not in El Salvador in December 1983, and I can prove it. Moreover, as General Bustillo can attest, I didn't meet him until January 1985, when we first shook hands in his quarters at Bolling Air Force Base just outside Washington, D.C.

The rest of Kohn's article contains errors of equal scope. Moreover, while *Rolling Stone* had hoped to make some headlines with the piece, publishing it just prior to Election Day, the story sank like a rock. It had no credibility at all.

I didn't fare a whole lot better in some of the books in which I've appeared either. Some were just plain wrong—almost maliciously so. A television producer named Leslie Cockburn distorted the facts in favor of the left-wing causes she espouses in a piece of trash entitled "Out of Control." She characterized me as a fanatical ayatollah of anticommunism "on close terms with Vice President George Bush." That of course is incorrect. She, like Kohn, describes me as a member of CIA "shooter" assassination teams directed against Castro. Her worst fiction is this: "Felix Rodriguez"—she quotes Edwin Wilson, a renegade CIA agent and known liar, as saying—"was a Batista Cuban, so he wasn't really liked by other Cubans."

This source of Cockburn's, remember, is the same sterling fellow whose sale of C-4 Plastique to Qaddafi has caused the deaths of Americans in terrorist incidents all over the globe. Wilson also told two gullible *Village Voice* writers in a 1987 interview that I "only left Cuba because Batista got thrown out." In fact, I left Cuba in 1954 at the age of fourteen to go to prep school.

While I could understand the attacks from left-wing writers, I found the erroneous citations in reputable books mystifying until I realized that few reporters actually take the time to do much original research.

Landslide, for example, was a well-received volume about the Iran/Contra fallout during Ronald Reagan's second term as President. It is touted as a well-researched book. Yet, in *Landslide* I am consistently referred to as an old friend of George Bush's—a highly inaccurate description. I can only surmise that the book's authors, Jane Mayer and Doyle McManus, referred to me in that way after having read General Gorman's February 14, 1985 memo to Ambassador Pickering, and relying on it alone.

Certainly they never sought to check the sources on my relationship with the Vice President, either with me or with him. This was strange, because during the course of the Iran/Contra investigation I spoke with McManus a number of times (McManus cites an April 1988 interview with me in one of his footnotes. That came as a surprise. I remember meeting with him, but he never told me I was being formally interviewed for a book). He never brought up the subject of how long I'd known the Vice President, as I recall. I can only imagine that the prospect of making some news—whether it was accurate or not—was more profitable than reporting the facts.

McManus and Mayer took the easy way out: they used clip files of old, inaccurate articles and did no original reporting when it came to my relationship with the Vice President. Neither did Steven Emerson, the alleged "investigative" reporter from *US News* whose book *Secret Warriors* has me in the Congo in the sixties when I was actually a principal agent in Miami (he probably pulled that "fact" out of the *Los Angeles Times* story on a data base) and "close" to General Richard Secord in Vietnam—which is not the case at all. Emerson never bothered to interview me or even request an interview. He, too, it would seem, wrote from clips.

The television news reporting about me was even worse than the print, on the whole. Three particularly outrageous examples come to mind. The first was during CBS anchor Dan Rather's frontal assault on Vice President George Bush on January 25, 1988.

Rather told viewers that his network had "spent more than a month" researching the taped piece that preceded the interview: an interview that turned into a historic shouting match between an unelected multimillion-dollar television personality and the Vice President of the United States.

Here are just a few of the errors:

• CBS reported that my TTF plan—the counterinsurgency concept for Central America I'd created in 1983—included targets in Nicaragua. As I have said repeatedly, that was never the case. They had only to read the TTF to see their error.

• CBS used the February 14, 1985 memo of General Gorman to assert I'd been "put into play by Ollie North" to help the Contras. Gorman had also written that I'd known North for a long time (which was incorrect) and that I'd known the Vice President since his days as DCI (also false).

Asked about Gorman's document on camera, Don Gregg told CBS, "I've heard about that memorandum, and I have no explanation for it." He was telling the truth—but the way CBS edited the footage made it look as if he were hiding something.

• CBS alleged—although its report never asserted outright—that I had spoken to Mr. Bush about Ollie North's resupply operations in the two short meetings we'd had at the White House in 1985 and 1986.

I had denied under oath during my Iran/Contra testimony that I ever spoke to the Vice President about North's operations. And CBS even had footage of that testimony. But Rather didn't broadcast my denial. In fact, the Vice President even told the hypercritical anchorman, "Felix Rodriguez testified under oath. He has been public, and you could at least have run a little of him saying that 'I never told the Vice President about the Contras.'"

Another of Rather's omissions was equally telling. He didn't bother to report that my testimony concerning the Vice President has never been successfully challenged or contradicted.

Why? I guess Rather chose not to include anything that might hamper his one-sided reporting. And besides, what's the use of allowing mere facts to get in the way of a dramatic piece of television.

Early in April 1988, Frank Snepp, a former CIA agent who was working as a producer for ABC, called me in Central America to ask if I knew anything concerning some stories circulating that the planes used to supply arms to the Contras from 1983 to 1985 had been also used to run drugs into the United States. I told him that I knew nothing. Then, a few days later, on April 7, a report on ABC's *World News Tonight* alleged that, as anchor Peter Jennings said, "Americans and Israelis provided arms to the Contras and then the same network smuggled drugs into the United States." ABC's chief correspondent, Richard Threlkeld, then picked up the story. "What was the American connection in all this? Our sources tell us it included the late William Casey's CIA and...Felix Rodriguez, a former CIA agent and counterinsurgency expert active in aiding the Contras."

Threlkeld's "sources"—and I use the term sarcastically—included a man to whom he referred as "Harry." Harry sounds just like Richard Brenneke—the man sure has a lot of aliases. His other major source was—of course—José Blandon.

Another of Threlkeld's experts was an Israeli professor named Benjamin Beit-Hallahmi, who told the ABC reporter that "Israel would never get involved in these kinds of things" without a go-ahead from the Reagan Administration. What Threlkeld never told viewers is that Hallahmi is an active critic of the Israeli arms industry. That's like allowing consumer advocate Ralph Nader to appear on a news spot on auto safety and referring to him as just a man on the street.

So much for sources. As evidence, Threlkeld showed an interview with José Blandon, who looked into the camera and said, "There was a man who worked in El Salvador, his name was Felix Rodriguez, who was in charge of all the operation and resupplied the arms to the Contras."

Blandon was right—in one narrow fact. I *was* in El Salvador—but I arrived on March 15, 1985, not even during the time frame of Threlkeld's arms-and-drugs story. All ABC had to do was ask, and I would have supplied them with adequate documentation as to where I was, and when.

But obviously my facts did not fit Threlkeld's preconceived ideas about the story. He reported that "Rodriguez denies" any connection with the drug operation—which is exactly what I'd told Frank Snepp. But then he went on to say that Manuel Noriega's former aide, Blandon, "confirms . . . Rodriguez was in fact a key figure."

I was also unable to pin ABC down on their sources for what Frank Snepp assured me was an "astounding story" in May 1988. According to Snepp, the network was planning to broadcast a story that I had met with drug pilots in Panama in August 1985 and had told them I—and they—had the blessings of Vice President Bush.

I was flabbergasted by the accusation. When Snepp told me ABC was planning to run this story, I volunteered to come to Washington. There I submitted to a three-hour, on-camera interview with Snepp. To its credit, after viewing the footage, during which I knocked down all their theories, ABC killed the story.

It is very disturbing to me that ever since my name and my words have started appearing in the press, the same sources of misinformation turn up repeatedly. Both ABC's and *Rolling Stone's* erroneous reports about my alleged connections to the arms for drugs scams appear to have centered on sourcing by Richard Brenneke and José Blandon, as well as information from Ramón Milian Rodríguez. A common thread ties Brenneke, Blandon and Milian Rodríguez together: each one has a connection to Senator John Kerry's subcommittee and its special counsel, Jack Blum.

Some of the rhetorical questions posed in the *Rolling Stone* article were identical to rhetorical questions posed by Blum during the course of the Kerry investigation. Were Blum's fingerprints on any of the reports? It cannot be proved. Yet circumstantial evidence certainly exists.

It is profoundly frustrating to try to fight anonymous accusations, leaks, and untruths without the same access to the press as a U.S. Senator and his freewheeling staff, or the millions of viewers a network's chief correspondent has. It is hurtful to see one's name linked to drug smugglers without any recourse for rebuttal.

Worse, there is virtually no remedy for anyone wrongly attacked in the press. Accusations often lead the nightly news, or appear as newspaper headlines. Clarifications and retractions get buried in the back of the paper if they ever get printed at all.

I used to believe what I read. These days, I have learned the hard way to be suspicious of everything. I have always thought that our American press is the best and freest in the world. I still believe that. But I have also learned from bitter experience that it can be erroneous and unfair.

19 Sometimes out of adversity comes good. Sometimes—just sometimes—strong and positive values prevail in politics, too. In my opinion, that is what happened in 1988, when Vice President George Bush won the Presidency of the United States.

I did not campaign actively for Mr. Bush, although I had been ready to do so if asked. Instead, I spent my time in El Salvador. Between February 1988 and late November, when I finally returned to the United States, I flew 298 missions with the Salvadoran air force.

Unfortunately, most of them were not anti-insurgency strikes. The majority were Medevac runs. I flew UH-1H choppers and brought out of the countryside the mangled, bloody bodies of young soldiers whose feet and legs had been blown off by one of the hundreds of thousands of land mines scattered indiscriminately by the FMLN throughout the area.

It is not just soldiers who are regularly maimed, either. Thousands upon thousands of civilians have been wounded by communist land mines in the past decade. Thousands of children without feet, legs, or arms are the innocent victims of the FMLN's random violence. It is a sorry fact, but one of the biggest industries in El Salvador today is the manufacture of prosthetic limbs.

Moreover, halfway through the election year, U.S. policy in El Salvador took a definite turn for the worse. In July 1988, Ambassador Edwin Corr ended his three-year assignment in the country. I'd grown to like Corr tremendously. We enjoyed a good working relationship: he respected my closeness with some of the Salvadoran military officers; I held him in esteem for the evenhanded way in which he dealt with all the Salvadorans he came in contact with. I also liked his open-minded approach toward Latin America. Corr is not an ideologue but a pragmatist—a necessary characteristic for anyone who hopes to succeed in those volatile regions. He is also tough but fair. The Salvadorans respected him for that toughness, even when he held their feet to the fire over his unswerving commitment to democratic principles.

Unfortunately, Corr's replacement, William Walker, turned out to be a liberal State Department bureaucrat of the old school. Almost immediately, Walker disenchanted the Salvadoran military establishment with his waffly approach to policy. Nor was he able to win any real respect from the nation's politicians. American officials like Walker are the reason the words YANQUI GO HOME get painted on walls all over Central America.

During Ed Corr's posting, the tide of war rolled against the communist guerrillas. After he left, the insurgents became bolder and bolder—even to the point of setting off civilian-killing car bombs in the capital on a regular basis.

Complicating matters even more was that, it being an election year back in the States, Latin American policy once again fell by the wayside. I found it frustrating as the campaign wore on that I often became an issue, while El Salvador and its very real problems did not.

At the end of 1988, I decided that it was time to return to Miami. My daughter, Rosemarie, was becoming engaged to a fine young man named Sylvain, a talented chef, and would be married shortly. Felix, Jr., told Rosa and me that he had plans to become engaged, too. Rosa, who has been patient about my being away from home for most of the twenty-seven years we've been married, finally put her foot down on the subject of long-term assignments.

Besides, with George Bush elected, there was ample reason to come home and celebrate. I decided to attend the Inaugural along with General Bustillo and his wife, Ana, Moisés Eshkenazi, a friend and one of the leaders of Miami's Cuban-Jewish community, and Jose Chao and Jorge Arrizurieta, active members in Miami Republican circles. For five days we partied at the crowded events and receptions, seeing old friends, meeting new ones, and taking part in the celebrations.

Americans who were born in this country perhaps tend to take Inauguration Day for granted. They should not. Inauguration Day is a celebration of freedom and democracy; it is visible evidence that leadership is passed not because of the power of the sword, but the power of law. To those of us for whom the United States has always been a beacon of freedom, Inauguration Day is a time to think and reflect.

As George Herbert Walker Bush placed his hand on the same Bible used by another George—Washington—and took the same oath as had Washington, exactly two hundred years before, a note Mr. Bush had written to me more than two years previously came to mind. "The truth," he wrote, "is a very powerful weapon. We have all been smeared by the lie and the insinuation; but the truth will prevail, it always does."

In Mr. Bush's case, the truth did prevail—and the evidence of it was being seen on television sets all across the nation as he took the oath of office.

As I watched, I saw other sights, too: the shadows of my ancestors who fought alongside General Máximo Gómez during the Cuban War of Independence. My mind's eye revisited Uncle Felix Claudio Mendigutia's farm, where I spent summer vacations as a child and ran down to the barns in the morning to splash milk fresh from the cows into my thick, sweet coffee.

I saw my beloved parents' faces and read in them the heartbreak and trauma of losing everything they had known to a brutal communist dictatorship. I remembered their fear and uncertainty of coming to a new country as immigrants—without anything but the one thing all new Americans possess in quantity: inexhaustible hope.

So, even as George Bush, standing tall and proud and ready to lead, vowed to "preserve, protect and defend" our Constitution, I silently took my own vows as well: vows I'd taken before, and will take again:

To my brothers and sisters living in slavery under communist oppression—I will continue to strive for your freedom.

To my adopted country—I will stand firm to my last breath to protect your precious values.

And to my beloved family—I will fight to the death to protect the things we treasure most—our honor and integrity.

INDEX

273